M000047180

EARLY REPUBLIC

Selected titles in ABC-CLIO's Perspectives in American Social History series

American Revolution: People and Perspectives
British Colonial America: People and Perspectives
Civil Rights Movement: People and Perspectives
Civil War: People and Perspectives
Industrial Revolution: People and Perspectives
Jacksonian and Antebellum Age: People and Perspectives
Making of the American West: People and Perspectives
Reconstruction: People and Perspectives

PERSPECTIVES IN
AMERICAN SOCIAL HISTORY

Early Republic
People and Perspectives

Andrew K. Frank, Editor
Peter C. Mancall, Series Editor

$50

 A B C  C L I O

Santa Barbara, California · Denver, Colorado · Oxford, England

Copyright 2009 by ABC-CLIO, Inc.

All rights reserved. No part of this publication may be reproduced, stored in a retrieval system, or trans-mitted, in any form or by any means, electronic, mechanical, photocopying, recording, or otherwise, except for the inclusion of brief quotations in a review, without prior permission in writing from the publishers.

Library of Congress Cataloging-in-Publication Data

Early republic : people and perspectives / Andrew K. Frank, editor.
      p. cm.—(Perspectives in American social history)
   Includes bibliographical references and index.
   ISBN 978-1-59884-019-3 (hardback : alk. paper)—ISBN 978-1-59884-020-9 (ebook)
1. United States—Social life and customs—1783–1865—Juvenile literature.   2. United States—Social conditions—To 1865—Juvenile literature.   3. United States—Race relations—History—18th century—Juvenile literature.   4. United States—Race relations—History—19th century—Juvenile literature.   5. Minorities—United States—History—Juvenile literature.   6. Social classes—United States—History—Juvenile literature.   7. Sex role—United States—History—Juvenile literature.   8. Political culture—United States—History—Juvenile literature.   I. Frank, Andrew, 1970–

   E164.E128 2008
   973.4—dc22

             2008044370

12 11 10 09   10 9 8 7 6 5 4 3 2 1

Production Editor: Cami Cacciatore
Production Manager: Don Schmidt
Media Editor: Julie Dunbar
Media Resources Manager: Caroline Price
File Management Coordinator: Paula Gerard

ABC-CLIO, Inc.
130 Cremona Drive, P.O. Box 1911
Santa Barbara, California 93116-1911

This book is also available on the World Wide Web as an Ebook. Visit www.abc-clio.com for details.

This book is printed on acid-free paper ∞

Manufactured in the United States of America

Contents

Series Introduction

Social history is, simply put, the study of past societies. More specifically, social historians attempt to describe societies in their totality, and hence often eschew analysis of politics and ideas. Though many social historians argue that it is impossible to understand how societies functioned without some consideration of the ways that politics worked on a daily basis or what ideas could be found circulating at any given time, they tend to pay little attention to the formal arenas of electoral politics or intellectual currents. In the United States, social historians have been engaged in describing components of the population that had earlier often escaped formal analysis, notably women, members of ethnic or cultural minorities, or those who had fewer economic opportunities than the elite.

Social history became a vibrant discipline in the United States after it had already gained enormous influence in Western Europe. In France, social history in its modern form emerged with the rising prominence of a group of scholars associated with the journal *Annales Economie, Societé, Civilisation* (or *Annales ESC* as it is known). In its pages and in a series of books from historians affiliated with the École des Hautes Études en Sciences Sociale in Paris, brilliant historians such as Marc Bloch, Jacques Le Goff, and Emanuel LeRoy Ladurie described seemingly every aspect of French society. Among the masterpieces of this historical reconstruction was Fernand Braudel's monumental study, *The Mediterranean and the Mediterranean World in the Age of Philip II*, published first in Paris in 1946 and in a revised edition in English in 1972. In this work Braudel argued that the only way to understand a place in its totality was to describe its environment, its social and economic structures, and its political systems. In Britain the emphasis of social historians has been less on questions of environment, per se, than on a description of human communities in all their complexities. For example, social historians there have taken advantage of that nation's remarkable local archives to reconstruct the history of the family and details of its rural past. Works such as Peter Laslett's *The World We Have Lost*, first printed in 1966, and the multiauthored *Agrarian History of England and Wales*, which began to appear in print in 1967, revealed that painstaking work could reveal the lives and habits of individuals who never previously attracted the interest of biographers, demographers, or most historians.

Social history in the United States gained a large following in the second half of the 20th century, especially during the 1960s and 1970s. Its development sprang from political, technical, and intellectual impulses deeply embedded in the culture of the modern university. The politics of civil rights and social reform fueled the passions of historians who strove to tell the stories of the underclass. They benefited from the adoption by historians of statistical analysis, which allowed scholars to trace where individuals lived, how often they moved, what kinds of jobs they took, and whether their economic status declined, stagnated, or improved over time. As history departments expanded, many who emerged from graduate schools focused their attention on groups previously ignored or marginalized. Women's history became a central concern among American historians, as did the history of African Americans, Native Americans, Latinos, and others. These historians pushed historical study in the United States farther away from the study of formal politics and intellectual trends. Though few Americanists could achieve the technical brilliance of some social historians in Europe, collectively they have been engaged in a vast act of description, with the goal of describing seemingly every facet of life from 1492 to the present.

The 16 volumes in this series together represent the continuing efforts of historians to describe American society. Most of the volumes focus on chronological areas, from the broad sweep of the colonial era to the more narrowly defined collections of essays on the eras of the Cold War, the baby boom, and America in the age of the Vietnam War. The series also includes entire volumes on the epochs that defined the nation, the American Revolution and the Civil War, as well as volumes dedicated to the process of westward expansion, women's rights, and African American history.

This social history series derives its strength from the talented editors of individual volumes. Each editor is an expert in his or her own field who selected and organized the contents of his or her volume. Editors solicited other experienced historians to write individual essays. Every volume contains first-rate analysis complemented by lively anecdotes designed to reveal the complex contours of specific historical moments. The many illustrations to be found in these volumes testify too to the recognition that any society can be understood not only by the texts that its participants produce but also by the images that they craft. Primary source documents in each volume will allow interested readers to pursue some specific topics in greater depth, and each volume contains a chronology to provide guidance to the flow of events over time. These tools—anecdotes, images, texts, and timelines—allow readers to gauge the inner workings of America in particular periods and yet also to glimpse connections between eras.

The articles in these volumes testify to the abundant strengths of historical scholarship in the United States in the early years of the 21st century.

Despite the occasional academic contest that flares into public notice, or the self-serving cant of politicians who want to manipulate the nation's past for partisan ends—for example, in debates over the Second Amendment to the U.S. Constitution and what it means about potential limits to the rights of gun ownership—the articles here all reveal the vast increase in knowledge of the American past that has taken place over the previous half century. Social historians do not dominate history faculties in American colleges and universities, but no one could deny them a seat at the intellectual table. Without their efforts, intellectual, cultural, and political historians would be hard pressed to understand why certain ideas circulated when they did, why some religious movements prospered or foundered, how developments in fields such as medicine and engineering reflected larger concerns, and what shaped the world we inhabit.

Fernand Braudel and his colleagues envisioned entire laboratories of historians in which scholars working together would be able to produce *histoire totale*: total history. Historians today seek more humble goals for our collective enterprise. But as the richly textured essays in these volumes reveal, scholarly collaboration has in fact brought us much closer to that dream. These volumes do not and cannot include every aspect of American history. However, every page reveals something interesting or valuable about how American society functioned. Together, these books suggest the crucial necessity of stepping back to view the grand complexities of the past rather than pursuing narrower prospects and lesser goals.

Peter C. Mancall

Series Editor

Introduction

The time of the early American republic (roughly 1783–1830) was an era of tremendous promise and seemingly insurmountable problems, an era of tumultuous changes and remarkable contradictions. During these decades, the United States extended its westward borders as millions of acres came under its control, at the same time new roads and canals bridged distances as never before. The new nation witnessed an expansion in the number of both slaves and slaveholders, even as many states and communities sought to end the institution. Conflicts with Native Americans intensified in many areas, as Indian peoples fled and fought against many of the changes that enveloped their lives. At the same time many Native Americans increasingly became interconnected in a rapidly spreading market economy. During those early years, a professional army slowly emerged, many religions flourished as white and black Americans flocked to new and old evangelical sects, and the nation's white women used republican rhetoric to create an increasingly public voice. Americans also faced a growing marketplace, one that threatened to transform a nation that was largely filled by independent farmers and craftsmen. Tradesmen organized, workers united, and consumerism increasingly transformed the daily lives of many Americans. As historian William Barney explained: "change was everywhere—in the departure of sons to the West, the growth of cities, the spread of factories, the inundation by immigrants, and the new steam-driven technology—and it was simultaneously exhilarating and frightening" (Barney 1987, 55). In short, the early republic was an era of contradictions and transformations, and Americans from all walks of life tried to control and adapt to the rapidly changing world.

The Traditional Early Republic

For generations, the history of the early republic has been told solely through the political lens. This narrative emphasized the writing of the Constitution, tensions and ideological differences between Federalists and Anti-Federalists, the presidency of George Washington (1789–1797), the rise and influence of Alexander Hamilton and Thomas Jefferson, and more generally the creation of an American nation. The traditional view of the early republic also contains a series of other standard events, comprised again of primarily diplomatic and political affairs. These events begin with the creation of a new federal government in the Constitutional Convention (1787) and extend through the diplomatic crisis with France in the XYZ Affair (1797), the geographic expansion of the nation through the Louisiana Purchase (1803), the Aaron Burr conspiracy to create a new nation in Texas (1805–1807), the War of 1812 with Great Britain, the 1820 Missouri Compromise that promised to resolve disputes over the slavery in the territories, the Monroe Doctrine that declared the Americas off limits to the European powers (1823), and the election of Andrew Jackson to the presidency (1828).

This often triumphant story of the early republic essentially explains the emergence of the American democratic experiment, the tensions between state and federal control, and the various landmark Supreme Court cases of the era, particularly cases like *Marbury v. Madison* (1803), the ruling that established the concept of judicial review and helped confirm the United States as a nation of laws. This narrative contained economic issues, especially tariffs and panics, but overwhelmingly the story was one of national progress. This was an era of industrialization, when factories, roads, canals, and large plantations all appeared seemingly at once. Other events certainly fill in the chronological gaps, and historians have offered various interpretations of these events. Yet the era itself was about the emergence of the nation and the creation of the republic. Indeed, in this literature, the early republic inevitably ended with the rise of President Jackson and the accompanying new, more democratic version of American politics and representation. Taken together, these events explain the process of coalescence that the United States underwent in this era, a path that began as 13 disparate states at the end of the American Revolution and ended in a single and coherent nation (Fiske 1888).

This standard historical narrative is not wrong per se; at its worst it is misleading and at its best incomplete. As much as these events and this political transformation undeniably shaped Americans and their history, the era that followed the Revolution contained much more than a political story. For a few decades now, historians have transformed the traditional version of the early republic—adding new topics, participants, and questions. This rewriting of the era has challenged all of the central themes and assumptions of the traditional story—questioning the chronological time frame, the focus on politics, the exceptionalism of the American experience, and the nature of capitalism and industrialization. Scholars of politics now recognize how voters were shaped by ideological concerns as well as by their ethnicity, community networks, and social backgrounds (Formisano 1984; Pasley et al. 2004). Economic historians have explored how capitalism was slowly created in the era, increasingly shaping the lives of Americans and redefining the nation (Clark 1990; Kulikoff 1992). Scholars of race, ethnicity, and gender have illuminated how the rise of the nation and its egalitarian rhetoric did not necessarily affect all Americans equally (Cott 1997; Nash 1988). In short, this literature demonstrates that in the early republic, as in all American eras that came before or after, everyday life for ordinary Americans was shaped but not defined by the political narrative. Political developments mattered, but for most Americans they took place in the background of the human experience.

The Chapters

Early Republic: People and Perspectives brings the perspectives and experiences of the American people to the forefront by examining their social realities through nine distinct essays, a chronology, a glossary of basic terms and events, and a series of primary sources. The nine essays form the heart of the volume, illuminating the multiple meanings and experiences of the era. Individual essays examine artisans, wage workers, Western settlers, soldiers and the military, women, African Americans, immigrants, Native Americans, and evangelicals. These essays inevitably overlap, as some chapters explore specific demographic groups and other chapters explore particular experiences that crossed racial, gender, or geographic boundaries. History is never so structured as to be divisible into discrete and self-autonomous categories. Women worked for wages in many of the new textile mills; African Americans occasionally entered the U.S. military, especially the navy; Western settlers and Native Americans frequently shaped the experiences of each other; and many European immigrants became Western migrants. Perhaps most significantly, evangelicalism in the early republic had perhaps its greatest success among African Americans. Indeed, independent black churches became common during the early republic, especially after the formation of the African Methodist Episcopal Church in 1816.

The volume begins with "A World of Independent Men: Artisans in the Early Republic." In it, historian A. Kristen Foster explores the transformation of craftsmen to wage workers in the early 19th century, demonstrating how the rise of capitalism and technological changes transformed the lives of many American workers. In Chapter 2, "Freeborn Americans: The Rise of the Urban Wage Earner and the Rhetoric of the Early Republic," Jessica M. Parr contrasts the varied experiences of wage workers with the ideology of republicanism. In the process, she reveals the struggles of workers to own their own labor and to find stability in an era of tumultuous change. In Chapter 3, "Seeking 'Men of Iron Sinew': Creating a Professional Military in the Early American Republic," Sally E. Bennett examines the rise of a professional army in the United States. In this essay, she describes the recruitment process, the daily struggles of soldiers, and the problems inherent in building a standing army in a society fearful of centralized power. In the following chapter, "Virtuous Expectations: Republican Motherhood and True Womanhood in the Early Republic," Dawn Sherman explores the experiences that united and defined the experiences of women from diverse racial, regional, and economic backgrounds. In each case, she demonstrates the difficulties they faced in living up to the era's gendered expectations. Jennifer Hull Dorsey, in Chapter 5, assesses the experiences of African Americans in the era. This essay—"States of Liberty, States of Bondage: African Americans in the Early Republic"—uses the words and experiences of various Africans Americans to illuminate how slaves and freedpeople endured the hardships of the era. In Chapter 6, "Colonizing the 'Western World': Western Settlers (1780–1830)," David Nichols explores the experiences on the rapidly expanding frontier, demonstrating how they increasingly became similar to those elsewhere in the United States. In Chapter 7, "'My Joy has Ebbed and Flowed, with the Complexion of the Times': Immigrants and Migrants in the Early Republic," Dawn Hutchins explores the mobility of the era. In the process, she reveals how immigrants from various European nations helped transform the period. In the following chapter, Andrew K. Frank assesses the experiences of the nation's Indian communities. In "Moving and Removing, Adapting and Adopting to the New Nation: Native Americans Respond to American Expansion," he explores the cultural, social, and political transformations in Native communities and various ways in which Natives tried to shape their new world. Finally, in the last chapter, Anna M. Lawrence details the spread of evangelicalism in the United States. In "The Fires of Evangelicalism in the Cauldron of the Early Republic: Race, Class, and Gender in the Second Great Awakening," she shows how Americans from many social groups experienced the era's religious revival.

Themes in the Early Republic

Along with the overlapping experiences among the nine topical chapters, three overarching themes unite these essays and the volume as a whole: market capitalism, the ideology of republicanism, and geographic expansion. Together, they create a coherent vision of the first few decades of U.S. history. Collectively, these themes reveal many of the nuances and contradictions of the early republic.

Market Capitalism

Many of the essays explore how Americans became increasingly defined by market capitalism. Although many Americans resisted this version of modernization and held on to traditional values in the face of what was often called the Money Power, the marketplace became an ever present influence in the era (Johnson 2006, 163). Whether they lived on farms or in towns or in the North, South, or West, Americans increasingly felt the impact of distant and often impersonal marketplaces. Slaves and slaveholders, farmers and factory workers, native or foreign-born, Indian traders and hunters all produced goods for distant markets and confronted the opportunities and pitfalls of a modern economy that based decisions on the impersonal forces of supply and demand. This changing reality also transformed how Americans lived, as a consumer culture with new ideas about refinement engulfed much of the nation (Breen 2004).

Market capitalism, as some of the chapters reveal, did not shape the nation uniformly. Economic developments created and magnified differences between Southern slave and Northern free states, especially as the North became associated more with factories than with fields (Chaplin 1993). Northerners built canals and moved into towns much faster than Southerners did. The emergence of cotton agriculture after the introduction of the cotton gin, though, helped reinvigorate the Southern economy and resulted in many Southerners implementing scientific methods in their fields and for their slaves. The backcountry was also shaped, albeit slightly differently, by the arrival of market forces. Native Americans resisted the impersonal demands of the marketplace, and in many ways the violence and revitalization movements of the early 19th century can be explained by the frustrations of Indians who saw the transformation of their communities and the loss of self-determination (Saunt 1999). Nevertheless, the pace of development kept up, though varied across the regions.

Some scholars, despite the uneven nature of the transformation, have used the rise of market capitalism to synthesize the early republic. A so-called market revolution—as the following chapters reveal—certainly transformed many elements of early American society. The rise of the market, at least according to many scholars, did more than transform the nation's economy. It fostered new political assumptions, religious movements, and gender norms. It resulted in the widespread building of roads and canals, what could be called a transportation revolution, and it created a consumer revolution that transformed the daily lives of most Americans. The market revolution separated the home from work, it linked local producers to distant markets, and it proverbially turned a nation of small-scale family farmers into a nation of factory workers and clerks. A rural nation was urbanizing, and many relatively self-sufficient communities became increasingly reliant on outsiders (Martin 2005; Sellers 1991; Stokes and Conway 1996).

The Ideology of Republicanism

The essays in this volume also demonstrate how concerns about representative democracy and the ideology of republicanism shaped the social realities of all Americans. During the nation's early decades, people from all walks of life fought and struggled to define the legacy of the American Revolution. Although the national ideals of life, liberty, and the pursuit of happiness were rhetorically established in the founding documents, the meanings of the terms and how much they would affect American society were largely left undefined. As historian Jacqueline Jones explains, "the genius of the American Revolution was its rhetoric of freedom and liberty that could be appropriated by so many different kinds of workers for so many different purposes" (Jones 1999, 56). As a result, independence and the revolution provided the context and a language for widespread challenges to an ever changing social order.

Many American women, for example, used the logic and rhetoric of republicanism to carve out new responsibilities in the new republic. As the raisers of the next generation of virtuous and disinterested citizens, motherhood took on fundamentally revised responsibilities in the early republic. After all, the founders of the nation frequently declared that the genius of democracy required a generation of virtuous men to engage in the public debates of politics. Who was better suited than the nation's mothers, many rhetorically asked, to socialize this founding generation? Sarah Hale, the editor of *Ladies' Magazine*, exemplified how some women drew upon the revolutionary ideology of the day to call for improvements for women, especially in regard to their education. "In this age of innovation," she wrote "perhaps no experiment will have an influence more important on the character and happiness of our society than the granting to females the advantages of a systematic and thorough education. The honor of this triumph, in favor of intellect over long established prejudices, belongs to the men of America" (Hale 1828, 1–2).

Women were not the only Americans to use the ideology of republicanism to advance their condition. On the frontier, American Indians confronted land speculators, prospective herders, and cotton farmers who coveted their lands and pressured elected politicians to make them available. As farmers used the rhetoric of republicanism to encourage the dispossession of Indian lands—only by adding additional lands could the nation ensure a generation of yeoman farmers—some Native Americans claimed that the honor of the nation required a different path. Even as discussions of Indian removal occurred in the shadows of republicanism, American opponents of removal often made the virtue of the nation an issue. Missionary Jeremiah Evarts, for example, declared in 1829 that "If the separate existence of the Indian tribes were an inconvenience to their neighbours, this would be but a slender reason for breaking down all the barriers of justice. . . . Many a powerful nation has felt it to be inconvenient to have a weak and dependent state in its neighbourhood, and has therefore forcibly joined the territory of such state to its own extensive domains. But this is done at the expense of honour and character" (Prucha 1981, 201–21). Even the creation of a professional U.S. military was shaped by concerns about what it meant to have a proper republican government. How could a nation that valued decentralized power, many Americans asked, embrace a standing peacetime army?

This volume also demonstrates how republicanism shaped the way Americans responded to capitalism. Perhaps most obviously, the early labor movements in the country drew on the revolutionary rhetoric to demand better working conditions. Seth Luther, a carpenter who helped created the Boston Trades' Union, made this explicitly clear when he declared that "The Declaration of Independence was the work of a combination, and was as hateful to the TRAITORS and TORIES of those days, as combinations among working men are now to the *avaricious* MONOPOLISTIC and *purse-proud* ARISTOCRAT" (Juravich et al. 1996, 14). For many Americans, republicanism provided a rhetorical tool to express the interests of masses and a critique of contemporary economic and political affairs. This was the case for one New England farmer who believed that there was a divide "between those that Labour for a Living and those that git a Living without Bodily Labour" (Kazin 1995, 13). The ongoing attempt to define the meaning of the Revolution certainly shaped life in the early republic.

Geographic Expansion

Finally, this volume illuminates how the geographic expansion of American society transformed the daily experiences of many Americans. The early republic consisted of a mere 13 states, but by 1830 it contained 24 states as well as several extensive territories. Much of this expansion came through the Louisiana Purchase of 1803, an area that Jefferson called an "empire of liberty" (Johnson 2006, 39). Geographic expansion also occurred through a series of lesser known and significantly smaller land cessions. Much of this expansion came through treaties and warfare with Native Americans; other cessions came from France, Spain, and Great Britain. By the end of the early republic, these land cessions allowed the United States to expand its western border more than 600 miles, from the western edge of the Appalachian Mountains to the valleys of the Missouri and Arkansas rivers. Explorers like Meriwether Lewis and William Clark explored the Rocky Mountains and saw the Pacific Ocean, opening the door to settlers, prospectors, and speculators who were often not far behind. By the end of the early republic, the American experience was hardly contained to the eastern shores and the original 13 states.

The geographic expansion of the nation created fundamentally new experiences for many Americans, especially as recent immigrants and other Americans flocked to the newly opened lands of the West. Settlers went through the often tedious and dangerous tasks of transforming forests into farmlands and connecting distant villages with Eastern centers. New towns like Rochester, New York, and Marietta, Ohio, formed in the American interior; internal improvements like the Erie Canal and the Federal Road were built to transport both people and trade goods; and the farms of the countryside often proved to be among the nation's most profitable. Although cities like New York and Philadelphia continued to grow, the nation's interior urbanized. New mill and factory towns emerged in Lowell, Massachusetts; Pawtucket, Maine; Slatersville, Rhode Island; and Rochester, New York. By the end of the early republic, the transformation of the West had already been completed in many areas, and the distinctions that separated the East from Trans-Appalachian West had largely disappeared.

Westward expansion also transformed the agricultural South. There, cotton agriculture rapidly moved west as lands in Alabama, Mississippi, and Louisiana were opened up to American settlers. As the Old South came into focus, the center of the Southern economy moved out of Richmond and to the frontier. Many of the new Western settlers, therefore, were African American slaves. As a result, slave populations went through tremendous growth and relocation. In 1790 there were fewer than 700,000 enslaved African Americans in the United States, with the largest populations in Virginia and South Carolina. By 1840, the enslaved population had increased to 2.5 million and most slaves now lived in the newly formed states. Indeed, many slaves from the upper South found themselves literally sold down the river to the auction blocks of New Orleans and elsewhere (Johnson 1999).

An Era of Contradictions

These three themes did not always create a unified early republic. Instead, the era in many ways can be defined by the contradictions and tensions among market capitalism, republicanism, and geographic expansion. Throughout the period, many Americans recognized the conflicts arising from growth, commerce, and republicanism. In fact, many of the founders believed that the rise of market capitalism would create a crisis of virtue in the early republic. John Adams, for example, asserted that "the Spirit of Commerce . . . is incompatible with that purity of Heart, and Greatness of soul which is necessary for an happy Republic" (Rahe 1994, 2: 23). Similarly, other Americans believed that the Louisiana Purchase would necessarily make it impossible for the republic to survive. The opening of these Western lands promised to provide families sufficient financial independence, but it also threatened Americans because it seemed like the nation may have become too large for a republican form of government. One critic, writing in a Boston newspaper made the purchase's threat to the republic clear. "Can an Empire so unwieldy, so nearly uncivilized, that will for a century or two require such heavy charge, and contribute so little towards degrading any part of it, will it be, can it be subject to *one* government?—And if it should, will that Government be republican?" (*Columbian Centinel*, July 13, 1803).

Other contradictions similarly characterized the early republic, and they form central parts of the volume. Abolitionists like George Buchanan recognized that national ideals contradicted national institutions. "While the Americans celebrate the anniversary of Freedom and Independence," he told a Baltimore audience at the start of the early republic, "abject slavery exists in all of her states but one" (Waldstreicher 1997, 311). The following decades did little to resolve this national contradiction. As the following chapters show, slavery became more marginalized and was gradually abolished in the Northern states, but its role in the Southern states and in the national economy became magnified. As the Atlantic slave trade came to a close in 1808, the nation's slave population grew exponentially through natural increase. Emancipation typically took place gradually in the North, and it corresponded with a contradictory colonization movement, a way to rid the United States of both slavery and large populations of free blacks. Similarly, the United States may have begun as a humanistic (nonreligious) nation, but evangelicalism increasingly turned Americans into a people of devout faith. Similarly, as Native Americans seemed to become more a part of the market economy and as many Indians embraced elements of so-called American civilization, they strengthened their demands for sovereignty and self-determination. As much as the expansion of the West promised to resolve land shortages in the East, it fostered political tensions nationwide over the expansion of slavery.

A Tumultuous Era

Industrialization also made the era a turbulent one. Technological changes and the emergence of factories resulted in the disappearance of career options for many specialized craftsmen and artisans. Apprentices became low-skilled wage workers, employees who worked rigidly defined hours, received meager wages, and typically had little chance for advancement. Similarly, thousands of farmers moved to cities to take jobs as wage laborers in new factories and mills. In short, work was fundamentally redefined in the early republic because the early years of industrialization offered little stability. As a result, family life was fundamentally altered, as industrialization separated work and home and redefined the household economy. The rise of factories also created a consumer revolution, one that resulted from increased productivity and that created an array of new products. Yet many workers found themselves marginalized from the consumer revolution that was reshaping American society. As English immigrant and labor organizer William Heighton stated, "The princely places, the magnificent mansions, the splendid equipages, the costly plate, the elegant and convenient furniture, with all the variety of rich and palatable viands, are solely the productions of the working class, who, after producing them, are legally but unjustly prevented from the enjoyment they yield" (Foner 1991, 69). In short, when the early republic ended, many of the contradictions and sources of anxiety remained intact. Yet the rapid transformations that reshaped American society had their effects, and a new American society had emerged (Larkin 1988).

Conclusion

For nine months in 1831 and 1832, French political theorist Alexis de Tocqueville toured the United States with the hope of learning about the young nation's political development and national character. De Tocqueville characterized the democratic United States in contrast to the aristocratic France of his birth, and the result was a series of rather optimistic observations about the young nation. "During my stay in the United States, nothing struck me more forcibly than the general equality of condition among the people," he writes. "I readily discovered the prodigious influence that this primary fact exercises on the whole course of society; it gives a peculiar direction to public opinion and a peculiar tenor to the laws; it imparts new maxims to the governing authorities and peculiar habits to the governed." In comparison to the monarchal world that he knew best, the results of the new republic were remarkable. Although de Tocqueville would reveal how race and gender created hierarchies and inequalities of their own, his observations reveal the tremendous transformations that the United States had undergone since the American Revolution. Its republic government and the widespread participation in free markets created a fundamentally new society, one that looked and felt remarkably different than the aristocratic Old World. "I soon perceived that the influence of this fact extends far beyond the political character and the laws of the country, and that it has no less effect on civil society than on the government," he explained. "This equality of condition is the fundamental fact from which all others seem to be derived" (De Tocqueville 1945). De Tocqueville may have overstated the "equality of condition among the people" as a universal social reality, but as the following chapters demonstrate, he certainly captured a recurring theme in the social ambitions of many early Americans. *Early Republic: People and Perspectives* explores the abilities and inabilities of Americans to achieve their ambitions and the turbulence that common Americans faced in this era of transformation. By the end of this era, as de Tocqueville himself understood, the lives of all Americans had been irrevocably changed.

Andrew K. Frank

References and Further Reading

Barney, William L. *The Passage of the Republic: An Interdisciplinary History of Nineteenth-Century America*. Lexington, MA: D. C. Heath and Company, 1987

Breen, T. H. *The Marketplace of Revolution: How Consumer Politics Shaped American Independence*. New York: Oxford University Press, 2004

Chaplin, Joyce E. *An Anxious Pursuit: Agricultural Innovation and Modernity in the Lower South, 1730–1815*. Chapel Hill: University of North Carolina Press, 1993

Clark, Christopher. *The Roots of Rural Capitalism: Western Massachusetts, 1780–1860*. Ithaca, NY: Cornell University Press, 1990

Cott, Nancy. *The Bonds of Womanhood: "Woman's Sphere" in New England, 1780–1835*, 2nd ed. New Haven, CT: Yale University Press, 1997

De Tocqueville, Alexis. *Democracy in America*. New York: Knopf, 1945 (Orig. pub. 1835)

Elkins, Stanley, and Erik McKitrick. *The Age of Federalism: The Early American Republic, 1788–1800*. New York: Oxford University Press, 1993

Fiske, John. *The Critical Period of American History, 1783–1789*. Boston, MA: Houghton Mifflin, 1888

Foner, Philip S. *William Heighton: Pioneer Labor Leader of Jacksonian Philadelphia. With Selections from Heighton's Writings and Speeches*. New York: International Publishers, 1991

Formisano, Ronald P. *The Transformation of Political Culture: Massachusetts Parties, 1790s–1840s*. New York: Oxford University Press, 1984

Hale, Sarah J. "Introduction." *Ladies' Magazine* 1 (January 1828): 1–4

Johnson, Paul E. *The Early American Republic*. New York: Oxford University Press, 2006

Johnson, Walter. *Soul by Soul: Life Inside the Antebellum Slave Market*. Cambridge, MA: Harvard University Press, 1999

Jones, Jacqueline. *A Social History of the Laboring Classes: From Colonial Times to the Present*. New York: Blackwell Publishers, 1999

Juravich, Tom, William F. Hartford, and James R. Green. *Commonwealth of Toil: Chapters in the History of Massachusetts Workers and Their Unions*. Amherst: University of Massachusetts Press, 1996

Kazin, Michael. *The Populist Persuasion: An American History*. New York: Basic Books, 1995

Kulikoff, Allan. *The Agrarian Origins of American Capitalism*. Charlottesville: University of Virginia Press, 1992

Larkin, Jack. *The Reshaping of Everyday Life, 1790–1840*. New York: Harper & Row, 1988

Martin, Scott C., ed. *Cultural Change and the Market Revolution in America, 1789–1860*. Lanham, MD: Rowman & Littlefield, 2005

Nash, Gary B. *Forging Freedom: The Formation of Philadelphia's Black Community, 1720–1840*. Cambridge, MA: Harvard University Press, 1988

Pasley, Jeffrey L., Andrew W. Robertson, and David Waldstreicher. *Beyond the Founders: New Approaches to the Political History of the Early Republic*. Chapel Hill: University of North Carolina Press, 2004

Perdue, Theda. *Cherokee Women: Gender and Culture Change, 1700–1835*. Lincoln: University of Nebraska Press, 1999

Prucha, Francis Paul, ed. *Cherokee Removal: The William Penn Essays and Other Writing*. Knoxville: University of Tennessee Press, 1981

Rahe, Paul. *Republics Ancient and Modern: Classical Republicanism and the American Revolution*. 2 vols. Chapel Hill: University of North Carolina Press, 1994

Saunt, Claudio. *A New Order of Things: Property, Power, and the Transformation of the Creek Indians, 1733–1816*. New York: Cambridge University Press, 1999

Sellers, Charles. *The Market Revolution: Jacksonian America, 1815–1846*. New York: Oxford University Press, 1991

Stokes, Melvyn, and Stephen Conway, eds. *The Market Revolution in America: Social, Political, and Religious Expressions, 1800–1880*. Charlottesville: University of Virginia Press, 1996

Waldstreicher, David. *In the Midst of Perpetual Fetes: The Making of American Nationalism, 1776–1820*. Chapel Hill: University of North Carolina Press, 1997

About the Editor and Contributors

Sally E. Colford Bennett is adjunct professor of English at Johnson County Community College, Overland Park, Kansas. She received her MFA in creative writing from Columbia College–Chicago. Her thesis work covered the Fort Dearborn Massacre at Chicago in 1812. She has published several essays and extended articles in various publications on American Indians and U.S. military history. She is a longtime participant in the War of 1812 in the West History Symposium. She is currently cowriting a regimental history of the First U.S. Infantry from 1796 to 1815.

Jennifer Hull Dorsey is Director of the Center of Revolutionary Era Studies at Sienna College in Loudonville, New York. Her primary research interest is the history of free African Americans in the early republic. Her current book project *The First Emancipation: African American Life on Maryland's Eastern Shore, 1783–1832* is under contract with Cornell University Press.

A. Kristen Foster is assistant professor of history at Marquette University. She is author of *Moral Visions and Material Ambitions: Philadelphia Struggles to Define the Republic, 1776–1836* (Lanham, MD: Lexington Books, 2004), assistant editor of *Voices from Vietnam* (Madison: Wisconsin Historical Society Press, 1997), and coeditor of *More than a Contest Between Armies: Essays on the Civil War Era* (Kent, OH: Kent State University Press, 2007).

Andrew K. Frank is assistant professor of history at Florida State University. He is the author of several books and articles on Native American and Southern history, including *Creeks and Southerners: Biculturalism on the Early American Frontier* (Lincoln: University of Nebraska Press, 2005), *The Routledge Historical Atlas of the American South* (New York: Routledge, 1999), and *American Revolution: People and Perspectives* (Santa Barbara, CA: ABC-Clio, 2007). He is currently working on *A Persistent People: The Seminoles and the Indians of Florida* (Chapel Hill: University of North Carolina Press, forthcoming), and *The Second Conquest: Indians, Settlers and Slaves on the Florida Frontier*. He received his PhD from the University of Florida.

Dawn Pauline Hutchins is a PhD student in history at the University of Tennessee. She has worked as a researcher for the Historic Preservation Office of the Seminole Tribe of Florida. She received her MA in history from Florida Atlantic University in 2007.

Anna Lawrence is assistant professor of history at Florida Atlantic University. She received her BA from Carleton College and her MA and PhD in history from the University of Michigan. She specializes in early American history, religious history, and gender history. She is currently working on a manuscript, "The Best of Bonds: Family, Sexuality and Revolution in Early Transatlantic Methodism, 1730–1815." She recently published "'A Most Solemn Season of Love': Charles Wesley and Marriage in Early Methodism," in *Charles Wesley: Life, Literature, and Legacy*, edited by Kenneth Newport and Ted Campbell, 465–485 (Wellington, NZ: Epworth Press, 2007). She is also the author of "'Both Parties Trembled for the Ark of God:' Transatlantic Methodism and the American Revolution," in *American Revolution: People and Perspectives*, edited by Andrew K. Frank (Santa Barbara, CA: ABC-Clio, 2007).

David Nichols is assistant professor of history at Indiana State University. He received his MA and PhD from the University of Kentucky and his bachelor's degree from Harvard University. In addition to several articles and other publications, he is the author of *Red Gentlemen and White Savages: Indians, Federalists, and the Search for Order on the American Frontier* (Charlottesville: University of Virginia Press, 2008).

Jessica M. Parr is a PhD candidate in Atlantic and early American history at the University of New Hampshire in Durham, where she is also an instructor. She holds an MA in American history and an MS in archives management from Simmons College in Boston. Prior to beginning work on her doctorate, she spent several years working in a number of museums and archives.

Dawn Sherman works at the National Archives and Records Administration in College Park, Maryland. She received her MA in history from Florida Atlantic University and is currently finishing her MLS at the University of Maryland at College Park. She is also the author of several articles on the experiences of American women in the 19th century.

Chronology

The Early Republic

1783

February England announces the cessation of hostilities with the United States and an end to the War of Independence.

April Congress declares victory in the War of Independence and ratifies a preliminary peace treaty. Thousands of loyalists from New York and other colonies flee for Canada and other British territories.

June The United States disbands the Continental Army. Unpaid war veterans protest, forcing Congress to take refuge in Princeton, New Jersey.

July The Supreme Court of Massachusetts rules that slavery violates the state's constitution.

September The United States and Great Britain sign the Treaty of Paris, bringing the war to a formal end.

October The House of Burgesses in Virginia emancipates African slaves who served in the Continental Army. Noah Webster helps standardize spelling and distinguish American English from its British counterpart by publishing the so-called blue-back speller (*A Grammatical Institute of the English Language*).

November George Washington delivers his Farewell Address to the Continental Army and declares his desire to return to private life at Mount Vernon in Virginia. The last British troops evacuate New York, their last military position in the United States.

December General Washington officially steps down as commander of the Continental Army. The Northern states ban the future importation of African-born slaves.

1784

January The United States Senate ratifies the Treaty of Paris with Great Britain; the Connecticut legislature passes a gradual emancipation act that declares an eventual end to slavery within its borders, and it prohibits its residents from future participation in the Atlantic slave trade.

February Rhode Island passes a gradual emancipation law to slowly eliminate the institution of slavery from the state.

June The Catholic Church appoints John Carroll as the Superior of the Missions for the Roman Catholic Church in America.

September The *Pennsylvania Packet and Daily Advertiser*, the first successful daily newspaper in the United States, begins distribution.

November Thomas Coke and Francis Asbury establish an American branch of the Methodist Church during a meeting at Barratt's Chapel in Frederica, Delaware.

1785

January The University of Georgia is chartered by the state legislature, making it the first state university in the United States.

March Thomas Jefferson replaces Benjamin Franklin as minister to France. The assembly of South Carolina issues a charter for the College of Charleston.

July Congress adopts the dollar as the official monetary unit for the United States.

October The American Shaker community forms in New Lebanon, New York.

1786

January Thomas Jefferson's Bill for Establishing Religious Freedom is passed by Virginia's legislature, effectively separating church and state.

August Frustrated farmers, many of them former soldiers in the Continental Army, begin Shay's Rebellion in western Massachusetts.

September Delegates from five states (Delaware, New Jersey, New York, Pennsylvania, and Virginia) meet at the Annapolis Convention in an unsuccessful attempt to revise the Articles of Confederation.

1787

February The state militia of Massachusetts brings Shay's Rebellion to an end. Thomas Jefferson publishes his *Notes on the State of Virginia*. Antislavery activists form the Delaware Society for the Gradual Abolition of Slavery.

April Richard Allen, Absalom Jones, and William White form the Free African Society in Philadelphia, Pennsylvania, creating what is perhaps the first independent voluntary association for African Americans in the United States.

May Fifty-five delegates from twelve states (all but Rhode Island) meet at the Philadelphia Convention, later known as the Constitutional Convention, to amend the Articles of Confederation or to create a new form of government entirely.

July The Constitutional Convention agrees to count slaves as three-fifths of a person for purposes of representation and taxation. The Continental Congress passes the Ordinance of 1787, creating the Northwest Territory and effectively banning slavery from its borders.

September 7 Barbados-born Prince Hall receives a charter for a Masonic Lodge for African Americans. Benjamin Franklin delivers the Rising Sun speech, and 39 delegates to the convention (one in absentia) sign the new U.S. Constitution.

October James Madison, Alexander Hamilton, and John Jay slowly release the essays that become *The Federalist Papers* in New York under the pseudonym Publius.

November The African Free School, started by Cornelius Davis, opens in New York City.

December Delaware becomes the first state to ratify the new United States Constitution.

1788

January Pennsylvanian members of the Society of Friends (Quakers) free their slaves. African American Andrew Bryan is ordained a minister, and the first African Baptist Church is certified in Savannah, Georgia; this is the first Baptist church in the state, predating the establishment of a white Baptist church by five years.

March Free blacks petition the state legislature of Massachusetts to protest the seizure and importation of emancipated slaves in the Caribbean.

September Congress chooses New York City to be the temporary seat of the newly formed U.S. government.

1789

January Father John Carroll founds Georgetown University, the first Catholic college in the United States.

February The State of Delaware prohibits the future importation of African slaves.

March The United States Constitution is ratified. Congress, meeting in New York City, convenes for the first time.

African American Olaudah Equiano publishes a first-hand account of slavery and the slave trade in *The Interesting Narrative of the Life of Olaudah Equiano: Written by Himself.*

April George Washington is elected and sworn in as the first president of the United States, and John Adams becomes vice president.

May The American Roman Catholic priests elect John Carroll to be their first bishop.

July Congress enacts a law regarding taxation for the first time. This 8.5 percent protective tax levies an additional fee on goods imported on foreign vessels as opposed to those that are imported on American ships.

September The Maryland Abolition Society forms. Congress submits 12 constitutional amendments to the states for ratification (ten of them will be ratified and become the Bill of Rights). Congress establishes the United States Army.

1790

February The Society of Friends (Quakers) petitions the U.S. Congress to ban the nation's participation in the slave trade.

March The Universal Friends found New Jerusalem, a millennialist utopian society. Congress authorizes the first national census. Judith Sargent Murray begins publishing "On the Equality of the Sexes," a woman's rights treatise, in the *Massachusetts Monthly.*

July Congress passes the Trade and Intercourse Act in order to regulate the Indian trade in eastern America.

August Creek Indians, led by Chief Alexander McGillivray, negotiate the Treaty of New York with the United States. The treaty cedes Creek lands in Georgia while recognizing Creek sovereignty in Georgia and Alabama.

December The first textile mill in the United States opens in Pawtucket, Rhode Island.

1791

January Free blacks in Charleston, South Carolina, protest the laws that limit their freedoms in a petition to the state legislature.

February Congress creates the Bank of the United States.

March Congress passes the Whiskey Tax, the first federal tax imposed by Congress directly onto the people.

August John Fitch receives the first U.S. patent for a steamboat.

November Little Turtle and the Miami Confederacy kill more than 900 U.S. soldiers in an overwhelming victory along the Wabash River in the Northwest Territory.

December The first ten amendments to the Constitution (the Bill of Rights) are ratified.

1792

March Overspeculation in stock of the Bank of the United States causes a nationwide financial panic.

July Samson Occom, a Mohegan and influential Christian missionary to other Native Americans, dies.

October The first edition of the *Old Farmer's Almanac* is published. Columbus Day is celebrated for the first time.

1793

January The Humane Society of Philadelphia, Pennsylvania, is established, making it the first aid society in the United States.

February Congress passes a Fugitive Slave Act, which prohibits the harboring of escaped slaves or interfering with their arrests.

March Eli Whitney obtains a patent from the United States for the cotton gin.

August John Woolman writes *A Word of Remembrance and Caution to the Rich*, in which he calls for a variety of social reforms, including the abolition of slavery.

November British ships begin seizing and impressing American ships and crews.

December The U.S. Congress authorizes the building of the first governmental road to connect Frankfort, Kentucky, with Cincinnati, Ohio.

1794

March Amos Fortune, a former slave, founds the Jaffrey Social Library in Jaffrey, New Hampshire; Congress prohibits U.S. ships from supplying other nations with African slaves.

June Philadelphian Richard Allen establishes the Bethel African Methodist Episcopal Church.

July Farmers and other rural Pennsylvanians protest the Whiskey Tax and initiate the Whiskey Rebellion.

August George Washington and 13,000 soldiers suppress the Whiskey Rebellion. The United States Army under General Anthony Wayne defeats a force of about 1,000 Indians who were led by Blue Jacket at the Battle of Fallen Timbers; this would be the final battle in the Northwest Indian War.

1795

June The United States and Great Britain sign the Jay Treaty, establishing rules for extradition between the two countries.

August The United States and 12 Ohio Indian tribes sign the Treaty of Greenville. The treaty cedes the region's tribal lands to General Anthony Wayne and the United States, thereby opening most of what is now Ohio to white settlement.

October The United States and Spain negotiate Pinckney's Treaty to resolve boundary disputes between the nations in the South and West and establishing the United States' right to ship goods down the Mississippi River.

1796

March The U.S. Supreme Court declares a state law unconstitutional for the first time in *Ware v. Hylton*.

August The Boston African Society is established.

September George Washington publishes his Farewell Address. In it, he states his reasons for returning to private life and deciding not to run for a third term as president.

October Public sentiment in Portsmouth, New Hampshire, prevents officials from returning a fugitive slave to his owner, President George Washington.

1797

June Charles Newbold receives a patent from the United States for the first cast-iron plow.

October The XYZ Affair occurs, and relations between France and the United States deteriorate.

1798

January A yellow fever epidemic spreads from Philadelphia, Pennsylvania, to Wilmington, Delaware.

April The Mississippi Territory (which includes Alabama) is organized out of Georgia's western lands.

June Congress passes the Alien Act, authorizing the president to deport immigrants who were believed to pose a threat to national security.

July Congress passes the Sedition Act, prohibiting "false, scandalous and malicious" writings about the United States government.

1799

February Pennsylvania farmers protest the first tax of 1798. John Fries, the leader of the rebellion, is convicted of treason and then later pardoned by President John Adams.

March New York's legislature enacts a gradual emancipation law.

June Handsome Lake initiates the Longhouse religion among Senecas, a revivalist movement that drew upon Christian and Native roots.

July Eliakim Spooner receives a patent for the first seeding machine. Eli Whitney signs a contract to produce 10,000 muskets for the United States government.

1800

April The U.S. Congress establishes a postal route along the Natchez Trace. It also authorizes and funds the creation of the Library of Congress.

August White Virginians uncover Gabriel's conspiracy to overthrow slavery in Richmond; 38 presumed conspirators are hanged.

October Spain returns the Louisiana Territory to France.

1801

January John Marshall becomes chief justice of the United States Supreme Court.

November Kentucky's legislature outlaws dueling.

1802

June The United States establishes the U.S. Military Academy at West Point in New York.

1803

February The U.S. Supreme Court, in *Marbury v. Madison*, declares that a law passed by Congress was unconstitutional, thus establishing the concept of judicial review, or the idea that the Supreme Court can rule a Congressionally passed law unconstitutional.

April For $15 million, the United States purchases the Louisiana Territory from France; the territory to be formally transferred in December.

1804

January The legislature of Ohio passes a series of regulations that restricts the movement of free African Americans in the state.

February New Jersey's legislature follows the lead of other Northern states and passes a gradual emancipation law.

May Meriwether Lewis and William Clark leave St. Louis, Missouri, on their expedition westward.

July Aaron Burr kills Alexander Hamilton in a pistol duel.

September A hurricane hits and devastates eastern South Carolina.

December The Walton War is fought between residents of Georgia and North Carolina.

1805

April Tenskwatawa, a Shawnee Indian, initiates a nativist religious movement among Native Americans in the Ohio Valley.

July The first Methodist camp meeting occurs near Smyrna, Delaware.

November The Lewis and Clark Expedition reaches the Pacific Ocean. The first woman's club in America—the Female Charitable Society—forms in Maine.

1806

August Aaron Burr plans to create an independent nation in the American southwest; he would be later tried and acquitted of treason.

September The Lewis and Clark Expedition returns to St. Louis, Missouri.

1807

March The U.S. Congress passes a law to prohibit the importation of African slaves into the United States, the law goes into effect the following year.

September Robert Fulton successfully operates the first steamboat. Fulton receives a patent a few months later.

1808

January The federal law banning the African slave trade goes into effect. The African Benevolent Society begins.

1809

July Shawnee leader Tecumseh, with the help of his twin brother The Shawnee Prophet, begins forming a pan-Indian coalition in the upper Mississippi Valley.

1810

February The first fire insurance joint stock company is organized in Philadelphia, Pennsylvania.

October The United States annexes the territory of West Florida from Spain.

1811

January Approximately 400 slaves revolt in two Louisiana parishes; United States soldiers and southern planters kill 75 slaves as they put down the rebellion.

October The first steam-powered ferry, the *Juliana*, begins operation between New York City and Hoboken, New Jersey.

November The Shawnee Prophet's warriors are defeated at The Battle of Tippecanoe by the forces under William Henry Harrison in Indiana. The construction of the National Road begins.

December The New Madrid Earthquake erupts along the Mississippi Valley. Aftershocks and additional tremors continue for more than two months.

1812

June The United States declares war on Great Britain, and the War of 1812 begins.

July The United States Army, led by General William Hull, invades Canada.

December Forty parishioners are killed in California when the Great Stone Church at Mission San Juan Capistrano collapses due to an earthquake.

1813

July The Creek Indians in Georgia and Alabama begin a bloody civil war at the Battle of Burnt Corn Creek.

August Red Stick Creek Indians attack and kill more than 500 Creeks who were loyal to the United States, white traders, and African American slaves who had taken refuge at Fort Mims in Alabama.

October Tecumseh is killed at the Battle of the Thames in Ontario, Canada.

December The British burn Buffalo, New York, and take nearby Fort Niagara during the War of 1812.

1814

March U.S. General Andrew Jackson and his Creek allies overwhelmingly defeat the Red Stick forces at the Battle of Horseshoe Bend.

August The defeated Creek Indians sign the Treaty of Fort Jackson; in it, they cede 23 million acres of territory to the United States. Peace negotiations begin in Ghent to bring the War of 1812 to a close. British forces destroy the Library of Congress. The United States economy suffers, and banks suspend specie payments.

September Francis Scott Key, at Fort McHenry in Maryland, writes and publishes "The Star Spangled Banner."

December The Treaty of Ghent is signed and the war between Britain and the United States formally ends. The Hartford Convention begins.

1815

January American troops defeat the British at the Battle of New Orleans. Thomas Jefferson donates approximately 6,500 volumes to rebuild the holdings of the Library of Congress.

February President James Madison redeclares an end to the War of 1812.

1816

April The African Methodist Episcopal Church is formally organized in Philadelphia, Pennsylvania. Congress passes the Tariff Bill of 1816 to protect the nation's industrial interests.

July United States troops destroy the so-called Negro Fort at Fort Apalachicola (Florida), as a punishment for the Seminoles' harboring of fugitive slaves.

December The American Colonization Society is founded in Washington, D.C.

1817

January African Americans in Philadelphia protest the efforts of the American Colonization Society to deport former slaves "back to Africa."

April Thomas Hopkins Gallaudet establishes a school for the deaf in Connecticut.

July Construction begins on the Erie Canal; detractors call it Clinton's Folly, after the governor of New York who authorized its creation.

August The *Zebulon M. Pike* reaches St. Louis, Missouri, making it the first steamboat to navigate the Mississippi River above the mouth of the Ohio River.

November The First Seminole War in Florida officially begins.

1818

April The United States Army defeats the Seminole Indians and their black allies at the Battle of Suwanee, effectively ending the First Seminole War. Sporadic fighting continues.

May General Andrew Jackson captures Pensacola in Spanish Florida.

October The United States and the Chickasaw Indians sign a secret treaty near Old Town in the Chickasaw Nation.

1819

March The United States Congress establishes the Indian Civilization Fund that authorizes the federal government to allocate money to teach Native Americans about agriculture, literacy, and arithmetic. Congress passes its first law to control immigration.

1820

February The first organized emigration of blacks leaves New York for Sierra Leone in Africa.

March Congress approves the Missouri Compromise, establishing the 36–30 parallel line as the dividing line between slave and free states. Maine breaks off from Massachusetts to become a free state; Missouri becomes a slave state.

May The United States Congress passes legislation that defines participating in the international slave trade as an act of piracy and one that is punishable by death.

Circa 1821

Sequoya creates the syllabary, a new alphabet that allows Cherokee to be the first written Native American language.

1821

June The African Methodist Episcopal Zion Church is founded in New York.

July Andrew Jackson becomes the first governor of the territory of Florida.

December Kentucky abolishes its debtor prisons.

1822

February Liberia is settled by freed American slaves under the auspices of the American Colonization Society; in 1847 it becomes a republic.

June Denmark Vesey and other African Americans are captured and later hanged for their presumed planning of a thwarted slave rebellion in and near Charleston, South Carolina.

1823

December President James Monroe details the Monroe Doctrine, which effectively declares that the United States wants to assume a significant diplomatic position in the hemisphere.

1824

March The United States Supreme Court, in *Gibbons v. Ogden*, establishes that the federal government has the authority to regulate interstate commerce.

November The United States eliminates property requirements for voting. The nation's first Reform Jewish Congregation forms in Charleston, South Carolina.

1825

January Robert Owen starts a secular utopian society in New Harmony, Indiana.

March John Marshall declares that the African slave trade is a violation of natural law.

October The construction of the Erie Canal, connecting the Hudson River with Lake Erie, is finished.

1826

February The America Temperance Society forms in Boston, Massachusetts.

1827

February Ballet is introduced to the United States at the Bowery Theater in New York City.

March The *Freedom's Journal,* the nation's first black newspaper, begins publication in New York.

July The Cherokees adopt a written tribal constitution as part of an attempt to strengthen their sovereignty and prevent their removal from tribal lands.

August Race riots erupt in Cincinnati, Ohio.

1828

February The Cherokee Indians begin using a printing press to publish materials with the syllabary.

April Noah Webster publishes the first American dictionary.

May Congress places restrictive taxes on imported raw materials in the so-called Tariff of Abominations.

December The legislature in South Carolina claims the right to nullify federal laws like the Tariff of Abominations.

1829

September Bostonian and free African American David Walker publishes his *Appeal to the Coloured Citizens of the World.*

October The Chesapeake and Delaware Canal is finished.

1830

May Congress passes the Indian Removal Act, authorizing the president to negotiate the removal of the tribes east of the Mississippi River.

September The first National Negro Convention meets in Philadelphia to improve the social condition of African Americans.

November At the first meeting of the Negro Convention of Free Men in Philadelphia, the attendees agree to boycott goods that are produced by African slaves.

A World of Independent Men: Artisans in the Early Republic

A. Kristen Foster

1

Introduction

From its inception, the early American republic was a nation of farmers. This fact, argued Thomas Jefferson, should define the nation—at least as long as possible. Sturdy yeomen farmers, he wrote in his *Notes on the State of Virginia*, "are the chosen people of God" (Jefferson 1853, 176). He hoped the United States, in fact, would always rely on Europe's craftsmen for most of its manufactured goods, arguing that manufacturing ultimately degraded human beings. It was not the work that corrupted men, he said, but the systematic abuse of the worker: "the want of food and clothing necessary to sustain life, has begotten a depravity of morals, a dependence and corruption, which render them [artisans] an undesirable accession to a country whose morals are sound" (Jefferson to Mr. Lithgow, January 1805, in Ford 1892–1899, 4: 563). As life in the United States unfolded over the course of the early republic, many artisans learned what Jefferson had predicted. Some became entrepreneurs, but most experienced uneasy changes in a way of life that had offered them self-esteem and promise for the future.

The years that followed the American Revolution proved to be watershed years for the early republic in many ways. Not yet seeing what Jefferson would predict in 1805, artisans in particular might expect that the Revolution offered them new opportunities to define America using their experiences as independent craftsmen. As a new nation, America contained possibilities not only for political change, but for social change as well. Revolutionary Thomas Paine argued in January of 1776 that common sense dictated that monarchies and aristocracies had no place in this new world. While he was in Paris during the war years, Paine's contemporary and one of colonial America's most famous artisans, Benjamin Franklin, also asserted the unlimited possibilities that America held for ordinary men. He explained to Europeans that it would not be worth their while to look to the United States for patronage as a birthright. "In Europe," he said, a birthright "has indeed its Value, but it is a Commodity that cannot be carried to a worse Market than to that of America, where People do not enquire concerning a Stranger, *What IS he*? but *What can he DO*?" In fact, argued Franklin, if a man has any skill, America will welcome him and respect him. Men who seek a salary because they are someone's son "will be despis'd and disregarded." Americans reward ordinary, independent yeomen, husbandmen, and mechanics, Franklin argued, because they are useful. "The People have a Saying," he wrote, "that God Almighty is himself a Mechanic, the greatest in the Universe; and he is respected and admired more for the Variety, Ingenuity, and Utility of his Handiworks, than for the Antiquity of his Family" (Franklin 1987, 976–77). In America a man would be judged by what he did, not by who his parents were, and such logic allowed many ordinary white men to think anew about their futures. If it was a revolution about equality and independence, then, some wondered, who better to help shape the ensuing changes than American craftsmen?

"Artisans," "craftsmen," "mechanics," and sometimes "tradesmen" were all early American monikers for independent men skilled in handicrafts of all sorts. Much like agriculturalists at the time, craftsmen enjoyed many levels of success and material comfort. The cordwainers who made shoes or the tallow chandlers who boiled soap seemed always to be on the edge of ruin; many often wondered if they would be able to feed their families. On the other end of the spectrum, silversmiths and cabinetmakers flourished as the princes of the artisan world. These men shared not, as some might expect, a class interest, but instead a belief that their skills were valuable, even essential, to their own well-being and to the health of their communities. These men were urban and rural, mostly white but some black, mostly free but some enslaved, Northern and Southern, wealthy and poor. Some boasted homes with multiple floors and rooms replete with luxury items, and others wondered from season to season if they would survive. They were not all workers by today's standards, but they all valued work.

In the end, whether rich or poor, these men, as long as they were free, worked not simply to live but to find satisfaction. Benjamin Franklin remembered in his *Autobiography* how important it was for his father to place him in a craft that was "agreable" to the boy. At first Josiah Franklin had hoped that young Ben might follow in his footsteps as a tallow chandler, but the father soon realized that his son did not find the trade to his liking. He thus took him through the busy streets of Boston to see "Joiners, Bricklayers, Turners, Braziers, &c. at their Work, that he might observe my inclination, & and endeavor to fix it on some Trade or other on Land." "[M]y father," noted Franklin, "was under Apprehensions that if he did not find one for me more agreable, I should break away and get to Sea" (Franklin

Shoemaker cutting out an upper leather of a shoe and journeyman joining the upper leather to the sole of a shoe. Illustrated in Jacob Johnson's *The Book of Trades* (1807). (*Library of Congress*)

1987, 1316). While Franklin became one of the most famous American printers and tradesmen, he was no different from any other boy in early 18th-century Boston hoping for excitement and adventure. To make something of his son, Josiah Franklin understood that he would need to apprentice Ben to a craft that would keep his adolescent interest and hopefully secure his future.

In this world of men and given the gendered divisions of labor at the time, it was almost exclusively a man's world, with skills and craft pride separating artisans from ordinary day laborers. When journeymen later had to work alongside women (for instance, seamstresses in the tailoring trade), the men protested this insult to their standing as journeymen, arguing that women degraded the craft system. Over the course of the early republic (roughly 1783–1830), however, revolutionary changes in market relationships, transportation, and manufacturing also brought significant change to how artisans did their work and how they thought about themselves as American citizens. Some lost ground and became wage laborers without craft protections, some rural artisans confronted competition often for the first time, and others found new opportunities to expand and become successful entrepreneurs.

American artisans worked in a craft system that was unprotected yet unfettered by the European medieval guild system. While the English guilds exerted a kind of quality control by carefully scrutinizing the skills of those who sought admission as members, the guilds did not make the Atlantic crossing with immigrant craftsmen. As Europeans sought new lives in the New World, men with trade skills commanded a seller's market because relatively few craftsmen labored in the colonies, and young America needed their skills to grow and prosper. Shoemakers, carpenters, and tailors could all find work in cities like Boston, New York, Philadelphia, and Charleston, as well as in rural America where a lack of transportation protected them from competition. Throughout the American countryside, men with handiwork skills often found themselves crafting and repairing what the country's yeomen farmers and their families could not do for themselves. Prior to the road, canal, and railroad booms that followed the War of 1812, each rural village had its own craft system of blacksmiths, tailors, and shoemakers for things that local farm families could not do themselves. Where farm women had traditionally sewn precut clothing, for instance, the market and transportation revolutions brought cheap, ready-made garments instead. While in the 18th century only about 5 percent of America's population lived in towns as large as 2,500 and by 1775 the largest city had 30,000 people, these urban areas led the young country through the transformations of the early republic. Artisans embraced and resisted change, lost ground and gained it, and helped shape the changes with their reactions.

Life in the Artisan Shop

American artisans worked according to a system dictated by long held craft practices that their forefathers had brought with them from Europe. These craftsmen knew they were part of a work hierarchy that included master craftsmen, journeymen, and apprentices regardless of the craft they practiced. Craftsmen supported this system because it allowed for both a measure of quality control and the promise of economic independence if one followed the rules. Apprentices and journeymen labored ultimately to become master craftsmen, to own their own shops, and to exert some control over their craft. For instance, in Boston in 1790, 45 percent of journey-

A man and three young apprentices setting type on a printing press in Philadelphia. Nineteenth-century woodcut from *Adams, Typographia*. (*Library of Congress*)

men had become masters in their crafts (Lubow 1997). Many journeymen, however, never became master craftsmen, and in crafts like shipbuilding, where an entrepreneur needed large sums of money to start a business, becoming a master was unlikely.

Every artisan began as an apprentice during his teenage years and spent three to seven years thereafter learning the mysteries of the craft from the shop's master craftsman, who often became a kind of surrogate father. Young boys like Ben Franklin, whose parents could not support all of their children or who could not guarantee all of their futures, willingly indentured their children to master craftsmen so that they could acquire a foundation for their adult lives. Under the terms of the indenture, in return for the labor of the apprentice, master craftsmen guaranteed their charges room, board, and a rudimentary education. As Franklin's experience suggests, unhappy apprentices ran away. Newspaper ads abounded in the early republic wherein masters sought news about and the return of their runaway apprentices. One Philadelphia master named Zachariah Lawrence was in search of 14-year-old runaway Ezra Westcot in February 1795 and offered "half a dollar reward" to anyone who returned the young tailoring apprentice to him, so that he could finish his indenture. The same day another master from Princeton, New Jersey, advertised for a very troublesome apprentice named John Clerk. Master John M'Clellen offered only "half a cent" for the return of "rude" John who apparently had a drinking problem and habits that "render[ed] him unsafe to be trusted where goods are easily embezzled." Although John was worth only half a cent, his master M'Clellen still sought the return of his apprenticed investment (Smith 1995, 98).

Apprenticeships could be difficult and unrewarding, but if boys successfully finished the terms of their contracts, they were ready to become independent journeymen who boasted skills and commanded respect. When a young man finished his years as an apprentice, the shop's master would give him new clothes and a set of tools to mark his entrance into the brotherhood of the craft. Now a journeyman, this skilled young man could sell his labor of his own free will and expect to be paid by the day or the piece. He would often contract with a single master, sometimes live in the master's house, and hope to accumulate enough wealth to begin his own shop in a few years, thus completing the journey from apprentice to master craftsman. As Boston's 45 percent success rate in 1790 shows, however, apprenticing in a craft and then working hard as a journeyman guaranteed nothing. When the economy was good, artisans might do well, but illness or an economic recession could throw many a skilled man's lot in with the unskilled and much reviled "lower sort."

The outcome, of course, was different for enslaved apprentices and journeymen. Although slaves also endured apprenticeships and learned the mysteries of various crafts, especially those useful to plantation life like blacksmithing and carpentry, their skills freed them only from fieldwork. Similarly, free white boys who did not finish their apprenticeships might expect to scrape by from season to season as wage-dependent day laborers with neither security nor respect.

The American Revolution changed the expectations and ambitions of artisans. As a country that openly broke free of the shackles of hereditary aristocracies, the American craftsman stood to gain a great deal of status in this yeoman's republic. Independence for skilled craftsmen also meant new opportunities to actively participate in the market. Between 1783 and 1830 changes in banking and credit targeted the hopes of these ordinary Americans. New York, in fact, chartered a bank for mechanics in 1810. After the American Revolution, artisans formed their own mutual benefit societies so that they could enjoy the fraternal bonds they had forged through their apprenticeships and in their shops. They also used this fellowship to control prices and craft production. These groups, however, never exerted the control of the English guilds, and this difference both helped and hurt American artisans. Artisans boasted skills and owned tools that generally elevated their status above the day laborers, servants, and slaves in their midst. These men sported leather aprons as a sign of their achieved status. They were neither too high nor too low in the social hierarchy. Prior to the Revolution, they had deferred to those above them on the social scale, but they always understood that their work was essential to their communities. After the war, artisans believed that they were the perfect citizens for the new republic, because they had earned their status by honest hard work, not because of their family name.

By the 1780s, changes arrived in the artisan shop. When Americans cut their political ties with Great Britain, they also lost the benefits and protections of the empire's mercantile system. Masters began to experiment with markets beyond their immediate communities, as the new federal government sought ways to support domestic economic growth. While some master craftsmen busily looked beyond their communities for business opportunities, many failed in their paternalistic craft obligations, often only feeding and housing apprentices without paying attention to their education or moral upbringing. As these urban masters were on the frontlines of the birth of a national market economy, they brought their goods into rural communities where artisans had previously proved indispensable for building and repairing almost everything. This change also disrupted the lives and livelihoods of rural artisans.

In spite of the inexorable changes that came with the birth of a national market economy, before the War of 1812 most journeymen worked as they had before the American Revolution. Although mass production, though not on the scale of the late 19th century, would make it more difficult for journeymen to become master craftsmen, for the time being journeymen still labored in small shops of three to five workers and enjoyed familiar daily routines. The workshops tended to be on the first floors of two- or three-story buildings and opened onto the street for business. The master's family generally lived on the upper floor or floors. These men worked together and continued to labor with their hand tools as artisans had done prior to the Revolution. They might enjoy one another's company as they worked to complete a customer's order. They chatted, drank beer and rum, took breaks for sweets, and worked hard. Tailors, for instance, might take an order from a lady for a riding coat; she would come to the shop for measurements, return for fitting and refitting, and then come one last time for the final touches. Part of the craft system allowed journeymen to enjoy a great deal of independence, because advancement to journeyman status meant that they had completed their training and the master could trust their skills. So journeymen worked with the respect they had earned as they completed whole projects and perhaps gained satisfaction from completing each step of the process while they finished a coat, a chair, or a pair of shoes.

Postrevolutionary artisanal pride manifested itself most broadly in New York City when in 1785 representatives from 31 crafts formed the General Society of Mechanics and Tradesmen (GSMT). This society, the first multicraft group of its kind, organized itself democratically with a president, vice president, secretary, and treasurer. Members elected their officers once a year by secret ballot. Like the smaller craft-specific benevolent groups, the GSMT charged dues to each member so that it could provide security and education to members and their children. They also used the dues for dinners and entertainment, certificates, and other sundry needs. This group, however, did not provide journeymen with the kinds of protection they later found they needed in their own societies and in later union organization. The General Society of Mechanics and Tradesmen, in fact, boasted a membership of New

Duncan Phyfe (1768–1854)

Perhaps America's best-known postrevolution-ary craftsman, Duncan Phyfe (1768–1854) is also considered the finest American cabinet-maker of his time. Phyfe's life experiences illus-trate the importance of skill as well as luck for every man who wanted to become a master craftsman in a trade like cabinetmaking where finished products could also be considered works of art. Phyfe was born Duncan Fife in Scotland but emigrated to America with his mother and sisters when he was 16. They set-tled in Albany, New York, where Duncan served a six-year apprenticeship with a cabinetmaker. In 1792, he decided to try his luck in New York City, where he changed the spelling of his

Considered by many as the greatest of all Ameri-can furniture makers, Duncan Phyfe was a princi-pal proponent/creator of the American Federal and the American Empire styles of furniture design. He also introduced the factory system into American cabinetmaking. (*Cirker, Hayward and Blanche Cirker, eds.* Dictionary of American Portraits, *1967*)

York's more prominent master craftsmen like cabinetmaker Duncan Phyfe. Although the society did not write journeymen out of their constitution, it was rare for lesser masters and journeymen to join. From its inception in 1785, however, through its heyday between 1801 and 1810, the GSMT lob-bied for things that all craftsmen found useful. With a membership between six and seven hundred around 1810, the society worked successfully for pro-tective tariffs, the defeat of a local workshop proposal, and the incorporation of the city's highest-capitalized bank. Although master craftsmen enjoyed the status of their exclusive society, they understood their importance as advo-cates for the artisan tradition prior to 1815 and market revolution.

"Great Transformations"

The economic warfare necessitated by the War of 1812, however, ushered in revolutionary market, transportation, and industrial changes and thus

name to Phyfe and set up shop on Broad Street, embarking on a journey in the furniture business. With limited prospects, Phyfe almost returned to Albany, but fortuitously the daughter of John Jacob Astor befriended him, and her patronage allowed him to stay in business. Because of his masterful skills and his strict Calvinist work ethic, he prospered thereafter, and his work reached both national and international markets.

As both artist and businessman, Phyfe, like other craftsmen in the early republic, found he had to balance his own craftsmanship with fashion. The styles of Englishmen George Hepplewhite and Thomas Sheraton influenced Phyfe's early neoclassical furniture. Using carved bows and eagles, Phyfe's work is noted for fine curves, its ornamental value, and the decorative use of the wood. By the end of the 1810s, however, Americans sought a heavier French Empire style. As a result, Phyfe the businessman complied with the demands of the market and made what some called butcher furniture because of its heavy, solid lines. Phyfe's business savvy was rewarded, however, as he became extremely wealthy himself. When he died, he had accumulated assets of over $500,000.

Of all the crafts in early America, cabinetmaking offered ordinary artisans little opportunity for advancement beyond journeyman status. The craft's many refinements required knowledge of drawing, proportion, style, woods and textures, veneering, gluing, varnishing, and joint construction. For a master craftsman like Phyfe, when the market and transportation revolutions expanded the possibilities for his furniture, he expanded business by supervising a large group of journeymen who worked on very specialized parts of the process from veneering to glazing. At the height of his business, Phyfe employed over 100 men. When he retired in 1847, he had three work buildings and a house, all on Fulton Street, and it was in this house that he died in 1854.

a new era for artisans. These "great transformations," as one historian has called them, ultimately did away with self-sufficiency and craft pride (Laurie 1989, 15). Through the final years of the early republic, artisans embraced opportunity, watched much of the craft system erode, organized protests and some strikes, became entrepreneurs and wage laborers, and began to express not an artisanal point of view but rather a number of class-conscious perspectives on the economy, politics, and social life in general.

Certainly Jefferson's Embargo in 1807 stimulated domestic manufactures, and American manufactories got their starts during these early years. Samuel Slater's textile mills in Pawtucket, Rhode Island, began manufacturing woolen cloth in 1815, and the Boston Manufacturing Company of Waltham, Massachusetts, began the most famous antebellum factory system at Lowell in 1826. While the stories of Slater and Lowell may be the most dramatic, these large-scale shifts from artisan shops to industrial wage labor were not the most common experience in the early republic. Changes in the mode of production within smaller shops, in fact, had the most profound effect on early American artisans.

As markets grew in the early 19th century, transportation improvements followed, and as transportation became cheaper and more efficient, manufacturing and agricultural production for the market grew. Although this market revolution had certainly begun by the 1780s, artisans felt its effects most strongly after the War of 1812. The market economy shifted domestic production initially from home-based need and a local barter economy to men and families consciously setting aside part of a crop or a few premade pairs of shoes for sale elsewhere. People began to consider making goods for future sale rather than for immediate consumption. Both urban and rural artisans were drawn into an impersonal market where their relationships were shaped less by community values and more by economic demands.

Transportation had been exorbitantly expensive prior to Robert Fulton's successful 1807 trip from New York to Albany in his steamboat *Clermont* and the canal boom that followed in the 1820s. With the canal age and the completion of the Erie Canal in particular in 1825, Americans connected the trans-Appalachian West to the major ports of the East and ushered in a new era for domestic trade. In the 1790s and 1800s Americans had paid to build turnpikes of plank wood and stone with drainage ditches on either side to protect the roads in foul weather. Although these turnpikes successfully connected seaport towns with their hinterlands prior to 1820, the canal phase of the transportation revolution brought about national, not local, changes. New York Governor DeWitt Clinton's Erie Canal drastically cut the cost of transportation to and from the New York interior. Freight rates from Buffalo to New York City, for instance, decreased from $100 per ton by land to only $10 per ton by the canal. New York's canal also opened up the Great Lakes and their far-reaching tributaries to easy trade with the East. By the 1830s, the nation had a complete water route from New York City to New Orleans, and by 1840 the nation boasted 3,300 miles of canals. Some, like Senator Henry Clay of Kentucky, dreamed of an American System where manufacturers in the Northeast would produce finished goods for the South and the West, the West would grow affordable foodstuffs for the Northeast, and the South would produce large-scale agricultural products like cotton and tobacco for export and use in other regions. The American economy of the 1820s and 1830s was increasingly national, even as most Americans lived rural lives and continued to rely on local production for most of their needs. Nine out of ten Americans lived on the land in 1790, and by 1860 eight out of ten still lived there.

The economic possibilities contained in the post–War of 1812 growth of America fueled a manufacturing revolution as well. The artisan shop could not survive in the face of the new entrepreneurial spirit of the 1820s and beyond. It seems that optimism and easy credit encouraged merchants, manufacturers like the Boston Manufacturing Company, farmers, and even artisans to devote more of their resources to investing in future production.

Entrance of the Canal into the Hudson at Albany (circa 1823), a depiction of boats traveling on the Erie Canal by historical artist James Eights. (*Whitford, Noble E.* History of the Canal System of the State of New York, *1906*)

By the time Andrew Jackson took the presidency in 1829, Americans in general seemed to accept the single-minded pursuit of profit as their birthright. This self-interest, however, did not always complement how artisans had historically organized production. Craft production had been based on a system of mutual benefit and considerations for the community. What some historians have called artisan republicanism seemed at odds with these market changes. According to the tenets of classical republican theory, the individual must always subordinate self-interest to the best interests of the community. Between the Revolution and the rise of Jackson, the artisan shop underwent changes that often divided the interests of masters and their journeymen, and these artisans interpreted and employed republican discourse to understand and mediate the changes.

Whereas some manufacturers had enough capital to invest in large factories like the shoe and textile manufactories of Lynn and Lowell Massachusetts or even the Tredegar Iron Works in Richmond, Virginia, most artisans endured the changes to their way of life as they participated in the move from the shop system of master-journeyman-apprentice to what was known as the sweating system, which kept labor in homes and in small shops but denied the laborers control of each step of the process. In Lowell and Lynn, the owners developed a managerial class to watch over the workers and dictate rules. They could expand production if demand increased simply by hiring more unskilled hands. Owners sought the labor of women because their wages were lower than those of men. Finally, the owners divided the manufacturing process into separate stages. These large manufactories certainly foreshadowed the future of production, but their methods would not dominate and define the ways that Americans worked until after the Civil War.

More commonly in the early 19th century, the sweating system proved the bane of the journeyman's existence. The businessmen who coordinated labor under this system were often former masters who sometimes formed partnerships with merchants. Without the large capital of the manufactories, these men could produce for the growing market by employing other methods. The resulting sweating system also facilitated the breakdown of mutually beneficial artisanal relationships and craft pride. Although workers "sweated" and continued to use hand tools in small shops and homes, the new system divided the labor into stages. Tailors, for instance, might have a skilled cutter cut many ladies' coats at once, but then the entrepreneur (perhaps a master craftsman) would send out different steps of the tailoring to different homes: the sleeves to one place, the buttons to another, and so on, until many jackets returned to his shop finished and ready for sale. Although the transition to manufactories and the sweating system did not happen overnight and even though, over the course of the early republic, many master craftsmen honored craft traditions, master and journeyman began to drift apart as employer and employee.

Confronting Change

As a group, journeymen realized that their chances of becoming master craftsmen were slimmer than ever in this new economy. During the give-and-take of the following decades, as journeymen became workingmen often without hope of owning land or their own shops, these artisans began to argue that they had a right to reliable wages that would allow them and their families a comfortable standard of living. At first, recognizing the growing divide between their interests and those of the master/employers, these journeymen formed mutual benefit societies to provide a sort of safety net in the case of illness or death and to aid in negotiations for wages and working conditions. They gave their groups names like Association of Journeymen Bookbinders, the United Society of Journeymen Tailors and the Practical House Carpenters' Society. In urban areas in particular, artisans from most of the larger trades formed fraternal organizations to pool resources for the sick or for families of deceased artisans, to join in social gatherings, and to maintain economic leverage in a changing market. Tailors, hatters, shipbuilders, carpenters, printers, butchers, bakers, and cabinetmakers all formed associations—some only for journeymen and some for masters as well. While artisan societies began to form in the 1780s and 1790s, the consciously separate journeymen's groups would become more important in the early 19th century.

During the Revolution, artisans had self-righteously appealed as ordinary citizens to the moral economy of their communities when they sensed injustice, but by 1830 their calls for a moral economy would be co-opted by the rough and tumble world of Jacksonian politics. In 1785, Benjamin Franklin, writing under the alias of Tradesman, angrily set the record straight in the

Certificate of membership in the General Society of Mechanics and Tradesmen, circa 1820. The Society was founded in 1785 as a mutual aid society for workmen and their families. The images illustrate the benevolent functions of society in the 1820s. A widow receives a money purse from a member while another shows an orphan the way to the school. In the background is a steamship and shipbuilding, both staples of the New York economy. In the four corners *putti* engage in manufacturing and agriculture. (*Library of Congress*)

Philadelphia papers when some of the city's well-to-do gentlemen argued that the wealthy had a greater stake in the city than the poor and that these working people could simply leave the city and start over in another place like Baltimore or on the frontier. Tradesman challenged all the old colonial notions of social deference and made it clear that wearing a leather apron or working with one's hands did not make a man expendable. He appealed, in fact, to the revolutionary-era assertions of republican equality, arguing that wealthy speculators were the worst social parasites. In Philadelphia a number of these businessmen suggested that mechanics who had fallen on hard times should simply sell their homes and move to another city or "go and buy lands amongst the savages." Tradesman believed these men used the misery of the poor to benefit themselves, saying:

> No—savage wretch as thou art, who would wish us all scalped that thou and thy greedy associates might enjoy our little patrimonies;—thou shalt never revel in our hard earned estates;—we will stay in defiance of thee and thy whole race. (*Independent Gazeteer*, January 22, 1785)

Tradesman spoke to a city whose residents understood—and some might even support—the idea of a moral economy in which the community acknowledged, among other things, the right of every man to make a decent wage. Those who subscribed to the tenets of the artisan shop, in theory, had understood these moral obligations. But as master craftsmen began to identify themselves more with a petty merchant class than with their journeymen, the artisan shop entered a transitional phase, and men like Tradesman became part of the transition to a market economy.

By the early 19th century, as masters aimed to keep their prices low to compete in the growing market economy, they often kept wages low or paid low rates for piecework. Based largely on the writings of the economist Adam Smith, one prevailing theory held that workers would prosper as long as worker organizations and the government allowed supply and demand to control the economy without interfering in business activities. But the journeymen did not seem to view the invisible hand so optimistically. Some believed they needed to take action. When the journeymen's societies could not negotiate what they believed was a fair agreement with master/employers, they might counsel their members to walk out on a single master, or they might try to organize a citywide walkout. They also tried to demand that masters hire only those who belonged to their societies. When masters in both New York and Philadelphia balked at this final demand in the first decade of the 19th century, journeymen staged significant walkouts and were taken to court for conspiracy in 1806 (Philadelphia) and 1809 (New York). In both of these trials, the court found the journeymen guilty of conspiring against other journeymen who wanted to work. Although the accused and their lawyers tried to show that all men had a right to protect themselves against unethical employers who violated community values and a moral economy, in the end the court found in favor of the prosecution, and the journeymen had to pay a fine. More importantly, however, these cases established limitations on the abilities of journeymen to organize and fight the impersonal changes of the market.

After the War of 1812, while the South lagged behind in the changes brought on by the market, transportation, and industrial revolutions, journeymen in Northern and Border states watched as their wages declined and their standards of living became more precarious. Many did not believe that the artisan system would protect them. By the 1820s, these changes, combined with a lack of faith that economic expansion would mean more and better opportunities for them, led journeymen and workingmen in general to organize and conceptualize the first labor movement in the United States. By December 1827, Philadelphia's journeymen had formed the nation's first collective trade association, hoping to protect their status and their wages. Unlike the craft-based associations of the postrevolutionary years, Philadelphia's Mechanic's Union of Trade Associations (MUTA) based membership not on craft—a criterion that would include well-to-do masters—but on status as wage-earning workers.

James Forten (1766–1842)

The life of sailmaker and abolitionist James Forten illustrates the possibilities for social mobility in early Philadelphia. He was born to free black parents on September 2, 1766, in Philadelphia, Pennsylvania. Although he and his parents were free, his father's father had been brought from Africa and made a slave, and Forten never lost sight of the importance of freedom for all men and women. His career began in a sail loft and ended in the halls of antislavery activism. He was an artisan, an inventor, an abolitionist, and one of the wealthiest Americans of his time. As a boy, young Forten benefited from the antislavery impulses alive in the city, taking advantage of Anthony Benezet's Quaker school for colored children. At 8, Forten began in the craft that would sustain him and make him a wealthy man; he began working alongside his journeyman father in the sail loft of Robert Bridges. When his father died in 1773 in a boating accident, young James took on more work and thus only attended school part-time.

During the American Revolution an exuberant 14-year-old Forten enlisted to help the patriot cause as a powder boy on one of the most heavily armed privateers out of Philadelphia, the *Royal Louis*. After his capture, Forten spent seven grueling months on board the British prison ship the *Jersey*. After the war, in 1785, Forten apprenticed himself to his former employer sailmaker Robert Bridges. He was 19, older than most apprentices, and advanced easily. By the next year, Bridges had made Forten the foreman of his sail loft and his handpicked successor. In 1798 Bridges retired from the loft and loaned Forten enough money to buy it for himself.

Eventually, master sailmaker James Forten became one of Philadelphia's wealthiest men. He used his money to advocate for abolition, temperance, and women's rights. As an employer he worked hard to secure black employment, but he was also committed to integration and kept all of Bridges white workers when he took over the loft. Forten personified the master artisan who not only worked with the men he employed, but also accepted the moral responsibilities of the craft system. His workers had to abide by his rules and values, laboring diligently and punctually, going to church, abstaining from drink, and always valuing thrift. By the time he died in 1842, Forten employed almost 40 men in his loft, worked hard for the cause of abolition, and contributed regularly to William Lloyd Garrison's *Liberator*. James Forten left behind a legacy that suggested the possibilities and disappointments of American independence and a vast market revolution.

By 1827, many Philadelphian workingpeople understood that the Revolution's egalitarian promises had not included them. The nation's laws evolved with the market economy, individual property rights continued to take precedence over more radical ideas of economic justice, and workingpeople began to see themselves not as day laborers and skilled craftsmen, but as workers with collective interests and collective rights. Out of Philadelphia's unsettled working district, a 27-year-old cordwainer named William Heighton emerged to lead and define the objectives of this workingman's movement. The dynamic Heighton was born in 1800 in Northamptonshire,

England, and grew up poor in Philadelphia's Southwark district. He committed himself as a young man to his own intellectual development. Although he worked hard to feed his family as a cordwainer, he found time to feed his curiosity through reading. Perhaps finding their calls for justice most compelling, he favored the Bible and English socialism. By the fall of 1827, he delivered a number of public addresses in which he laid out his plan to release wage workers from the "iron chain of bondage" (Foner 1991, 69).

In November 1827, Heighton delivered a prolabor speech in Philadelphia's Southwark neighborhood. He asked his listeners to think about their futures in the context of the Revolution's egalitarian promises and certain new theories on the social and economic value of labor. Heighton had been reading the works of British economist David Ricardo and socialist John Gray. Like many early 19th-century labor organizers, he was particularly taken by Ricardo's labor theory of value, which asserted that labor gave value to raw materials and thus should determine the price of any product. In his speech, he called on the city's workingpeople to demand a redistribution of the city's wealth based on this compelling idea. "[W]e labor hard in producing all the comforts of life for the enjoyment of others, while we ourselves obtain but a scanty portion," he told his audience. Making clear the injustice of it all, he attacked the wealthy:

> The princely places, the magnificent mansions, the splendid equipages, the costly plate, the elegant and convenient furniture, with all the variety of rich and palatable viands, are solely the productions of the working class, who, after producing them, are legally but unjustly prevented from the enjoyment they yield. (Foner 1991, 69)

Heighton blamed not only the wealthy, but also the laws that Americans had passed for what he called "legal extortion." By the end of the speech, he urged his listeners to fight injustice themselves.

Over the next two years, Heighton and his followers defined the early American labor movement by seeking tangible change through education and organization. They established the *Mechanics' Free Press* to educate the evolving working class on important social, political, and economic issues. As did other cities, they also supported a separate mechanics' library, wherein workingmen could take time to uplift themselves. Why was education so important to these labor leaders? They argued that historically workingmen had relinquished their power and their wealth out of ignorance. Heighton even argued that wealthy politicians used laws to chain the working class to poverty. As a result, this early labor movement eschewed radical social upheaval for calculated political change. Its proponents argued that workingmen should slowly gain enough political power to win the rights, economic and political, that the Revolution had promised them. And Heighton understood the power of numbers. He urged Philadelphia's workers to move away from individual trade-based organizations and toward a unified and generalized citywide trade union. This time organizers clearly advocated not a beneficial society like the one New Yorkers had established in 1785, but a union that would act for economic change.

This was the first time in American history—reflecting the changes that the new market economy brought to the artisan way of life—that workingmen, regardless of skill level, were called on to think of themselves as worker-producers with a common interest that stood in direct contrast to that of the nonproducers who profited from their hard work. Localized, craft-specific strikes like those of 1806 and 1809 in Philadelphia and New York had only disappointed artisans and had made them wary of using the strike to achieve their goals because it seemed to lead to loss rather than to gain. One all-encompassing union, instead, would provide workingmen with a powerful counterforce to early 19th-century economic oppression. "We must no longer cherish the vulgar idea," said Heighton, "that one occupation is more respectable than another." Philadelphia workingmen must have agreed with him to some extent, because in early December 1827 they met at Tyler's Tavern to form the country's first labor union. They argued in their associative constitution that they had less than they deserved and that "feeling our inability, individually, to ward off from very excessive accumulation of wealth and power into the hands of a few, are desirous of forming an Association" ("Preamble of the Mechanics Union of Trade Associations' Constitution," October 25, 1828). Thus, a diverse group of skilled and unskilled workers formed the Mechanic's Union of Trade Associations, also known as MUTA. The next year they helped form a Workingmen's Party in the city, but by 1830 the party had endorsed not its own candidate but candidates from the mainstream Whig and Democratic parties.

Conclusion

By 1830, economic and technological forces had laid siege to the craft system and the artisan shop in America. A discouraged William Heighton left Philadelphia after watching the Democrats in particular co-opt the ideas of his beloved Workingmen's Party. The growth of a market economy after the War of 1812 had already jeopardized Thomas Jefferson's dream of a yeoman farmer's republic. Domestic manufactures increased every decade as artisans continued to labor as apprentices, journeymen, and master craftsmen. Many of these craftsmen might have wondered at Jefferson's prescience as he predicted that a manufacturing system would degrade workers and thus the republic. These men already understood that they were becoming just workers.

References and Further Reading

Blewett, Mary H. "Work, Gender and the Artisan Tradition in New England Shoemaking, 1780–1860." In Peter N. Stearns, ed. *Expanding the Past: A*

Reader in Social History, 119–146. New York: New York University Press, 1988

Foner, Philip S. *William Heighton: Pioneer Labor Leader of Jacksonian Philadelphia. With Selections from Heighton's Writings and Speeches.* New York: International Publishers, 1991

Ford, Paul Leicester, ed. *The Writings of Thomas Jefferson.* 10 vols. New York: G. P. Putnam's Sons, 1892–1899

Foster, A. Kristen. *Moral Visions and Material Ambitions: Philadelphia Struggles to Define the Republic, 1776–1836.* Lanham, MD: Lexington Books, 2004

Franklin, Benjamin. *Writings.* Edited by J. A. Leo Lemay. New York: Library of America, 1987

Gilje, Paul, ed. *Wages of Independence: Capitalism in the Early American Republic.* Madison, WI: Madison House, 1997

Jefferson, Thomas. *Notes on the State of Virginia.* Richmond, VA: J. W. Randolph, 1853

Laurie, Bruce. *Artisans into Workers: Labor in Nineteenth-Century America.* New York: Hill and Wang, 1989

Lubow, Lisa Beth. "From Carpenter to Capitalist: The Business of Building in Post-Revolutionary Boston." In Conrad Edick Wright and Kathryn P. Viens, eds. *Entrepreneurs: The Boston Business Community, 1700–1800,* 181–209. Boston: Massachusetts Historical Society and Northeastern University Press, 1997

Rock, Howard B. *Artisans of the New Republic: The Tradesmen of New York City in the Age of Jefferson.* New York: New York University Press, 1979

Rock, Howard B., ed. *New York City Artisan, 1789–1825: A Documentary History.* Albany: State University of New York, 1989

Rock, Howard B., Paul A. Gilje, and Robert Asher, eds. *American Artisans: Crafting Social Identity, 1750–1850.* Baltimore, MD: Johns Hopkins University Press, 1995

Schultz, Ronald. *The Republic of Labor: Philadelphia Artisans and the Politics of Class, 1720–1830.* New York: Oxford University Press, 1993

Smith, Billy G., ed. *Life in Early Philadelphia: Documents from the Revolutionary and Early National Periods.* University Park: Pennsylvania State University Press, 1995

Smith, Billy G. *The "Lower Sort": Philadelphia's Laboring People, 1750–1800.* Ithaca, NY: Cornell University Press, 1990

Sutton, William R. *Journeymen for Jesus: Evangelical Artisans Confront Capitalism in Jacksonian Baltimore.* University Park: Pennsylvania State University Press, 1998

Wilentz, Sean. *Chants Democratic: New York City and The Rise of the American Working Class, 1788–1850.* New York: Oxford University Press, 1984

Freeborn Americans: The Rise of the Urban Wage Earner and the Rhetoric of the Early Republic

2

Jessica M. Parr

Introduction

In 1836, 12-year-old Lucy Larcom began working in the textile mills of Lowell, Massachusetts. Larcom's path to the mills was in many ways the culmination of an era of change, during which thousands of other Americans moved to the nation's towns and engaged in wage work for the first time. Born in Beverly, Massachusetts, Lucy's decision to become a millworker was born in tragedy. After her father died at sea when she was 10, her widowed mother moved Lucy and her three sisters to Lowell to take a position managing a boardinghouse for the Lawrence Manufacturing Company. Young Lucy was, at least initially, fascinated by the mill girls: "their independence, their pride in their ability to earn money and control their lives, impressed her far more deeply than she realized at the time" (Marchalonis 1989, 28). Despite her mother's intentions, Lucy would soon join those whom she admired. When Mrs. Larcom's wages could not sustain the family, she turned to her young daughters to make up the difference. Lucy Larcom and her sisters became mill girls soon after they arrived in the mill town.

For her part, Lucy largely enjoyed the new arrangement. At first, she worked changing the bobbins on the spinning frames, work that was frequently reserved for young children. Like other working mill children under the age of 13, Lucy worked nine months out of the year. The other three months, she attended school as was required. Workers in the mills received wages that ranged between \$1.85 and \$3.00 a week. Although these rates were considered high for the time, they were significantly less than what men made and hardly enough to support a family. Children, not surprisingly, received less than adults. In their first year of working at the mill, the four Larcom girls collectively earned only about $230 (Dublin 1993, 98). Gradually, Lucy grew restless with the mill life and dreamt of a career writing and teaching, a profession she would eventually practice as an adult (Larcom 1973, 161).

Although thousands of Americans moved to towns and took wage work in the early republic, the experiences of the Larcom sisters were unusual in a significant way. Despite the upheaval of their lives, they remained together as a family. As is evident in Sarah Hodgdon's story, most mill girls were separated from their families when they took their jobs. Moreover, the Larcoms were from a seafaring family, whereas most mill exployees came from farms. However, the basic story of children going to work to help support their families was not at all unusual in the early years of the American Industrial Revolution. Lucy's 10-year stint as a mill girl is just one story of many. She lived and worked during an important period of labor history, in which the American economy and labor system underwent a dramatic transformation from an agricultural to an industrialized society. In 1790, approximately 90 percent of the population was comprised of farmers, the majority of whom grew crops for their own subsistence, rather than for market (Appleby 2000, 63). Following on the heels of the American Revolution, the economy began the gradual change toward industrialization that continued well beyond the early republican era. By 1830, the percentage of farmers was on an endless decline as the nation increasingly became a land of wage workers and urban dwellers. In the early republic alone, the major cities saw tremendous growth, with Philadelphia's population increasing by 114 percent, New York's by 191 percent, Boston's by 84 percent, and Baltimore's by 156 percent.

This chapter expounds on the experiences of urban wage earners like Lucy Larcom and offers a glimpse into everyday life in the early republic. It discusses the social, economic, and political forces behind the experience of the urban wage earner, as well as exploring the influence of workers themselves on industrialization in early America. In many ways, this is the history of the working class and their toils to support themselves, but it is also about their efforts to assert control of their lives and labors and to carve a place for themselves in a tumultuous American society. Much as the legacy of the American Revolution informed the American national consciousness, it also informed the class consciousness that is an important piece of the story of the rise of the urban wage earner. Indeed, as historian Jacqueline Jones observes, "ordinary workers served as the backbone of the rebellion, especially in the cities" (Jones 1999, 56). The participants of Boston's famous Tea Party included sailors, coopers, blacksmiths, printers, rope makers, and other colonial urban workers. Jones continues that "the genius of the American Revolution was its rhetoric of freedom and liberty that could be appropriated by so many different kinds of workers for so many different purposes" (Jones 1999, 56). When the war ended, these workers sought to make their new nation in their own image.

Sarah Hodgdon

Sarah Hodgdon was born in 1814 in Rochester, New Hampshire, to Abner and Mary Hodgdon. She was the oldest of four children. The Hodgdon family was well respected in the community. Sarah's father was a trustee of the local Methodist church. In 1830, at the age of 16, Sarah left home to work at the Merrimack Company in Lowell, Massachusetts, along with her friend, Elizabeth, and a neighbor, Wealthy Page.

Several of her letters home have survived, documenting Sarah's 10-year stint as a mill girl. Her sense of separation from her family is evident in her letters, although she repeatedly reassured her family that she was safe and content. Letters from Wesley Page to the Hodgdon family also reassured them of Sarah's good health. Later letters exchanged between Sarah and her sister, another Elizabeth, also indicated that from time to time she expressed an eagerness to return home. Even then, she does not appear to have ever mentioned this desire in her letters to her parents.

During her tenure at the Merrimack Company, Sarah lived in a company-owned boardinghouse, along with Elizabeth and Wealthy. The three friends worked together in the same weaving room of the factory, an average of approximately 11 hours a day, 6 days a week. On Sundays, many millworkers attended church, although the letters note Sarah's reluctance to pay the pew rental fee, common in urban churches. Sarah's earnings amounted to $1 a week. Although paltry by contemporary standards, the average mill worker in 1830 made just half that. Indeed, Sarah's earnings are generous by comparison and in all likelihood were tendered in addition to room and board.

Eventually, Sarah went on to work at the Great Falls Manufacturing Company, though the exact date is unknown. Like many of her female contemporaries, Sarah did not spend the rest of her life working in the mills. In 1845, she married Rochester shoemaker William Jenness. Little is known about her life after the mills, but the couple is believed to have remained in Rochester for at least 15 years after their marriage.

As will become evident in this chapter, Revolutionary ideology, industrialization, consumer consciousness, and class consciousness were all interlinked. In the early republic, scholars have concluded that there was "a powerful link between political and economic freedom" and between "the commercialization and democratization of the United States" (Appleby 2000, 56, 58). Even before the Revolution, there was a drive toward individual economic independence. In 1768, for example, Philadelphia shopkeeper Charles Thompson wrote a letter that asserted the necessity of the cooperation of the city's merchants in the battle against new British importation taxes. Thompson signed his letter "A Freeborn American" (Schultz 1993, 3). Through the War of Independence, the United States attained political freedom from Britain. For many Americans, true independence from Great Britain also required that the United States attain full economic freedom. Naturally, this rhetoric placed a heavy burden on the successful development of American commerce.

Urban Regionalism

The United States did not develop or industrialize evenly across the states. The South's economy remained significantly more rural and agricultural than the North's. The South would urbanize, but urban manufacturing centers, such as the textile mills of Lowell, Massachusetts, developed much earlier in the North than in the South. Not surprisingly, most of the major urban manufacturing centers were also port cities; New York, Boston, Baltimore, and Philadelphia were among the largest centers. Shipping naturally led factory owners to be in close proximity to the ports. As a result, Philadelphia was the largest and wealthiest urban manufacturing center in the latter half of the 18th century. Its busy ports were the largest source of employment, and they further created an expanding market for luxury goods and services from a variety of workers. As a result, Philadelphia filled with coachmen, booksellers, and jewelers (Smith 1990, 67).

New York, Baltimore, and Boston rivaled Philadelphia as important port cities. In addition to its status as an important port city and emerging financial center, New York boasted printing, construction, and modest textile and clothing industries. In fact, New York's ready-made clothing industry was a mainstay of "sweated labor" by the 1820s (Wilentz 1984, 39). For its part, by 1800, Boston had largely recovered from the significant economic damage that was caused by the wartime British occupation. Many of Boston's popular occupations—like shipwrights, ship carpenters, and sailmakers—were connected to Boston's maritime world, and these jobs continued to return after the war. Boston was also home to large printing and building construction industries and to a thriving service industry (Carr 2004, 148–49, 152). In 1790, Baltimore was the fourth largest city in the United States, after Boston, Philadelphia, and New York (Steffen 1984, 3). In addition to its status as an important trade port, Baltimore boasted large industries in shoemaking, clothing, and construction. Between 1794 and 1815, the three occupations combined comprised 52 percent of all crafts (Steffen 1984, 30). In the postwar years, the city experienced an influx of workers who flooded the market.

Wage workers did not reside only in larger cities. The young nation also contained smaller urban centers, such as the Massachusetts towns of Lynn, Lawrence, and Lowell. Lynn, as previously noted, boasted important shoe and barrel-making industries. Lawrence and Lowell had burgeoning textile industries that were fed by the mass production of Southern cotton, a development made possible by the invention of Eli Whitney's cotton gin in 1793.

In all of these areas, industrialization began to shift the labor focus from individual households to outside the household (Jones 1999, 38). In his analysis of the rise of New York City's working class, historian Bruce Laurie notes the first major rural-to-urban migration as occurring between 1780 and 1810 (Laurie 1997, 36). Between 1790 and 1800, New York City's population increased by over 80 percent. An outbreak of war, an embargo, and multiple outbreaks of yellow fever did not quell the rabid population boom;

Buildings of a cotton mill line the banks of the Merrimack River in Lowell, Massachusetts, during the Industrial Revolution of the 19th century. (*Library of Congress*)

between 1800 and 1820, New York's population nearly tripled (Wilentz 1984, 25). Migration was driven, in part, by a sense that the it would afford new economic possibilities for the worker (Jones 1999, 93).

Democratic Ambition

As suggested in the introduction, the legacy of the American Revolution was a formidable force in transforming all aspects of American culture and society, including the American labor system and the rise of urban wage earners. An important part of this rhetoric, as it pertains to industrialization, was what historian Joyce Appleby calls the "democratization of ambition" (Appleby 2000, 133). This phrase describes the notion that social mobility could be attained by the common man; anyone had the opportunity for success, and no one was inevitably trapped into the social standing of his or her birth. This ideology did not match reality, particularly for nonwhites, but social mobility was an important part of the contemporary rhetoric. As a result, "class standing, economic position and occupation" replaced birthright as important measurements for an individual's standing in society (Nash 1986, 4). The perceived attainment of social mobility led people to move in search of better economic opportunities. It also led them to purchase material representations of social standing. As a result, the Revolution helped bolster the rise of consumption and consumer credit. In many ways, this was the beginning of the proverbial American dream, as the social equality of urban centers was measured by an individual's ability to attain that dream (Nash 1996, 5).

Benjamin Franklin stands as one of the most prolific examples of what the American was supposed to be. The son of a humble candlemaker who ran away from his printing apprenticeship in Boston to Philadelphia, Franklin used the printing skills he had acquired in his erstwhile apprenticeship along with his science background to create a successful business for himself (Jones 1999, 35). He became the proverbial American success story: a man of humble origins, who, through the fruits of his own labor, became not only his own boss (and as such controlled his own labor) but also a wealthy man and a political force in the creation of the new republic. He stood as proof positive that, in Philadelphia at least, it was indeed possible to attain control over one's own labor and achieve both social respectability and economic stability.

The Varieties of Labor

To better understand the world of urban wage earners, it is necessary to step back and take a moment to understand exactly who they were during the early republic. The social tier structure in early American society was the product of a system that had gradually evolved since the first European settlements. Wealthy and powerful landed interests occupied the top tier. Ship captains, merchants, and some types of artisans occupied a nebulous middle tier, or "middling sort." For the most part, urban wage earners occupied the lower echelons of society, just above slaves and indentured servants. Though there were different degrees of social respectability among individuals, they were often referred to as the lower sort by their contemporaries (Smith 1990, 1). These tiers were hardly fixed by birth, but few Americans at the time experienced rapid transformations of status.

The labor system of the early republic, as historian Jacqueline Jones notes, cannot be reduced to the simplistic free-labor-versus-slave-labor divide. The changes in free labor in the industrial period essentially complicated free labor, making it rather incoherent as a category. Prior to industrialization, free laborers were often usefully divided into skilled and unskilled groups. Unskilled laborers included washerwomen, porters, woodcutters, and factory workers. Skilled laborers included sailors and some lesser artisans, such as tailors, shoemakers, and coopers (Smith 1990, 4). With the exception of sailors, skilled labors were usually afforded a higher degree of social respectability than the unskilled. As in many other societies, there was a hierarchy among the workers, with master craftsmen ranking above journeymen and journeymen ranking above apprentices and common laborers. Certain types of craftsmen also held a higher social standing than others. As Charles Steffen notes, "those who fashioned products from clay or stone and those who manufactured luxury items were at the bottom" (Steffen 1984, 14).

During the early republic, occupation and class standing became increasingly related to one another. In Philadelphia, for example, workers were taxed in accordance with "the value of their occupations, in addition to their taxable goods and earnings" (Innes 1988, 225). Class standing was also related to one's ability to assert independence over their labor. Prior to American industrialization, labor was simply divided into free labor versus bound labor. Bound labor included slave labor, indentured servitude, and apprenticeships, even though slavery was usually a lifetime condition, and indentured servants and apprentices were bound to their masters for a limited period of time. The idea was for indentured servants and apprentices to one day transcend their existence under a bound labor system and become masters of their own labor. They were to do as Franklin had done.

The Rise of the Worker

Industrialization and the rise of wage work brought tremendous social changes to the workplace. During the preindustrial era, hopeful craftsmen followed a prescribed path from apprentices to journeymen to master craftsmen. Apprentices could expect, at least eventually, to become masters of their own shops. The progression toward industrialization made that prospect less of a certainty. During the last decades of the 18th century and the earliest decades of the 19th century, the demand for the skills of craftsmen decreased. The skills of artisans were gradually replaced by advancements in technology. As a result, many aspiring master craftsmen became trapped in what were once temporary journeyman roles. They became permanent wage earners or employees, rather than masters or masters-in-training. Thus, the distinction between craftsman and common laborer slowly disappeared, with fewer artisans in a position to become their own boss and exercise control over their own labor. In New York City, for example, artisans accounted for a very small part of the labor force by the 1820s (Laurie 1997, 28). To add insult to injury, the workday became more formal and structured than it had once been. Gone were the rum-laced breaks and camaraderie shared among the workers, journeymen, and masters. Master-journeymen tensions and resentments reigned in its place (Juravich et al. 1996, 2). These resentments, which are explored in more detail later in the chapter, came to a head in the 19th-century labor movements.

Improvements in technology account for many of the changes in the experiences of the urban wage earner, but other factors also shaped the lives of workers in the early republic. In Baltimore, as it did elsewhere, demographic growth and the democratic ideology put a strain on the apprentice system. The democratic impulse led many communities to limit the privileges afforded to well-connected long-term residents of the community. In short, local and state governments recognized that those with familial, business, or social connections had significant advantages when it came to securing a desirable apprenticeship. As historian Charles Steffen notes, the Maryland Assembly changed the laws to "bring coherence to the informal and unsystematic way that apprentice contracts had long been handled"

(Steffen 1984, 28). This informal system—common in the era—directly conflicted with the democratic rhetoric of the day. In Boston, for example, 13 of the 19 American-born master printers had connections to the Green family. The Green family, who were descended from Cambridge printer Samuel Green, had powerful business connections in government and industry that afforded lucrative printing contacts (Reese 1989, 344). Thus, those with ties to the Green family were at a considerable advantage. The new Maryland legislation was designed to circumvent such problems of privilege and give a larger percentage of the population a chance for better opportunities. Not surprisingly, other states sought similar forms of regulation.

The Age of Refinement

The expansion of consumer culture—the emergence of what has been recently called the Age of Refinement—was another important factor that drove the changes in the American labor system and that contributed to the decline of the artisan. Refinement had its roots in the end of the 17th century, but it escalated during the 18th century. Refinement was marked by a drive to infuse gentility into colonial life, the intent to make American communities more polished like the European cities, particularly London (Bushman 1993, 414–15). British-made consumer goods, particularly luxury goods, flew out of colonial and early American shops at a rapid pace. Little in the way of finery was produced domestically, and the consumer preference tended strongly toward what was manufactured in Britain anyway. On occasion, booksellers even falsified the book imprints of books published in the colonies to attract consumers. In the pursuit of refinement, Americans also purchased Wedgewood ceramics, fine silks, lace and damasks, and furniture (Breen 2004, 39–42, 168–69).

In the colonial era, the possession of imported goods became linked to social mobility; ownership of British goods was an outward indicator of success, as they were more or less "social props" (Breen 1988, 83). In other words, they were a visible measure of an individual's ability to attain his aspirations. Among the upper echelons of society, larger elegant homes boasted spacious entrances and richly decorated formal sitting parlors that were designed to impress visitors and emphatically state the social worth of the family. Those of more modest means hoped to merely upgrade their possessions. For instance, a humble farmer family might hope to upgrade their table service from crude wooden plates to pewter (Jones 1999, 36–37). Many of the architectural details (pillars and moldings) and furnishings of this period were reminiscent of the civilizations of ancient Rome and Greece. Among Wedgewood's first and most popular designs was a pattern with white statuesque classical figures on a blue field. Art historians refer to this style as neoclassical. It may seem surprising that the aesthetic trends of the day tended toward those of classical Rome and Greece when the colonists'

Architectural drawing of the interior of a proposed house in Virginia, by Benjamin Latrobe, circa 1795–1799. In the 18th century, refinement became associated with sumptuous possessions and large, elegant homes. Latrobe introduced the Greek revival syle into American architecture. (*Library of Congress*)

aim was to be more British. However, much of the political rhetoric that drove the American Revolution and, later, working class consciousness also invoked classical Greece and Rome. The aesthetics, the political ideologies, and social sensibilities were all connected.

Post-Revolutionary Consumerism

As mentioned previously, few of the products that were consumed in the pre-Revolutionary world were actually produced in the colonies. The American colonies had little capacity for the manufacture of goods. This changed in the early republic. After the war, the desire for the goods and refined status remained, but American nationalism and strained relations with Britain created a new economic and social environment (Faler 1981, 12). As a result,

Joseph Buckingham Tinker

Joseph Buckingham Tinker was born in 1779 to a poor, rural family. Following an apprenticeship to a farming family, he broke into the printing industry at the age of 17. Over the next four years, he served in a series of apprenticeships in Walpole, New Hampshire, and Greenfield, Massachusetts. He joined the Boston printing firm of Thomas and Andrews as a journeyman in 1800 and worked his way up to superintendent of mechanical operations in 1804.

Traditionally, printers were artisans who had the opportunity to eventually become master craftsmen and own their own shops. This system was dying out with the advent of new technology, and, as already noted, there was less of a distinction between the artisan and the common laborer. Tinker's career spanned an important period of transition in which it was increasingly difficult to break out of a laborer's role in every type of artisan's shop: "masters became 'bosses' and journeymen became 'hands'" (Juravich et al., 1996, 1–3). Thus, Tinker managed to transcend the "hands" role that

awaited many journeymen of that era. That his career began just ahead of the peak years of this labor transition was no doubt to his benefit.

The same year as his promotion, he changed his name to Joseph Tinker Buckingham to commemorate his success and new, hard-won "social autonomy" (Kornblith 1995, 124). He may not have owned his own shop, but his position did afford a degree of control over his life and labor that many in his position did not have. The following year, he married Melinda Alvord, with whom he had 13 children. The couple lived "in modest comfort," in a rented house. Like other men in his position, he did not expect to become rich, but he was very much concerned with attaining this "modest comfort" (Kornblith 1995, 125). To many Americans of this era, excessive wealth or its display was considered vulgar and carried undertones of aristocracy (Vickers 1990, 3–29). Buckingham's use of the rather ambiguous term "modest comfort" indicated that he was well aware of the sensibilities of the period. He wanted enough material comfort to

post-Revolutionary rhetoric placed a high premium on ending American dependence on British goods. Anti-British sentiment resulted in repeated boycotts, and it put pressure on the United States to meet consumer demands domestically. The exact nature of the goods that Americans purchased did not change after the Revolution, but the emphasis moved to buying goods manufactured in the United States. Americans, as Timothy Breen has written, were forced to "re-imagine themselves within an independent commercial empire" (Breen 1993, 492). The consumption of American goods remained a means by which the common man could express his political independence. By participating in consumer culture, individuals were "feeding themselves through their wages and thereby participating in the system of natural liberty" (Appleby 2000, 168). It was a great democratizer.

In the early American republic, consumption took on another meaning when placed in the context of the tension between federalism and antifederalism. Federalists were those who envisioned a strong federal government, presumably run by learned (namely, upper-class) men. Antifederalists sup-

indicate that he was not of the much maligned lower class, but he did not wish to be seen as ostentatious in his lifestyle. In essence, he hoped to join the ranks of the middling sort.

In 1810, Buckingham and a partner purchased Thomas and Andrew's shop for $4,500. Within five years, Buckingham was bankrupt, and it took him two years to recover his master status. In pursuit of this goal, in 1817, he established *New England Galaxy*, a weekly pamphlet. Within six years, he expanded his publishing interests to include a daily newspaper, *The Boston Courier*. Like his printing shop, his newspapers ran into a series of financial difficulties in the 1830s. He sold *New England Galaxy* to Boston abolitionist Samuel Gridley Howe and John O. Sargent in 1834. In the fall of 1837, he was forced to sell one-third interest of *The Courier* to Eben B. Foster in a desperate attempt to recover the precarious nature of his finances. Unfortunately, both efforts proved futile.

As a printer and publisher, Buckingham was among the more respectable wage earners. In spite of the ultimate failure of his businesses, Buckingham was a model of the republican notion of virtue among his contemporaries. As noted in this chapter, there was a significant focus on the virtue of success through hard work, or the self-made man. Buckingham even promoted himself as such: by his own account, he worked 12 to 16 hours a day. No doubt Buckingham saw himself as the virtuous republican worker and consciously worked to cultivate that image and project it to others.

Through hard work, he overcame his humble origins and became a member of the respectable "middling sort" (Kornblith 1995, 125). In other words, Buckingham attained a degree of social respectability that a poor, rural farmer would not have had, even if that rise in social and economic standing was precarious. As biographer and historian Gary Kornblith notes, the instability that Buckingham experienced was not unusual; rather, it was very much a part of the experience of the proverbial self-made man.

ported states' rights and feared that a strong federal government would impede the right of the individual, much as the British monarchy had done. In 1787, the leadership of the newly minted United States revised the Articles of Confederation, its first governing document. The United States Constitution, which was ratified in 1789 along with the Bill of Rights, marked an attempt to carefully balance the rights of the government with the rights of the individual. Material wealth had long been the domain of the wealthy elite, and the evolving capitalist system gave the illusion, at least, that Americans were on a more equitable social plane. Within that context, it is easy to see how allowing for broad participation in a consumer culture might help assuage fears of an American aristocracy. Americans sought not only commercial independence from Great Britain but also economic freedoms for the individual.

While seemingly unrelated to the rise of the urban wage earner, refinement was an important driving force in the industrialization of the early United States. In short, consumer demands, combined with post-Revolutionary rhetoric, forced American craftsmen and manufacturers to find a way to meet their demands without engaging in trade with Britain. The burgeoning shoe industry in Lynn, Massachusetts, exemplifies the rise of American production. Lynn shoemakers seized on the vacancy created by the boycott of British shoes and made great headway in the market during the American Revolution. After the Revolution, shoemakers and merchants faced fears that British goods, which were perceived to be superior, would regain their stranglehold on the American consumer market (Smith 1990, 13). Thus, they were selling not only their labor, but also the American *product* to the American *people*. A related consequence was that, in post-Revolutionary America, in addition to the physical products that American workers and laborers produced, American labor itself became a product for sale (Wilentz 1984, 5, 28).

Republicanism

Other common threads between refinement, Revolutionary ideology, and the rise of urban wage earners were the republican notions of equality and virtue. Most histories of labor action focus on the strikes and violence of the late 19th and 20th centuries. However, though early Republican workers and later workers shared many concerns, like the length of the workday and working conditions, the climate was not quite as intense as in later periods, and the extent of labor activism was not quite at the same level. It is important to remember that social, political, and intellectual movements develop and change over time, often increasing in intensity. The well-studied labor movements of the 19th and 20th centuries did not erupt out of the blue. Much of what occurred within the early republic served as a staging ground for labor activism and working class consciousness in the decades to come.

One of the most prolific labor leaders of this period was Seth Luther, a Rhode Island journeyman carpenter whose experience culminated in his being a key figure in the formation of the Boston Trades' Union in the mid-1830s. Drawing from the rhetoric of the Revolution, he declared that "The Declaration of Independence was the work of a combination, and was as hateful to the TRAITORS and TORIES of those days, as combinations among working men are now to the *avaricious* MONOPOLISTIC and *purse-proud* ARISTOCRAT" (Juravich et al. 1996, 14). Luther saw the unions as patriots who were opposed to the business owners, judges, lawyers, and other elites of the period. If necessary, workers, just like Revolutionary soldiers, had the right to use force against Tories to defend their rights. The battle between Luther's workers and the local government was tense at times but ultimately did not dissolve into violence (Juravich et al. 1996, 14). Instead, the struggle ran its course and resulted in *Commonwealth v. Hunt*, a feted 1840 conspiracy trial in which bootmaker Jeremiah Horne brought charges against the Boston Trades' Union for persuading his employer to fire him after he refused to pay a fine for violating the union's rules. Eventually, the Massachusetts Supreme

Judicial Court ruled in favor of the Union and effectively affirmed the right of Americans to unionize (Juravich et al. 1996, 13, 18).

As the story of the Boston bootmaker suggests, republicanism took on many meanings for different people in the early republic. Most commonly, it referred to rule, or control, by the common man. Equality and virtue were two desirable attributes with links to Enlightenment philosophy commonly found in the rhetoric of early American republicanism. This egalitarianism "placed tradesmen on equal footing with other citizens" (Rock 1979, 27). In the first years of the 19th century, tradesmen drew a sense that they could attain "the esteemed and responsible position in society that they sought" (Rock 1979, 45). No doubt empowering, this ideology helped to feed an emerging class collectivism in the early republic. When economic realities contradicted the rhetoric of republicanism, frustrations often mounted. In Philadelphia, for example, members of the laboring class took notice of the enormous inequity in the distribution of wealth. As Robert Schultz observes, "they saw men like themselves scrambling for work, accepting wages below custom, working outside their trades, and sacrificing their dignity to feed their families" (Schultz 1993, 30).

The Commodity of Labor

In the early republic, work was no longer a mere means of subsistence. Tradesmen demonstrated that they were increasingly unwilling to accept what they viewed as substandard working conditions and began to collectively negotiate for desirable wages and for the protection of their jobs from unqualified, cheaper workers. They saw their labor as a marketable commodity, and they sought control over that commodity. To that end, unions made use of public propaganda both against business with which they held grievances and in support of businesses whose labor practices the union deemed fair. Early union campaigns were rather common, albeit short-lived, in the early republic. For instance, on November 23, 1804, the Union Society of Journeyman Taylors [sic] printed an open letter to the public in New York City's *Evening Post*. In it, the tailors sought public support for their unionization, provided a list of businesses that employed its members, and asked readers to support these businesses (Rock 1989, 222–25). In 1819, the Journeyman Taylors placed an advertisement in the *Evening Post* asking for public support against the inclusion of women. The society argued that women could be hired at a lower rate and would thus undermine the male membership's ability to negotiate for higher wages (Marchalonis 1989, 26–27; Turbin 1987, 48–49).

The length of the workday was another important cause early in the labor movement. The average American worker in the early republic worked 6 days a week, at least 10 and sometimes as many as 14 hours a day. As the apprentice system deteriorated, "workers found themselves toiling much

A LIST OF PRICES

TO BE

GIVEN TO JOURNEYMEN,

AGREED ON BY

THE SOCIETY OF MASTER TAYLORS,

Of the City of New-York,

TWENTY-SECOND JANUARY, 1805, VIZ.

	S. D.
MENS' Coats, with quilted collars and paded,	19
Do. do. plain collars,	18
Do. do. of Mens' cloth or double milled kersimere, turned in, with quilted collars and paded,	20
Do. swelled edge,	22
Do. of kersimere, Ladies' cloth, coating, frize, and every other description of thin woolen, turned in, with quilted collars & paded,	19
Do. do. with plain collars,	18
Mens coats, edged,	21
Do. Coattees of every description, 2s less than long coats,	
Do. Pea Jackets,	16
Do. Spencers, quilted collars and paded,	12
Do. do. plain collars,	11
Do. Round Jackets, quilted collars,	13 6
Do. do. plain collars,	12 6
Do. Great Coats, without capes,	18
Do. do. with one cape,	19 6
And for each additional cape,	6
Mens' Cloaks,	16
Do. Long Regimental Coats,	30
Do. do. do. holes on both sides,	32
Do. do. do. laced,	36
Do. Short Regimental Coats,	27
Do. Horsemens' do.	30
Do. Dressing Gowns,	10
Do. do. Surtout fashion,	14
Mens' Pantaloons, with strings or buttons,	9
Do. do. without either,	8
Do. do. with tongues or feet and buttons,	10
Do. do. do. without buttons,	9
Do. Sherry Vallies,	12
Do. do. leathered,	14
Do. Breeches,	10

	S. D.
Mens' Long Gaters,	8
Do. short do.	6
Do. Waistcoats,	8
Do. do. with skirts,	9
Do. Uniform, do. with skirts, flaps & holes,	10
Do. Flannel Vests,	3
Do. do. with sleeves,	5
Do. do. faced,	6
Do. do. do. with sleeves,	8
Do. Drawers,	3
Youths' Long coats,	16
Do. Coattees,	14
Do. Great Coats,	16
Do. Waistcoats,	6
Do. Pantaloons, plain,	6
Do. do. with strings or buttons,	7
Do. do. with tongues and buttons,	8
Boys' Coattees, with a collar,	12
Childrens' do. without do.	10
Boys' Great Coats,	12
Childrens' do.	10
Do. Dress, first size,	12
Do. edged, do. do.	14
Do. Dress, second size,	14
Do. edged, do. do.	16
Ladies' Plain Habits,	16
Do. with skirts,	24
Do. Great Coats,	18
Do. Spencers,	12
Girls' Great Coats,	12

All tryed on Garments, one shilling extra,
All outside Breast Pockets, one shilling extra,
*   except when there is no other pockets in*
*   the coat.*

For and in behalf of the SOCIETY,

ROBT. COCKS, *Chairman.*

J. SCOFIELD, *Sec'ry.*

A list of prices to be given to journeymen, agreed on by The Society of Master Taylors, New York, January 22, 1805. (*Library of Congress*)

harder, with less control, and for significantly less pay" (Juravich et al. 1996, 19). Technology was intended to make production more efficient and thus more profitable, and in the race to produce greater profits, workdays grew longer and demands rose for the production of ever larger quantities. The workers occasionally resisted, protesting the length of the days and also linking the long days to "the growing problem of child labor." The concern was that, in many cases, children were being exploited and denied an education. Once again, this seemed to betray the post-Revolutionary ideals of creating a new generation of informed and virtuous voters. Proponents of child labor laws asserted that "if they were to fulfill their responsibilities as citizens they needed, 'an education suitable to the character of American freeman.' Without such preparation, they would be ill equipped to maintain their independence in the face of upper-class manipulation" (Juravich et al. 1996, 20). In other words, the workday needed to be limited so that children could attend school and become active citizens.

The pursuit of the 10-hour workday was perhaps the central goal of labor activists in the early republic. This campaign lasted throughout the era and culminated in many ways in Seth Luther's "Ten-Hour Circular." This 1835 pamphlet informed workers of their rights and apprised them of the physical and mental dangers of "excessive toil." Like many other labor propaganda pieces of the period, Luther's strongly worded "Ten-Hour Circular" invoked republican rhetoric and asserted the virtuosity of the workingman's cause. Luther referred to "the blood" of "Fathers shed on our battle-fields in the War of the Revolution" and asserted that "no earthly power shall resist our righteous claims with impunity" (Juravich et al. 1996, 24). This pamphlet helped to incite workers in the early years of labor organization, even as the young country faced an economic depression beginning in 1837. Luther's vision did not encompass all workers. Women were an important force in the early labor movement, but they frequently operated separately from the men's labor organizations (Juravich et al. 1996, 22).

Over the course of the 19th century, fewer women organized than men. Many historians believe that this difference partially resulted because many women saw their work as an afterthought, as a temporary means of subsistence, rather than as an important part of their identities (Juravich et al. 1996, 9). Some women, however, did organize to protest their mistreatment. As early as the 1820s, female millworkers unionized to protest unfair wages and other undesirable working conditions. The women, like other workers before them, made use of the rhetoric of the Revolution, referring to the mill owners as "Tories" who "placed return on investment before considerations of justice and equality" (Rock et al. 1995, 255–256). They also made use of this rhetoric to rail against their male counterparts. In response to the aforementioned letter from the Journeyman Taylors, they published an open letter that defended female labor and their right to equitable work. Interestingly, the women also asserted that tailoring was properly women's work (Rock et al. 1995, 255–256). In doing so, they asserted their right to work, but within conventional gender roles. As historian Linda Kerber observed, the women interpreted the republican values, which were connected to the labor movement as a whole, "in terms of what it meant to them as women." Women within the labor movement merged "the domestic domain of the pre-industrial woman with the new public ideology" (Kerber 1980, 269). In other words, they did not view themselves as subversive, but rather as citizens acting within what they believed to be appropriate gender boundaries. Women's labor reform leader Sarah Bagley noted that "free institutions," such as labor, were "based upon the virtue and intelligence of the American people, and the influence of the mother form and mould the man" (Juravich et al. 1996, 23). Scholars call this rhetoric "republican motherhood." These women claimed labor rights, and later their right to suffrage, not necessarily as equal citizens, but because their involvement in labor, education, and politics would make them better wives and mothers.

Individual Virtue

Another aspect of republicanism, which was related to social mobility, was about the virtue of the individual. The virtuous republican urban wage earner should be honest, hard-working, and free from vice. In addition, his labors were considered "noble" (Foner 1970, 12). In sum, the virtuous republican worker was "well-rewarded and independent, socially mobile, virtuous and enlightened, a worthy citizen of the republic," a self-made man (Siracusa 1979, 106). His social mobility and personal economic growth were viewed as reward for his virtue. America's economic growth as a whole was seen as reward for a fruitful, productive work force. As suggested earlier, the ultimate goal was not to become rich. Rather, it was to attain economic stability, and join the ranks of the middling sort. In short, this was the beginning of the meritocracy that has long pervaded American mentality.

Rhetoric Versus Reality

The new system of republican wage work was designed to be egalitarian, but the reality was often sharply different. Racism proved to be a significant obstacle to republican ideas of equality. A disproportionate number of black workers were included in the ranks of Northerners who were caught up in the last vestiges of bound labor. Free blacks and sometimes slaves were relegated to low-level jobs, such as caulkers in the shipyards. Ship captains were often reluctant to hire black sailors, and white sailors were frequently hostile toward them. There were numerous instances of assaults on black sailors by white sailors. Even Northerners who claimed to be abolitionists commonly refused to hire blacks for higher, more respectable positions as clerks or bookkeepers. This behavior flew in the face of the rhetoric of democratic ambitions and virtue in the marketplace.

Middle-class economic stability eluded many, regardless of race. Every-day life in the laboring class neighborhoods was neither comfortable nor easy for many urban wage earners. The life expectancy was 45 for white men and 20 for women. It was 35 for African Americans, with infant mortality of black infants double that of white infants (Appleby 2000, 63). Material comfort eluded many of those who survived. The average common laborer earned only approximately $120 a year. In large cities, such as Philadelphia and New York, laborers lived in small, crowded, rented tenements; occasionally multiple families shared the same tenement apartment (Smith 1990, 9; Wilentz 1984, 27). Furthermore, laboring neighborhoods were often plagued by disease and violence. Influxes of French, Scottish, German, and Irish immigrants brought diseases, such as dysentery, typhus, and typhoid fever, and crowded and unsanitary conditions made containment of these diseases difficult. One of the most notable examples of the problems caused by disease is Philadelphia's 1793 yellow fever outbreak, which killed 4,041 people between July and October (Wheeler and Becker 2002, 108). The majority of the outbreak's victims lived in working-class neighborhoods, within close proximity to the docks.

For those who could not survive on their wages or who struggled to find work, the early republic had new institutions to deal with them. It was not uncommon for the poorest of families to serve stints in debtor's prison or to wind up in poorhouses (Smith 1990, 18). In New York City, the population in the city's poorhouses tripled between the mid 1790s and 1817; by 1817, one-seventh of the city's population required some form of charitable assistance (Wilentz 1984, 26). Few urban wage-earning families had the resources to provide their offspring with the means to a better life (Smith 1990, 12).

Most workers also struggled to enjoy the consumer culture that their labor helped create. Even with the availability of generous credit, many of the laborers who worked producing consumer goods and services could not afford to partake of these products themselves. The standard of living kept rising, and urban wage earners were unable to keep up (Fried 1973, 9). In New York, less than 1 percent of the population earned the equivalent of $7,000 annually in 1980 dollars. The basic costs of living, such as food and shelter, took 80 percent or more of the worker's wages (Appleby 2000, 63). By contemporary standards, this meant that they were unable to fully participate in the drive toward economic independence from Great Britain. More than any other class tier, working-class laborers were also at the mercy of the ebb and flow of the economy.

As a result of the uneven economic development, life in the early republic was often unpredictable for American workers. Even the most basic needs went unfulfilled. Such was the case for Peter and Hannah Carle, a young Philadelphia working-class couple. In 1799, they desperately tried to provide their infant daughter with a proper funeral and burial. They wanted her buried in the cemetery of Gloria Dei, but Peter's employment had been sporadic for the prior several months. The $500 fee was more than the couple

Almshouse on Spruce Street, Philadelphia, 1800. (*Library of Congress*)

could afford, but the alternative was burial in Potter's Field, the place reserved for unmarked graves in many communities. Fortunately for them, the pastor took pity and agreed to reduce the fee to a cost the Carles could manage; many were not so lucky (Smith 1990, 8).

Conclusion

American society and culture have evolved dramatically since the early republic, yet there are distinct elements of continuity. The urban wage earners' battles to achieve ownership of their labor only strengthened through the 19th and 20th centuries, with actions like the Hampstead Strike and the Bread and Roses Strike. Social mobility and the attainment of economic stability also remain important parts of American culture. Indeed, the cliché of the modest but comfortable little white house and picket fence has become an important image, an icon of the proverbial American dream. Consumption also remains an important part of American culture, with consumers urged to buy American. Some of the conflicts of labor in the early republic remain. The problems of race and gender have yet to be resolved, particularly in terms of equitable wages. Nevertheless, the early stages of the Industrial Revolution set an important framework for the future.

References and Further Reading

Appleby, Joyce. *Inheriting the Revolution: the First Generation of Americans.* Cambridge, MA: Belknap Press, 2000

Bolster, W. Jeffrey. *Black Jacks: African American Seamen in the Age of Sail.* Cambridge, MA: Harvard University Press, 1999

Breen, T. H. "'Baubles of Britain:' The American and Consumer Revolutions of the Eighteenth Century." *Past and Present* 119 (May 1988): 73–104

Breen, T. H. *The Marketplace of Revolution: How Consumer Politics Shaped American Independence.* New York: Oxford University Press, 2004

Breen, T. H. "Narrative of Commercial Life: Consumption, Ideology, and Community on the Eve of the American Revolution." *William and Mary Quarterly*, 3rd ser. 50 (July 1993): 471–501

Brewer, John, and Roy Porter, eds. *Consumption and the World of Goods.* New York: Routledge, 1993

Bridenbaugh, Carl. *The Colonial Craftsman.* New York: Oxford University Press, 1950

Bushman, Richard L. *The Refinement of America: People, Cities, Houses.* New York: Vintage, 1993

Butler, Jon. *Becoming America: The Revolution Before 1776.* Cambridge, MA: Harvard University Press, 2000

Carr, Jacqueline Barbara. *After the Siege: A Social History of Boston, 1775–1800.* Boston, MA: Northeastern University Press, 2004

Corfield, Penelope J., ed. *Language, History and Class.* Cambridge, MA: Basil Blackwell, 1991

Dublin, Thomas, ed. *Farm to Factory: Women's Letters, 1830–1860*, 2nd ed. New York: Columbia University Press, 1993

Faler, Paul G. *Mechanics and Manufacturers in the Early Industrial Revolution.* Albany: State University of New York Press, 1981

Foner, Eric. *Free Soil, Free Labor, Free Men: The Ideology of the Republican Party Before the Civil War.* New York: Oxford University Press, 1970

Fried, Marc. *The World of the Urban Working Class.* Cambridge, MA: Harvard University Press, 1973

Fruchtman, Jack Jr. *Atlantic Cousins: Benjamin Franklin and His Visionary Friends.* New York: Thunder's Mouth Press, 2005

Gilje, Paul A., and Howard B. Rock, eds. *Keepers of the Revolution: New Yorkers at Work in the Early Republic.* Ithaca, NY: Cornell University Press, 1992

Green, James R., and Hugh Carter Donahue. *Boston's Workers: a Labor History.* Boston, MA: Trustees of the Public Library of the City of Boston, 1979

Groneman, Carol, and Mary Beth Norton, eds. *"To Toil the Livelong Day": America's Women at Work, 1780–1980.* Ithaca, NY: Cornell University Press, 1987

Innes, Stephen, ed. *Work and Labor in Early America*. Chapel Hill: University of North Carolina Press, 1988

Jones, Jacqueline. *A Social History of the Laboring Classes: From Colonial Times to the Present*. Malden, MA: Blackwell Publishing, 1999

Juravich, Tom, William F. Hartford, and James R. Green. *Commonwealth of Toil: Chapters in the History of Massachusetts Workers and Their Unions*. Amherst: University of Massachusetts Press, 1996

Kerber, Linda K. *Women of the Republic: Intellect and Ideology in Revolutionary America*. Chapel Hill: University of North Carolina Press, 1980

Kornblith, Gary. "Becoming Joseph T. Buckingham: The Artisanal Struggle for Independence in Early-Nineteenth Century Boston." In Howard B. Rock, Paul A. Gilje, and Robert Asher. *American Artisans: Crafting Social Identity, 1750–1850*, 123–134. Baltimore, MD: Johns Hopkins University Press, 1995

Larcom, Lucy. *A New England Girlhood*. Gloucester, MA: Peter Smith, 1973

Laurie, Bruce. *Artisans into Workers: Labor in Nineteenth-Century America*. Chicago: University of Illinois Press, 1997

Layer, Robert G. *Earnings of Cotton Mill Operatives, 1825–1914*. Cambridge, MA: Harvard University Press, 1955

Marchalonis, Shirley. *The Worlds of Lucy Larcom, 1824–1893*. Athens: University of Georgia Press, 1989

McGaw, Judith A. *Early American Technology: Making and Doing Things from the Colonial Era to 1850*. Chapel Hill: University of North Carolina Press, 1994

Nash, Gary B. *The Urban Crucible: The Northern Seaports and the Origins of the American Revolution*. Cambridge, MA: Harvard University Press, 1986

Reese, William S. *The First Hundred Years of Printing in British North America: Printers and Collectors: From the Proceedings of the American Antiquarian Society*, Volume 99, Part 2. Worcester, MA: American Antiquarian Society, 1989

Rock, Howard B. *Artisans of the New Republic: The Tradesmen of New York City in the Age of Jefferson*. New York: New York University Press, 1979

Rock, Howard B., ed. *New York City Artisan, 1789–1825: A Documentary History*. Albany: State University of New York Press, 1989

Rock, Howard B., Paul A. Gilje, and Robert Asher. *American Artisans: Crafting Social Identity, 1750–1850*. Baltimore, MD: Johns Hopkins University Press, 1995

Schultz, Ronald. *The Republic of Labor: Philadelphia Artisans and the Politics of Class, 1720–1830*. New York: Oxford University Press, 1993

Siracusa, Carl. *A Mechanical People: Perceptions of the Industrial Order in Massachusetts, 1815–1880*. Middletown, CT: Wesleyan University Press, 1979

Smith, Billy G. *The "Lower Sort": Philadelphia's Laboring People, 1750–1800*. Ithaca, NY: Cornell University Press, 1990

Steffen, Charles G. *The Mechanics of Baltimore: Workers and Politics in the Age of Revolution, 1763–1812.* Chicago: University of Illinois Press, 1984

Tunis, Edwin. *Colonial Craftsmen and the Beginnings of American Industry.* Baltimore, MD: Johns Hopkins University Press, 1965

Turbin, Carole. "Beyond Conventional Wisdom: Women's Wage Work, Household Economic Contribution, and Labor Activism in a Mid-Nineteenth-Century Working-Class Community." In Carol Groneman and Mary Beth Norton, eds. *"To Toil the Livelong Day": America's Women at Work, 1780–1980,* 47–67. Ithaca, NY: Cornell University Press, 1987

Vickers, Daniel. "Competency and Competition: Economic Culture in Early America." *The William and Mary Quarterly,* 3rd Ser. 47 (January 1990): 3–29

Wheeler, William Bruce, and Susan D. Becker, eds. *Discovering the American Past: A Look at the Evidence,* Volume 1, 5th ed. Boston, MA: Houghton Mifflin Company, 2002

Wilentz, Sean. *Chants Democratic: New York City and the Rise of the Working Class, 1788–1850.* New York: Oxford University Press, 1984

Cinco Ranch High School Library
23440 Cinco Ranch Blvd.
Katy, TX 77494

Seeking "Men of Iron Sinew": Creating a Professional Military in the Early American Republic | 3

Sally E. Bennett

Introduction

In the early republic, the United States military offered options that many citizens eagerly took advantage of, such as food, access to land, respectability, and a salary. For others, especially when economic times were good, the military offered little incentive to join. In these instances, the local militia seemed to be a better option; they could serve near and care for their families and farms. The militia also seemed to be a better option to the new nation, because Americans feared that a peacetime standing army threatened liberty. Yet pressures to defend the nation eventually outweighed other concerns, and the country moved from relying on a militia to a dual system that combined a militia and a professional military and then finally to a military that relied almost exclusively on a professional fighting force. To create that professional force, captains in the new military worked to recruit "men of iron sinew," train them, prevent them from deserting, and keep their companies operating on Western borders far from supplies (*Pennsylvania Gazette* August 9, 1799).

Transition to a Professional Standing Army

Between the Revolutionary War and the end of the War of 1812, the United States wrestled with the benefits and dangers of a peacetime standing army. To many citizens of the new republic, a standing army did not protect but rather only threatened their civil liberties. This was a holdover from the Revolutionary era, when British regulars were seen as agents of British tyranny.

Certificate of membership in the Second Regiment, Hudson Brigade, First Division, Hudson County State Militia, circa 1800–1810. (*Library of Congress*)

A peacetime standing army also appeared dangerous because it placed too much power in a centralized authority and thereby challenged republican ideology. Many colonists preferred to develop their own state militia that would muster only when needed for local and sometimes national defense. This solution seemingly worked in the colonial era, when local militias responded to local threats in ways and at speeds that British regulars could not. Also, citizen soldiers of the militias could serve locally and return to their homes to plant or harvest crops. The public image of liberty made many Americans prefer the citizen-soldier of the militia rather than a soldier in a professional army.

Congress had its own set of concerns about a standing army. Debates between Federalists and anti-Federalists over the military and civil liberty prevented Congress from creating a sizable permanent standing army until the early 1800s. Congressional representatives feared that the army would be loyal to military leadership rather than to civil authority or that it could turn against the government. At the same time, George Washington and many other military leaders recognized that state militias lacked professional training and were difficult to unify into a national force. Many military professionals bemoaned the quality of the soldiers even among the regulars. In 1797, for example, General James Wilkinson complained, "The condition of the army stationed at [Fort Wayne] is a frightful picture to the scientific soldier. . . . [I]gnorance & licentiousness have been fostered while intelligence &

virtue exiled." Wilkinson further lamented that what the army needed most was "subordination and discipline to banish that disorder, vice, and abuse [which has] infected every member of the *corps militaire*" and to "clear this Aegean stable of anarchy and confusion, to extract order from chaos" (*American State Papers, Miscellaneous* 1834, 1: 586). If it were up to military leaders like Washington and Wilkinson, the nation would turn to career soldiers.

During the Revolutionary War, Americans used a dual army structure; it relied on local volunteer militias as well as on a small national professional army. Long before the war, citizen-soldiers organized themselves into part-time militias for local defense against both Native Americans and colonial powers. Before the war, they stockpiled weapons and increased their training. Congress, after considerable debate, developed its own professional army in 1775. After the 1783 Treaty of Paris ended the war, Congress disbanded all but a small portion of the Continental Army and created the first peacetime standing army, a group of 700 men that combined militia and some regulars under congressional control.

For three decades, the new nation repeatedly organized and reorganized its military and adjusted the balance between militia and regulars. In 1791, less than a decade after disbanding it, Congress rebuilt the national army in the form of the Legion of the United States. Little Turtle's War in the Northwest Territory made it clear that the state militias could not effectively defend American national interests. In 1796, Congress disbanded all but a few regiments and dragoon companies of the Legion only to find that it needed to rebuild the army yet again. This time, because the U.S. feared it could no longer maintain its policy of neutrality in the war between Britain and France, Congress built up the national army by establishing a navy. Over the next 10 years, Congress and President Thomas Jefferson scaled back the size of the forces, though they expanded arsenals and fortifications. By 1812, when the U.S. declared war against Great Britain, it had to rebuild its military once again, this time more permanently. The War of 1812, despite ideological objections, made it clear that a regular army had an established and accepted role to play. American citizens ultimately recognized the value of a professional national fighting force and began creating one. The nation now had to develop methods of recruiting, training, and providing for its new, standing, professional army.

Recruiting a Professional Army

In the early republic, captains recruited their own companies or ship's crews. Recruiters tried to counter popular preferences for the militia and entice men to enlist for professional military service. The recruiting party generally consisted of a first lieutenant or other officer, a model sergeant, a corporal, musicians (typically a fifer and a drummer), and at least six enlisted men.

The parties recruited in towns, cities, and rural areas according to increasingly centralized standards and regulations. For example, the United

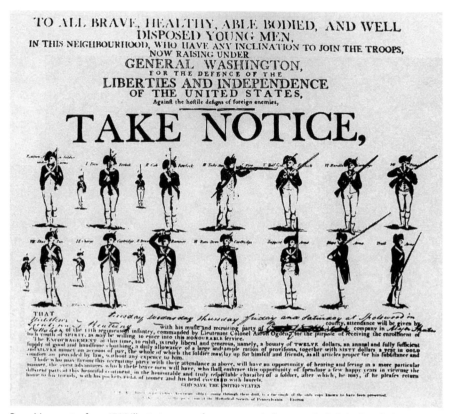

Recruiting poster from 1799 illustrates poses from a manual of arms typical of the Revolutionary period. (*Grafton, John*. The American Revolution, A Picture Sourcebook, *1975*)

States issued *Rules and Regulations Respecting the Recruiting Service* in 1798 and *Additional Rules and Regulations for Recruiting the Army* in 1814. Many of these rules were designed to protect the civil liberties of Americans. Recruiters, for example, were expressly prohibited from using indirect methods to "inveigle" men to enlist or to enlist anyone who was intoxicated (Adams 1798, 4). Recruiters, however, offered bounties or lands to obtain enlistees. Bounties were typically between $12 and $24, half of which was paid upon enlistment and the rest upon fulfillment of duty. Enlistments lasted from three to five years or for the duration of a war, and pay rates were $3 per month in the 1790s and $5 per month in the early 19th century. At the end of his enlistment period, a recruit could receive a land grant of up to 160 acres.

In their efforts to encourage enlistment, company captains printed handbills and advertised in newspapers. The language of recruitment was replete with inspiring phrases about the good benefits and exciting and pleasant service. Recruiters directed a 1791 *Pennsylvania Gazette* advertisement at local youth "who wish[ed] to become adventurers in a new country." It touted inducements, such as "a generous bounty," and promised that following a "short" term of service they might "set down on their own farms, and enjoy all the blessings of peace and plenty." Other recruiting ads and broadsides assured the interested and impoverished that, "the duties will be pleasant, the payment prompt, the cloathing elegant, and the provisions good" (*Pennsylvania Gazette* March 23, 1791).

Although many men were attracted by the salaries and land grants, others were eager to meet their more mundane needs. For some men, the clothing allowance proved to be a key incentive; recruits at one post arrived almost naked (Coffman 1986, 16). In a time when many families still practiced primogeniture, leaving the family farm to the eldest son, younger sons did not always have the option of obtaining their own land, particularly in the Northeast and Mid-Atlantic. Furthermore, by doing military service on the frontier, a soldier could see firsthand the quality of the lands available and learn about specific options for moving west. As a result, many soldiers moved west after their terms of enlistment ended.

Industrialization also helped recruiters. As farmers increasingly struggled to make ends meet, some families enlisted their underage children. In these cases, the army became a substitute for an apprenticeship and a means to avoid poverty and starvation. These young boys often worked either as drummers or fifers or as powder monkeys, positions that often turned into becoming artillerists. Sponsors of children into the army, whether parents or guardians, often took half of the bounty for themselves and essentially sold the children as indentured servants to the United States military.

Parents could freely give their consent for young boys to enlist but found it was not so easy to get them discharged. On August 7, 1809, soldier and father Allan Rigsby enlisted his two sons, ages 12 and 10, for five years of service. Their soldiers' rations meant survival for the boys, but survival came at a cost. Rigsby signed a statement promising that he would "not use any argument or means to dissuade or prevent my two sons Samuel or John Rigsby from re-enlisting when their period of service expires" (Rigsby 1809). Occasionally, parents had second thoughts and petitioned the government to have their children returned to them. For instance, William Mason enlisted in Philadelphia in 1811, but in 1813 his uncle wrote on his behalf to the secretary of war requesting Mason's discharge. He claimed the boy was underage and already apprenticed at the time of his enlistment. Despite all the uncle's efforts—no doubt encouraged by fears over the approaching war with Britain—William Mason did not get out of the army (James Gibson to General Armstrong, May 11, 1813, in *Letters Received by the Office of the Adjutant General 1805–1821*, 27). Young soldiers were not the only ones who wanted out of their service. In prosperous times, men of all ages deserted or looked for opportunities to leave. Similarly, many of the recruits who wanted food, clothing, or the bounty money tried to desert during the march to their first postings (Coffman 1986, 18; Heidler and Heidler 2004, 177).

George Davenport (1783–1845)

Born in England in 1783 to a seafaring family, the educated George Davenport became an American soldier literally by accident. Beginning at age 17, he worked on his uncle's merchant ship. In the course of his adventures aboard ship, he visited such places as France and Spain. While in St. Petersburg, Russia, he and his fellow sailors were taken prisoner. Kept in demeaning conditions with little food, Davenport, freed a few months later, learned firsthand the tyranny of monarchies.

In 1804, while his uncle's ship prepared to return to England by taking up anchor in New York harbor, Davenport broke his leg rescuing a seaman who fell overboard. The captain of the ship brought him to medical care with the intention of picking him up on a return trip. During his convalescence, he was encouraged to take to the countryside to improve his health. Near Carlisle, Pennsylvania, a recruiting officer of the 1st U.S. Infantry acknowledged Davenport's ability to read and write and

offered him a noncommissioned appointment to corporal if he would enlist. Davenport signed on for a five-year enlistment, during which he was promoted to sergeant. He reenlisted in 1809 at Fort Belle Fontaine near St. Louis, Missouri, and again in 1814.

In the ensuing years, Davenport became a professional soldier of the United States Army. He performed a variety of duties from assisting in the recruiting service, to being an express rider, and to overseeing grave digging at Fort Adams, near New Orleans, where he had to use his spade to keep floating coffins down while his fellow soldiers quickly tried to shovel dirt on top of them. He soldiered on the Sabine Expedition against the Spaniards and helped build Fort Clark on the Illinois River during the Peoria Indian Campaign of September 1813. By the summer of 1814, he and his company, under Captain Thomas Hamilton of the 1st U.S. Infantry, arrived in Buffalo, New York, just in time to be sent over to fight in the Battle of

The Recruits

At the turn of the 19th century, Secretary of War James McHenry reminded recruiters that they were building a professional army and that a "faithful army is to be preferred to a numerous one" (*Pennsylvania Gazette* June 6, 1799). The men of quality needed for the new professional army were to be healthy, white, often skilled, native-born men of good reputation. For most branches of the developing professional military, recruits also had to meet height and age requirements; they had to be at least 5 feet 6 inches and between the ages of 18 and 40. They also had to undergo a medical examination. Regulations required the recruiter "not to suffer any man to pass who has not been stripped of all his clothes, to see that he has no rupture . . . has the perfect use of his eyes and ears, and the free motion of every joint and limb . . . no tumors nor diseased enlargements of bones or joints; no sore legs nor marks of an old sore . . . that his appearance is healthy . . . that he is not consumptive (tubercular) nor subject to fits" (*Additional Rules* 1814). If a

Lundy's Lane on the Niagara frontier, followed by the siege of Fort Erie.

At some point near the end of his military career, he married a widow, Margaret Lewis, who was some 16 years older than he and who had two children. Davenport did not, however, remain a sergeant. Having been demoted to a private three times during the course of his career for insubordination, he could no longer be promoted again to that position. At the end of the war, the army was reduced, and Davenport mustered out to take on the role of a civilian.

In 1816, Colonel William Morrison, an army contractor, hired him to deliver supplies. From success in this position, he obtained a permit to be a sutler at a new army post, Fort Armstrong, on the Mississippi River, now known as Rock Island Arsenal. He settled down and received permission for a preemption of land near the post, where he built a house for his family. Oddly, due to the advanced age of his wife upon their marriage, Davenport had two sons by his stepdaughter Susan (1817 and 1823) and a daughter (1835) by his indentured servant, Catherine Po, or Pouitt. He grew prosperous enough to make a return trip in the spring of 1827 to England to visit family.

During the Blackhawk War in 1832, he acted as quartermaster general for the Illinois Militia. He engaged in trade with the local Indians, especially the Fox. In the later years of his life, he went by the title of colonel.

Davenport's life ended tragically on July 4, 1845. On that day, he remained at home while his family went on a picnic to celebrate the holiday. A gang of outlaws, known as the Banditti of the Prairie, who menaced the Mississippi and Rock River valleys during this era, tortured and murdered Davenport during a robbery. He died later that night. Davenport was given two funerals: one by the whites and another ceremony by the Fox Indians, chiefs, and warriors, who put a cedar post in the ground by his grave, painted white and inscribed with Fox symbols.

recruit was not healthy or of the proper age, the army docked the recruiting officer an amount equal to the bounty paid out to the recruit.

Secretary of War McHenry's notion of faithfulness and quality also included citizenship or at least residency in the United States. The *Rules and Regulations Respecting the Recruiting Service* defined the favored recruit. "Natives of fair conduct and character are to be preferred; but foreigners of good reputation for sobriety and honesty may also be enlisted" (Adams 1798, 5). Recruiters, however, did not always follow these guidelines. In several companies, at least one quarter of the recruits were foreign-born. Men seeking to enlist had to prove some length of residency by producing a certificate of naturalization plus at least two affidavits from so-called respectable citizens from their county.

African Americans and Native Americans did not enjoy the same opportunities as white recruits inasmuch as participating in the military was a marker of social status and respectability. The *Rules and Regulations Respecting the Recruiting Service* emphatically stated that, "Negros, mulattoes, or indians are not to be enlisted" (Adams 1798, 5). At first, the infantry did not recruit men of color. Nevertheless, men of African or Indian descent may well have served. Enlistment forms recorded skin tones as well as eye and hair color, and they may indicate that some soldiers were African American or Indian. These descriptions are hardly smoking guns, but after 1812 black and mulatto soldiers certainly served. As the fears of war increased, so did the recruitment of African Americans. During the War of 1812, for example, Captain William Bezeau's 26th Regiment of U.S. Infantry had up to 200 men, most of African heritage. The 27th Regiment had a musician, John Miller, who was born in Santo Domingo. Private James Shirley, a 24-year-old slave and seaman from Boston, enlisted in the 40th Regiment as a drummer on September 23, 1814. His owner, according to regulations, likely received his pay and bounties (*Register of Enlistments* 1798–1815).

African Americans had a better experience in the U.S. Navy. Despite regulations to the contrary, the navy accepted men of African descent between 1783 and the 1820s. The difficult conditions of naval service made it less attractive to most recruits, and captains had difficulty attracting crews. The navy also had to compete for recruits with the more highly paid merchant and fishing ships. As a result, African American sailors and seamen found more cultural acceptance than they experienced on shore. They lived and messed with whites, they worked and fought battles alongside whites, and their officers often respected them and the service they gave. They also occasionally celebrated victories together. Following his August 1812 victory over the *Guerriere,* U.S.S *Constitution* Captain Isaac Hull praised the conduct in battle of his black sailors, saying they "fought like devils" (Miller 1913, 520). Elsewhere during the War of 1812, a New York theater honored the service of all the members of a particular ship. The crew "marched together into the pit, and nearly one half of them were negroes" (Bolster 1990, 1179).

Although recruiters probably did not enlist known Native Americans as common soldiers, Natives of mixed ancestry often became military officers. After the 1803 Louisiana Purchase, the United States Military Academy at West Point accepted many of the first sons of the newly acquired territory. One of them, Louis Loramier, had a Native mother and French father. Objections to Loramier's acceptance came from Captain Amos Stoddard, an artillery officer stationed at St. Louis, who complained that Loramier "exhibited too much of the Indian color" (Stoddard May 7, 1804). Nonetheless, Loramier graduated from the Academy in 1806 and was probably one of the first Native Americans to do so. After he graduated from the Academy, he served at the westernmost outpost of the U.S. Army at the time, Fort Osage, near present-day Kansas City, and he resigned in 1809 to return to farming near Cape Girardeau, Missouri.

As recruiting companies struggled to make their quotas, the character of enlistees became increasingly questionable. Recruiters sought men of quality, but beggars could not be choosers. Despite calls for "sturdy young men, of reputation for industry and morals," recruiters often recognized that they needed to attract a larger group of volunteers (*Pennsylvania Gazette* August 9, 1791). One recruiting ad, for example, made this clear. "No soldier can be arrested on account of debt or contract," the posting declared. Yet, in a contradictory manner, it also stated that the "object of raising an army is to defend our country, not to rob the gallows—lazy, drunken, thievish rascals need not apply" (*Pennsylvania Gazette* June 6, 1799). All too often recruiters attracted men with undesirable characteristics.

Complaints about recruits were common in the early republic. Ohio land speculator John Cleves Symmes feared that if soldiers were not chosen with more care they might become like the hastily recruited group that plagued General St. Clair in 1792, who were "totally debilitated" and possibly "incapable" of doing their military duty. He further speculated that their characters were lacking because recruiters found these men in "prisons and . . . brothels" (Prucha 1969, 26–27). In 1802, an army captain expressed similar concerns about new recruits. Perhaps colored by attitudes about ethnicity or industrialization, he recommended that recruiting parties should not venture into port cities like Baltimore, Boston, Philadelphia, or New York, because "soldiers recruited in those places are far inferior to those recruited in the country places"; men from port towns, he said, were very likely to desert (Wingate, 1802, in *Letters Received by the Office of the Adjutant General 1805–1821*). John Randolph, a Virginia Congressman, likewise viewed common soldiers as "loungers, who live upon the public [and] consume the fruits of [citizens'] honest industry, under the pretext of protecting them from a foreign yoke." He noted, "The military parade which meets the eye in almost every direction excites the gall of our citizens. They put no confidence in the protection of ragamuffins" (Miller 1913, 202–24).

Recruits with skills were eagerly sought by the military. Although the United States remained largely a nation of farmers in the early republic, many soldiers brought with them a host of nonagricultural skills. New soldiers were former carpenters, distillers, harness makers, cordwainers, coopers, cobblers, saddlers, barbers, currier/tanners, bakers, hatters, painters, clerks, printers, tailors, and blacksmiths. Captains sought men with the talents that they expected to need once the company was stationed at a post, often in the West where skilled workers might not be easy to find among the population. This was especially true for recruits who could read and write. Literate men frequently became corporals or sergeants, who often did work similar to clerks, writing down the daily garrison orders into the order books, keeping records of supplies issued to new recruits, and performing other duties that required a fine and legible hand.

Life in the Professional Army

The soldier in the new military was, first and foremost, a free citizen of the republic, as were his officers. Before the Revolutionary War, the British did

George Burnett (b.?–1812): An Old Soldier

On a sultry August morning in 1812, George Burnett, a fifer in Captain Nathan Heald's company of the 1st U.S. Infantry Regiment, marched up the slight incline of low sandy dunes along the shore of Lake Michigan. Here, Burnett fifed his way into the War of 1812.

Barely two months previously, the United States declared war against Great Britain. Along with his company, he headed toward the sprinkling of cottonwoods, windblown grass, and scrub pines to the prairie where hailed the reports of rifle fire. Behind him, along the shore, stood the wives and children of the regulars and militia, with two baggage wagons: one with children, including the very pregnant wife of a soldier, and the other containing provisions to feed the departing force on their jour-ney to Fort Wayne, some 250 miles to the east-southeast. The wagon guard and militia awaited the outcome of the U.S. regulars' show of force to the unseen enemy. Only then could the party resume their march.

No doubt Burnett had reason to be proud to participate in one more battle of one more war, for he had served in American forces for over 35 years. Beginning his service in 1777 during the American War of Independence and continuing beyond the 1790s as a musician in the 1st U.S. Infantry Regiment, Burnett wit-nessed General Josiah Harmar's defeat by the forces led by Little Turtle of the Miami Nation, served among the troops stationed at Fort Detroit, and was finally posted to Fort Dear-born, a distant outpost at Chicago.

not treat citizen-soldiers in the militia or their officers with the respect that a free citizen expected. In the years following the end of the American Rev-olution, journalist and publisher of the *Philadelphia Aurora*, William Duane, noted that the public perception of the officer corps was that they treated their soldiers with "terror, cruelty, and degradation" (Duane 1813, 13). Offi-cers of the old school remained aloof from their men in the garrison, follow-ing the pattern established by British officers. In the new military, however, there could be no justification for such treatment of fellow citizens. In the new military, U.S. leaders sought to avoid the condescension the British had displayed toward American colonists and officers, as well as the absolute dis-cipline and severe treatment of the militia.

The men who joined the military in the early republic discovered that American notions of liberty translated into a new focus on their needs; even their feelings mattered in the new military. New, young officers followed what General James Wilkinson called scientific training and disciplinary methods to create professional soldiers (General James Wilkinson to Captain James Bruff, June 17, 1797, *American State Papers* 1834, 1: 586). Baron von Steuben's 1794 instructions, in *The Soldier's Monitor,* charged company cap-tains to keep as their first objective, "to gain the love of [their] men, by treat-ing them with every possible kindness, and humanity, enquiring into their complaints, and when well founded, seeing them redressed." He should also "visit those that are sick [and] speak tenderly to them" (Steuben 1814, 65).

Burnett, an ordinary citizen of the new republic, became a career soldier in a time when the politics of his country looked down on serving in the standing army. Records do not indicate whether Burnett married or had children. It was not uncommon to find men serving a lifetime in the military without families. In 1811, a fellow soldier wrote on Burnett's behalf to Jacob Kingsbury, the colonel of the 1st U.S. Infantry Regiment, to request help for Burnett so he could retire from the service, asking whether Burnett could be granted land near the fort where he could settle down?

Burnett never received a reply to his request; so on July 1, 1811, despite being an old soldier at about 45 years of age, he reenlisted for another term of five years. However, unknown to Burnett, this was to be his last battle.

The U.S. regulars lost nearly half their company in the first volley from the more than four hundred weapons of Potawatomi, Winnebago, and other tribes. Burnett was wounded. After the commanding officer surrendered his men to save their lives, the survivors were marched back to the garrison by their captors. That evening, along with some seven other wounded soldiers, Burnett was put to death before his commanding officer and the other survivors.

The contrast with the traditional British method of leadership could not be more stark. Duane's 1813 infantry handbook repeated this advice; captains should be "a father, friend, and protector to his men: duty should be inflexibly enforced; but kindness and care, in promoting proper gratifications of his soldiers should be his constant study" (Duane 1813, 110). Although the new professional military required a new kind of officer, it could not train these officers until the United States Military Academy at West Point officially opened in 1802.

The professional officers of the early republic had to be able to foster a new kind of relationship with the men they trained. Discipline was as necessary "for him that teaches, as for those that are taught." In other words, an army officer was to model everything in his own demeanor toward his men that he himself required of them. An officer was not to intimidate his soldiers with an atmosphere of "terror and hatred" (Duane 1813, 12). This included changes in punishments. At first, officers avoided whipping and other forms of corporal punishment on their own initiative, and eventually, in 1812, the military outlawed whipping.

Military leaders expected that this new style of management and leadership would lead to better and more loyal companies. Steuben explain that "[t]he attention that arises from . . . attention to the sick and wounded, is almost inconceivable; it will moreover be the means of preserving the lives of many valuable men" (Steuben 1794, 135). Similarly, Duane believed that,

Engraving of the U.S. Military Academy at West Point, New York, 1831. (*Library of Congress*)

"when [an officer] treats those over whom he is placed, as men whose happiness and credit he studies, rather than as slaves over whom he has the right to tyrannize [sic]," the men perform better (Duane 1813, 12). New training could not, however, guarantee loyalty, and the new recruits did not always fare very well when they went into battle. In 1790, for example, Lieutenant Colonel Josiah Harmar's combined force of militia and regulars hardly followed their orders, as the military theorists would have predicted. Instead, as they fought against the Indians of the Northwest Territory, they scattered against orders to search for plunder, they refused orders to advance, and otherwise forced Harmar to retreat (Hassler 1982, 52).

Discipline and Daily Life

Recruits first learned about military discipline when they gathered at central rendezvous points. There they were issued uniforms and equipment, and they had their personal information recorded by a clerk. They also began training in the *Manual of Exercise* and the *Rules and Regulations of the Army*, and they studied the *Articles of War* that would govern their lives in the professional military. For a recruit to be considered a true soldier of his company, he first had to master his drill, learn how to use his weapon, and take care of his clothing. Officers could not take recruits on as servants or waiters until the recruit had learned every part of his duty. Recruits were considered full soldiers only when they could successfully demonstrate their ability to aid in protecting the company, whether in the field or in garrison. Experienced—or old—soldiers frequently mentored new recruits in these details, and they often did so according to *The Regulations*, which required mentors to use patience and leniency in teaching the "duties of a soldier," including how to "clean himself, arms & accoutrements" (Adams 1798, 5).

Although many recruits signed up for adventure, they often found their duties mundane. Whether in garrison or on the march, a scheduled regimen ordered their daily lives. Infantrymen went through drills at least twice a day, once in the morning and again in the afternoon. They learned their "exercise"—caring for and loading their muskets, marching in formation, understanding drum calls—and they followed the daily routine of reveille, roll call, guard mount, fatigue duty, dinner call, evening parade, retreat, and tattoo. Those who were stationed on the frontier (a majority of soldiers in the early republic) also spent significant time building fortifications and roads. They cut and hauled firewood, repaired the garrison, raised and harvested crops, cut and stored ice, built roads, cooked and served food, and maintained officers' equipment. Service in the navy was often equally tedious, especially as ships spent months at sea. Sailors cared for every aspect of the ship, whether it was the rigging, the sails, or the wood. In wartime, the men also served on gun crews (Millett 1984, 36). After the War of 1812, the navy protected travelers to Latin America, fishing ships in the North Atlantic and Pacific, and merchant ships from pirates in the Caribbean. It also sought to enforce the ban on the Atlantic slave trade and to complete river and harbor surveys (Hassler 1982, 122).

Soldiers, especially those stationed in the West, had opportunities to add to their military income. Some used their peacetime skills to tailor uniforms for other soldiers, and the military paid others to do extra duty or to build fortifications. Army regulations required that soldiers get their uniforms and clothing tailored before they could be worn. Men who had been tailors, hatters, and cobblers frequently used these skills to earn extra pay. The 1801 *Standing Orders of the 1st U.S. Infantry* even specified the rates they could charge, the breaks they were allowed to take, and the fines they paid if they damaged uniforms or clothing. Regulations also included extra pay, up to $1 per day, and extra rations for men who helped with construction projects (Coffman 1986, 15–16). Some posts hired out soldiers to the local U.S. government Indian Trade Factory for the unpleasant job of cleaning and packing hides for shipment and actually shipping out the hides (Griswold 1927, 268–69). Though military pay could be lower than civilian pay, it was steady, and the chance to earn extra income, with room, board, and clothing supplied, made the military an attractive option for some.

Soldiers in the new professional standing army followed strict rules of sanitation and enjoyed, at least on paper, relatively high levels of nutrition and medical care. Standards varied, but they became increasingly uniform in the early republic. At one garrison, for example, soldiers had to shave at least every three days, have laundry washed twice per week, and air out their bedding every Sunday morning (Griswold 1927, 152, 184, 289). Thursday and Sunday were clean linen days: Each soldier had to have on a clean shirt, overalls, and stockings. After 1801, the *Standing Orders* also required that soldiers cut their hair short and stopped requiring that soldiers powder their hair. Sideburns were not allowed to grow down below the lower part of the ear. The army also prohibited men from urinating on the garrison walls, and some forts provided ports, similar to outhouses, in the walls between barracks for men to use (Griswold 1927, 270, 298). The 1809 garrison order book for Fort Wayne in Indiana Territory included regulations for bathing in the river (Griswold 1927, 240, 271). Personal cleanliness extended to the mess, where regulations required men to use the community washbasin and towel and to clean their hands before they could set the table and eat their meals. They also required men to use a tablecloth and utensils, including knife, fork, and spoon, to eat their one-pot meals and bread. For a man who might have grown up in impoverished conditions, learning proper hygiene and table etiquette must have been a novel experience.

Garrisoned soldiers were often well fed. They all received daily rations of food that included a pound of beef or three-quarters of a pound of pork, along with 18 ounces of flour or a pound of bread. In Western forts—where provisions often arrived late or were of poor quality—commanders supplemented military provisions by requiring soldiers to tend gardens or to hunt. When units were stationed near rivers or other waterways, fishing nets were frequently available for the soldiers. For instance, at Fort Massac on the Ohio River, a bar was extended over the river with lines and fishhooks to catch catfish and other types of fish. When available, fresh vegetables were included in the daily ration. In their absence, vinegar helped to stave off scurvy. Naval rations were even more generous than those received by the land forces. Depending on the ports, sailors occasionally bought fresh fruits and vegetables as well as fresh fish from the sea, in addition to the standard ration of bread or sea biscuits and salted meat. Commanding officers often ordered subordinates to purchase these items. At times, however, attempts to make a post self-sufficient did not work. In 1819, when supplies could not get through to Camp Missouri, everyone was placed on rations and scurvy abounded. Even though many sick soldiers were relocated to Fort Osage, many died at that post (Coffman 1986, 19–21; Heidler and Heidler 2004, 184–85).

Women contributed to camp hygiene, medical care, and morale. They offered companionship, provided medical care, and even engaged in combat when necessary. Military regulations allowed four washerwomen to a company and hospital matrons on an as-needed basis. These authorized workers received rations and pay, but wives not appointed to these tasks, as well as children in general, did not. At times, the lives of these women could be isolated and dangerous. Women were required to obey the same rules and regulations that their husbands did. If they failed to do so, they could find themselves thrown out of the protection of the garrison to fend for them-

During the Battle of Fort Niagara, a pair of uniformed soldiers and two civilians (one a woman) load and fire a cannon during the War of 1812, Fort Niagara, New York, December 18, 1813. (*Hulton Archive/Getty Images*)

selves and their children outside the stockade. Women and children died in attacks and accidents, children had little access to school or playmates, and class distinctions often kept women separated from officers' wives. Also, the military offered only limited pensions or assistance to widows (Coffman 1986, 25–26, 35–38; Hassler 1982, 51; Heidler and Heidler 2004, 186).

Conclusion

During the early republic, the United States created a professional army to serve in both peacetime and wartime. Thousands of soldiers were recruited to serve in this new army. Many of the new recruits found themselves far from home at Western garrisons and encampments. They trained under recruiting officers with new ideas about discipline and morale, and they often struggled to perform their duties under difficult conditions. Many companies had to build their own forts in places where supplies, food, materials, and pay were often uncertain. Soldiers also suffered from disease as well as poor living conditions. Eventually, captains posted and enforced hygienic standards, and conditions slowly improved. Wives, children, and camp followers offered some relief; they helped to improve morale and to care for the men. Throughout this period, officers and their soldiers helped to define what it meant to serve in the professional army. Though a peacetime standing army had not yet acquired the patriotic connotations it would have in later years, by the mid-1800s the United States had reorganized its military into a system based on the professional soldier.

References and Further Reading

Adams, John. *Rules and Regulations Respecting the Recruiting Service, 1798.* George Washington Papers, 1741–1799: Series 6. Military Papers. 1755–1798, Library of Congress, Washington, DC

Additional Rules and Regulations for Recruiting the Army, 1814. Army Papers. Missouri Historical Society, St. Louis

American State Papers, Miscellaneous. 2 vols. Washington, DC: Gales and Seaton, 1834

Appleby, Joyce. *Inheriting the Revolution, the First Generation of Americans.* Cambridge, MA: Belknap, 2001

Birtle, Andrew J. "The Origins of the Legion of the United States." *Journal of Military History* 67 (October 2003): 1249–62

Bolster, W. Jeffrey. *Black Jacks: African American Seamen in the Age of Sail.* Cambridge, MA: Harvard University Press, 1997

Bolster, W. Jeffrey. "'To Feel Like a Man': Black Seamen in the Northern States, 1800–1860." *Journal of American History* 76 (March 1990): 1173–99

Coffman, Edward M. *The Old Army: A Portrait of the American Army in Peacetime, 1784–1898.* New York: Oxford University Press, 1986

Corbin, Henry, and Raphael P. Thian, eds. *Legislative History of the General Staff of the Army of the United States (Its Organizations, Duties, Pay, and Allowances), 1775–1901.* Washington, DC: Government Printing Office, 1901

Cress, Lawrence Delbert. *Citizens in Arms: The Army and the Militia in American Society to the War of 1812.* Chapel Hill: University of North Carolina Press, 1982

Cusick, James G. *The Other War of 1812: The Patriot War and the American Invasion of Spanish East Florida.* Gainesville: University Press of Florida, 2003

Donaldson, Gary A. *The History of African-Americans in the Military.* Malabar, FL: Krieger, 1991

Duane, William. *A Handbook for Infantry: Containing the First Principles of Military Discipline.* Philadelphia: Author, 1813

Estes, J. Worth. *Naval Surgeon: Life and Death at Sea in the Age of Sail.* Canton, MA: Science History Publications, 1998

Griswold, Bert J., ed. *Fort Wayne, Gateway of the West, 1802–1813: Garrison Orderly Books; Indian Agency Account Book.* Indianapolis: Historical Bureau of the Indiana Library and Historical Department,1927

Guthman, William H. *March to Massacre, a History of the First Seven Years of the United States Army.* New York: McGraw Hill, 1975

Hassler, Warren W. Jr. *With Shield and Sword: American Military Affairs, Colonial Times to the Present.* Ames: Iowa State University Press, 1982

Heidler, David S., and Jeanne T. Heidler. *Daily Life in the Early American Republic, 1790–1820: Creating a New Nation.* Westport, CT: Greenwood Press, 2004

Kohn, Richard H. *Eagle and Sword: The Federalists and the Creation of the Military Establishment in America, 1783–1802.* New York: Free Press, 1975

Letters Received by the Office of the Adjutant General, 1805–1821. Microcopy 566, Roll 27. National Archives, Washington, DC

Letters to the Secretary of War. Microcopy 370, Roll 1. National Archives, Washington DC

Miller, Marion Mills, ed. *Great Debates in American History.* 14 vols. New York: Current Literature Publishing Company, 1913

Millett, Allen R. *Semper Fidelis, the History of the United States Marine Corps.* New York: Free Press, 1991

Millett, Allan R., and Peter Maslowski. *For the Common Defense: A Military History of the United States of America.* New York: Free Press, 1984

Nichols, Roger L. *General Henry Atkinson: A Western Military Career.* Norman: University of Oklahoma Press, 1965

Pennsylvania Gazette. 1791–1799.

Prucha, Francis Paul. *The Sword of the Republic: The United States Army on the Frontier, 1783–1834.* New York: Macmillan, 1969

Register of Enlistments, 1798–1815. Microcopy 233. National Archives, Washington, DC

Rigsby, Allen. Thomas Adams Smith Papers, 1809. Western Historical Manuscript Collection. University of Missouri Archives, Kansas City

Rowe, Mary Ellen. *Bulwark of the Republic: The American Militia in Antebellum West.* Westport, CT: Praeger, 2003

Skeen, C. Edward. *Citizen Soldiers in the War of 1812.* Lexington: University Press of Kentucky, 1999

Skelton, William B. "The Confederation's Regulars: A Social Profile of Enlisted Service in America's First Standing Army." *William and Mary Quarterly* 3rd ser. 46 (October 1989): 770–85

Stagg, J.C.A. "Soldiers in Peace and War: Comparative Perspectives on the Recruitment of the United States Army, 1802–1815." *William and Mary Quarterly* 3rd ser. 57 (January 2000): 79–120

Steuben, Baron de. *The Soldier's Monitor: Being a System of Discipline for the Use of the Infantry of the United States; Comprising Chiefly the Regulations of Baron De Steuben.* Rutland, VT: Fay & Davison, 1814

Stoddard, Amos. Papers, 1796–1812. Missouri Historical Society, St. Louis

Virtuous Expectations: Republican Motherhood and True Womanhood in the Early Republic

4

Dawn Sherman

Introduction

In the early republic, the daily lives of American women remained defined by many of the same traits and constraints that characterized life in the colonial era. Although differences separated white women from women of color, Northerners from Southerners, urbanites from farmers, and the rich from the poor, a few common themes united their experiences as women. These experiences included the necessity of work and participating in the marketplace, the centrality of family life, the obtaining of formal and informal educations, the influence of religion on their lives, and their participation in various reform movements. Women found themselves engaged in a wide array of tasks that frequently required them to place the interests of their husbands, fathers, and children before their personal desires. Their experiences also included an inability to live up to the pervasive and yet typically unrealistic gendered expectations of the era, ideas that were established by two popular concepts of the period: what scholars have called republican motherhood and true womanhood. These ideologies were challenged during the nation's first decades, especially as industrialization transformed much of society and new ideas about democracy and freedom permeated society. Yet, at the end of the era, the meaning of womanhood for most Americans remained remarkably intact.

Gendered Social Expectations

During the late 18th century, a nascent United States was trying to define itself as a nation. As the shape of the nation slowly evolved, American men and women from all walks of life defined and redefined the roles that women would play and the expectations that they would live with in this new democratic republic. With the abandonment of the British hierarchy and the accompanying social customs, many Americans envisioned and advocated a social upheaval, one in which the so-called natural social laws could be challenged. This social revolution, at least in the eyes of many, never materialized, and the patriarchal norms of the colonial world remained largely intact. As much as societal norms embraced the belief in an economic meritocracy and as much as it emphasized a democracy of ambitions, the new social code included strict social expectations for men and women. The revolution, in other words, hardly revolutionized what it meant to be a man or a woman.

The women of the early republic, the period between 1783 and 1830, were governed largely by two concepts: republican motherhood and true womanhood. These ideologies encompassed a range of expectations that overlapped one another and that adhered to many of the gendered norms of the colonial world, yet they also embraced many of the new concerns of the young republic. In many ways the concepts were amorphous fictions, but, taken as a loose set of complex ideals, the concepts defined women's proper place in American society. Based largely on the rhetoric of the Revolution and on the presumed demands of a democratic republic, patriotism and loyalty were the essence of the ideology of republican motherhood. This ideology established that women of America's new republic, through their maternal instincts and familial roles as mothers, would raise their sons to be virtuous and loyal citizens of the republic. As republican mothers, women were conveyors of truth, loyalty, and virtue, and, by rearing a loyal generation of children, they ensured the future of the democracy.

By 1820, republican motherhood had morphed into the closely defined ideology of true womanhood, a popular term used in trendy 19th-century advice magazines and religious literature. The value of women remained rooted in virtue and in their centrality to creating a nation capable of a successful democracy, but their importance transcended their role as mothers. The ideology of true womanhood also embraced women as daughters, sisters, and wives. This ideal deemed piety, purity, submissiveness, and domesticity as key attributes of a true woman, who was both a good wife and a good mother. The concept emerged in part due to the slow transition from a dominant agrarian economy to an increasingly industrial economy. As the American economy became more diversified, men were drawn away from their homes and family farms, and into either a wage labor force or a professional occupation (such as a lawyer, office worker, factory manager, or doctor). Through the establishment of a professional work force in American society came the emergence of a middle class, whose rise allowed the woman to assume the role of the dominant and most influential parent in the realm of the family, redefining her as wife and mother.

Image of a woman with three children from a membership certificate from the Independent Benevolent Society of Philadelphia, 1811. (*Library of Congress*)

The common theme linking these models was the separation of spheres: private and public, women's and men's. Relegated to the domestic realm, women were guardians of virtue, piety, and morality. Women, it was presumed, were too fragile and delicate to participate in public arenas such as business or politics. Men, presumed to be less pious than women, were considered more capable of handling the evils presented by business and political matters. In this worldview, the home became a refuge and women served as the protectors. While women were ideally prevented from direct participation in public affairs, they possessed a certain amount of authority over the family and thereby had an indirect influence on society and politics.

The ideologies of republican motherhood and true womanhood could rarely be pursued, let alone achieved, by the least privileged women. These notions, however, continued to define women of elite and bourgeois status, women who possessed the time and means to dedicate to the precepts of this rhetoric and imagery. Economic status, racism, and ethnocentrism prevented many women from living up to the gendered norms of the early republic. Other women rejected these expectations entirely, refusing to submit to such an austere existence.

The Economic Transformation

The Industrial Revolution in the Northeast ushered in a significant shift in the nature of women's work and their participation in the marketplace. Although the nature of women's work often did not necessarily change during the early years of industrialization, the location in which their work took place was frequently new. The transition in milieu greatly affected how women's labor was regarded and how working women fit into the social expectations encompassed in the popular images of republican mother and true womanhood.

Family Life

The family was the defining institution for women of the early republic. This criterion proved to be true for all women, regardless of race, class, or region. In 1787, a young adolescent girl, Betsy Purviance of Maryland, was informed by her father that women were ordained to care for and manage their family, whether wealthy or of meager means. This was the traditional belief about a woman's duty and responsibility throughout the 18th and 19th centuries in America. Purviance received advice that women across the young nation would have recognized. A few years earlier, Christopher Marshall of Philadelphia, for example, recorded in his journal that his wife was "constantly employed in the affairs of the family." These affairs, especially in the agrarian world, consisted of an endless list of tasks and responsibilities that enabled households to survive. Marshall noted that his wife tended to the kitchen, baked bread and pies, and cooked meat. He noted her "cleanliness about the house" and observed "her attendance in the orchard, cutting and drying apples . . . making of cider without tools . . . seeing all our washing done . . . all smoothed by her; add to this, her making of twenty large cheeses, and that from one cow, and daily using with milk and cream, besides her sewing, knitting, &c" (Duane 1877, 157–58). These were just a few of the tasks and responsibilities that the women of America's early republic undertook and that young girls like Betsy Purviance were expected to master. Unfortunately, Mrs. Marshall, like many women of her time, was identified only by her husband's name—Mrs. Christopher Marshall—because her given name, like that of other women in the era, went unrecorded as the result of patriarchy.

As Betsy Purviance's father and Mrs. Marshall demonstrated, the responsibilities associated with family dominated the life of women, especially married women, in the early republic. Marriage was a central and defining aspect for the majority of women in 18th- and 19th-century American society. Girls were raised and educated with the ultimate ambition of finding and serving a husband and raising a family. This frequently required that women sacrifice their own interests on behalf of the needs of their family. Upon her marriage, for example, Sarah Hill Fletcher moved to

Illustration from *Narrative of the Life and Adventures of Henry Bibb, an American Slave* in which a baby is auctioned away from his mother, 1849. (*Library of Congress*)

Indianapolis to join her husband and set up her own household. In diary entries for 1821, Sarah included that she spun wool, washed all day, baked, and spun candlewicks. Sarah, like countless other early American women, left behind her family and friends in Ohio to accommodate her husband's opportunities.

Enslaved women faced even more challenges when it came to marriage and family building. Slave women needed permission from their owners to marry because their marriages were informally recognized by society but not formally sanctioned by law. In addition, enslaved women had remarkably limited choices for a husband because they were usually expected to find a mate on the same or neighboring plantation. For bondwomen, marriage did not secure them permanent residency with their husbands or with their children for that matter. At any time their owner or the owner of their husbands, if different, could sell members of the slave family and separate them. This had tremendous effects on the slave community. Elizabeth Keckley, for example, had little memory of her father, George Pleasant, because he lived on another plantation. His master allowed only semiannual visits to see Elizabeth on Easter and Christmas. When George's owner decided to leave Virginia for the greener pastures of the West, Elizabeth and her mother Agnes Hobbs faced a permanent separation. George Pleasant saw neither his daughter nor his beloved wife ever again. Elizabeth would go through other separations from family of equal, if not greater, psychological effect. In 1863, Old Elizabeth, as she was called, could still remember the forced separation from her family in 1777 Maryland, an event that took place when she was just 11

Old Elizabeth (1766–1866)

The life stories of slaves are typically anonymous generalities applicable to the slave experience en masse. Few slaves possessed the ability to record their own life experiences; however, the former slave known as Old Elizabeth is a rare exception. At the ripe old age of 97, she shared the story of her religious struggle and enlightenment.

Born in Maryland in 1766, she lived a childhood of sorrow but found hope and spirituality in her adolescent and later years. Her parents, also slaves, instilled a great sense of religion and spirituality in Elizabeth and her siblings. Nightly her father read from Scripture. At age 11, Elizabeth was separated from her family and sent to work on another plantation. Depressed and overwhelmed by loneliness, she ran away back to her family. Her escape was short-lived. Left desolate of spirit, Elizabeth turned to God for comfort, praying constantly throughout each day. Her state of misery lasted about half a year, when at last she experienced spiritual enlightenment and salvation through a revelation sent by God. Elizabeth took solace in her daily worship, but, taunted by others for her emotional devotion, she abandoned her constant homage. At this point, she felt the spirit of peace and joy leave her.

For a short period, Elizabeth returned to the farm with her mother, but twice more she was sold and forced to move. She began to pray

years old. When her master sent Elizabeth to live on another farm, she was devastated by the separation from her family and trekked 20 miles without permission to be reunited with her mother. For her violation, she was bound by a rope and severely lashed. Sustaining a traditional family structure was complicated and nearly impossible for slave families (Gutman 1976).

Marriage and family structure and function for Native American women greatly differed from other women's in the early republic. Traditionally, many Indian nations were matrilineal and matrilocal. In these societies, families were traced through the woman's line, female relatives structured their households around each other, and women controlled property. In addition, elder women frequently initiated the courtship rituals for their families. Among the Cherokee, and most southeastern nations, a married man left his village and household and took up residence with his wife and her clan. He could not become a member of her family, and their children would become part of the women's family. Similarly, Choctaw women were responsible for the choice of their marital partner. During the ceremonial courtship ritual, a Choctaw man chased the woman he desired in a public performance. If she allowed herself to be captured, she affirmed the commitment. By avoiding capture, the Choctaw maiden denied the marriage pledge. Many eastern Indians also practiced polygamy, reserving the practice of multiple wives as a privilege for powerful men. Cherokee men usually married a sister of their first wife so that they would not have to leave the village and any children would belong to the same clan. This practice further extended the clan's lineage and enhanced the women's personal autonomy.

again, yearning for the inner peace she had previously felt, yet she felt a calling to bring salvation to others as well. At age 30 Elizabeth began to seek this calling when she was freed from bondage. Once granted her freedom, Elizabeth took a more active role in her religion by attending different meetings but still struggled with her purpose and her role in spreading the Lord's word. Elizabeth encountered many challenges because she was neither generally educated nor ordained by any church to preach. The zealous nature of her meetings caused great concern. Moreover, she was a woman and, what's more, a black woman. She faced not only racism but also sexism among her fellow Christians. However, Elizabeth was not swayed from her path. She persisted in her mission, traveling throughout the United States, including Maryland, Virginia, Pennsylvania, and Michigan, where she founded a school for colored orphans.

In her travels, she challenged the boundaries of gender, race, and religion. Although faced with adversity, Elizabeth also met with great success. Whether worshiping with an entire town or just a few people, Elizabeth brought the spirit of the Lord to many a soul. Her dedication and faith led her across borders and into the hearts of many. At the age of 87 Elizabeth retired to Philadelphia, physically burdened by illness but spiritually harmonious.

Women raised the children collectively among their clans; fathers had little influence on their own offspring. The practice of multiple marriages among these tribes allowed for strong kinship ties and facilitated trading relations with white men who participated in intermarriage. Through these marital connections, traders obtained access and their wives' assistance in multiple villages, clans, and sometimes even tribal nations (Perdue 1998).

Single Women

Not all women in the early republic viewed marriage and family as their ultimate ambition in life. Some young women recognized that marriage had its disadvantages and even advocated the sensibility and benefits of remaining single. Unmarried women, whether single or widowed, held an advantage that married women did not: They could own property, and they possessed their own labor. New Englander Eliza Southgate expressed this advantage in a letter to her cousin in 1800:

> I do not esteem marriage absolutely essential to happiness. A single life is considered too generally a reproach; but let me ask you, which is the most despicable—she who marries a man she scarcely thinks *well* of—to avoid the reputation of an old maid—or, she who with more delicacy than one she could not highly esteem, preferred to live single all her life." (Goodfriend and Christie 1981, 91)

Although Eliza indeed married just a few years later to Walter Brown, she still asserted her belief in the growing trend toward prudence of choice and contemplated the notion of remaining single.

While many women of America's early republic began to exercise discretion when choosing marriage partners, some refused to marry at all. Catharine Sedgwick, daughter of a prominent Massachusetts family, chose to remain unwed. She remarked in 1828 that "so many I have loved have made shipwreck of happiness in marriage or have found it a dreary joyless condition where affection has died of starvation, so many have been blighted by incurable and bitter sorrows" (Cott 1997, 49). Although presented with numerous requests for her hand, Sedgwick refused because no one reflected her notion of perfection. However, as years passed, Sedgwick became dissatisfied with her solitary state. She began to regret foregoing her many chances at the contentment that marriage offered. While the love and affection from her siblings persisted, she no longer held the spotlight in their hearts. Husbands, wives, and children replaced her. Although she accepted her state, even relishing the independence, she resented the loneliness and "would not advise anyone to remain unmarried" (Sedgwick 1997, 165). As Sedgwick's experience indicates, the decision to marry or remain unwed held an unpredictable future for many.

Many poor girls similarly delayed their nuptials. As opportunities for wage work became available for women in urban factories, many girls of meager means chose to work a few years before choosing the limitations of marriage and family. Many of these spinsters took work at the textile mills in the Northeast or at one of the other new workplaces of the early republic. These women craved the experience of independence, both physical and financial. These working girls, often for the first time, lived away from home and parental constraints. Most of them spent about two years in the factories or mills before eventually taking what was seen as their proper place in the domestic realm. While liberty from the patriarchy of marriage and family was a growing trend during the 18th and 19th centuries, marriage remained the portal to a woman's identity and family the aspiration of the masses (Chambers-Scheller 1984).

The Household Economy

Household production was essential to the financial survival of most families living in the early republic. Martha Ballard and Elizabeth Meredith represent the role of typical white women living during the early republic. Conservative ideologies of the 18th and 19th centuries suggested that women confine themselves to domestic bliss and the joy of child care, buttressing the illusion of petticoats and afternoon tea in the parlor. However, the reality for most women entailed full days of constant, strenuous, and tedious toil, striving to maintain a subsistence existence for their families; this reality applied to the Ballards and Merediths.

Martha Ballard, in Hallowell, Maine, could hardly be defined by her marriage or family. Fortunately for the historian, she filled her diary with a slew of mundane occurrences as well as with payments and exchanges for goods and services that she offered on the frontier of Maine. Even at a glance, Martha Ballard's life appears exhausting. Often left alone for long periods (her husband was a frontier surveyor), the survival of the Ballard household economy and family rested on Martha's shoulders. She served a plethora of functions in her effort to support her family. Martha was wife, mother, teacher, cook, baker, spinner, weaver, and gardener, and she tended an array of farm animals: turkeys, chickens, pigs, and sheep. Her most lucrative and perhaps most strenuous duty was that of midwife and community medical caregiver. As her daughters grew older and were able to spin or weave without supervision, Martha dedicated more time to her work as a midwife, and her family benefited from this increase in household income. Armed with her paddle, Martha braved the local waters and navigated her trusted canoe to attend laboring mothers or sick and ailing neighbors. Often Martha received payment in kind for her medical services. Rather than shillings and pence, she accepted coffee, tea, cheese, butter, vegetables, farm animals, or cloth. An array of various goods sufficed as payment. In essence, Martha Ballard was an independent entrepreneur. Although Martha certainly functioned within the confines of the defined domestic realm, she also penetrated the boundaries of the republican mother and the true woman as an economically independent woman (Ulrich 1990).

Elizabeth Meredith also challenged the ideologies of her day. Elizabeth emigrated from England and made her home in Philadelphia, Pennsylvania. Elizabeth played a key role in her husband's businesses and investments, and she was quite confident in her abilities. She wrote to her son in 1796, in a rather puckish manner, that at the time she served as the clerk to her husband's tannery business, seeing as no one else could fill the position. Indeed, she proved essential to her husband's business. She functioned as bookkeeper, collected debts, and acquired financing. These functions did not eliminate her obligations as a mother to raise dutiful sons and to prepare her daughters for their future duties as housewives. However, Elizabeth's correspondence demonstrates her importance as mother and household manager as well as a partner and consultant in the family business and investments. Like Martha Ballard, Elizabeth existed outside the periphery of contemporary ideals regarding the appropriate activity of women (Branson 1996).

Women living in urban areas also made their financial contributions to family economics, and theirs was just as necessary as those of their countryside counterparts. Urban dwellers in the early republic were often immigrants—English, German, and Irish—who were looking for a new start. The dawning of the Industrial Revolution allowed urban women to tap into a new market of exchange: the wage labor system. These women were not limited by the boundaries of the home; their neighborhoods became their spheres. Immigrants lived in close proximity to each other in small tenement

Textile workers at spinning machines, from an 1836 engraving. (*Library of Congress*)

quarters. Women in these neighborhoods formed close bonds and assisted one another in the chores and tasks that needed tending, such as babysitting and preparing meals. Urban women participated in a multitude of occupations. Those with room to spare rented to boarders. Many took advantage of the large, single male population working in the city. Women hired themselves out to launder, press, and darn clothing as well as to prepare meals for men with no families. Urban women also found work in factories and mills as seamstresses, pressers, and laundresses. Many of these tasks were performed by women in rural areas, but urban women were paid for their work.

Women of the South

Most white Southern women were nothing like Margaret Mitchell's mythic creations in *Gone with the Wind*. Mary Mason of Raleigh, North Carolina, explained the very nature of a good Southern housewife. She provides a long laundry list (no pun intended) of a housewife's responsibilities and duties. These tasks included but were not limited to weekly pantry cleaning, ironing, washing dishes, food preparation, laundering (clothes, bed coverings, and bed linens), tending to the dairy (making milk, cheese, and butter), gardening (which vegetables to plant, when and where), and caring for the poultry (chickens, geese, ducks, and turkeys). In addition to all these chores, Mason addressed methods of care for children with particular maladies such as worms, vomiting, colic, measles, mumps, scarlet fever, and numerous other ailments. She also discussed child management and teaching good morals and manners (Mason 1875). One of Mason's most interesting topics was the appropriate treatment of slaves. She declared that, for slaves to act appropriately, a mistress must be kind yet firm. According to Ms. Mary Mason, a smooth day's work depended on the early rise of the slaves. To appease them and to gain their respect, Mason indicated that a good mistress should take a genuine interest in their lives: including their health, hygiene, and overall appearance. She also insisted that slaves be praised for their good work in an effort to inspire them and to keep them honest. She recommended that slaves be made comfortable and be provided with abundant food. Mason drew special attention to the good health of servants. She suggested that the house kitchen be in close proximity to the main house to prevent servants from exposure to bad weather, which might cause serious illness. According to Mason, all of her advice drew on the tenets of a good and right Christian mistress. Southern mistresses such as Mason set the tone for the vision of the South, but these women were merely an exaggerated representation of the regional ideal (Mason 1875).

The life of a bondwoman was markedly different from that of her mistress, for obvious reasons. Whereas plantation mistresses led lives of relative seclusion due to the distances between neighboring properties and family members, bondwomen benefited from the close-knit community of slaves, who were concentrated in the slave quarters of plantations. Bondwomen frequently had more opportunities than their white counterparts to socialize and to communicate with other women. Of course, this opportunity to socialize and form relationships with other slaves does not diminish the fact that these women were held in bondage and considered property. George Bourne illustrated this point when he created his 1834 print depicting the exchange of a female slave for a sheep and a ram (currently located on the New York Public Library Digital Gallery). An Englishman who immigrated to the United States and lived briefly in Virginia's Shenandoah Valley, Bourne was also a Presbyterian pastor and an abolitionist. His engraving exemplified the status of slaves as no better than property, relegating bondwomen and all slaves to the status of domestic animals, their lives dependent on the mercy of their owners.

Female slaves led the most laborious and difficult lives of all the women discussed. While women like Mary Mason described their lofty expectations of housework, African American slaves actually performed most of the tasks themselves. House slaves performed traditional domestic maintenance chores in the plantation house, including cooking, cleaning, laundering, and

Women work in a field alongside men, harvesting grain. Illustration from *The Columbian Magazine*, published in Philadelphia, 1788. (*Library of Congress*)

caring for the mistress's children. Elizabeth Keckley, for example, cared for her mistress's daughter. Elizabeth was only 4 years old when she took on this task, but she recalled her confidence in her ability. She was also happy to move from the slave cabin to the main house. Dressed in a short frock and white apron, Elizabeth was instructed to keep the flies at bay and to prevent Mrs. Brunell's baby from crying. She rocked the child while she attended her duty; however, she rocked a bit too energetically, and the baby tumbled to the floor. Bewildered and frightened, Elizabeth grabbed the fire shovel in an effort to rescue the infant. This did not go over well with Mrs. Brunell. For her folly, Elizabeth received numerous heavyhanded lashes—a punishment she never forgot. Even young children were subject to brutal corporal punishments.

In addition to household duties, female slaves also performed hard labor, usually associated with but not limited to fieldwork. Bondwomen fertilized fields by hand with manure, felled trees with axes, and drove animal plows. When pregnant, women continued to perform a wide range of albeit lighter tasks, such as hoeing, raking, and pulling weeds. Slave women also worked the dairy and tended to farm animals and gardens. Whether domestic or field hands, slave women also necessarily fulfilled their duties as wives and mothers. Once their day of forced labor was complete, bondwomen tended to their own families. They prepared meals, cultivated their garden plots, stored what food was available to them, mended worn clothing, cleaned their living quarters, and cared for the elders. Slave women, like white women, spun, wove, and sewed. They also functioned as midwives, not only within the slave community but also for white women. The toil of slave women was endless.

The wives of yeomen farmers endured a more arduous life than their plantation sisters experienced, yet they maintained the free will that bondwomen did not possess. Few yeomen owned slaves, and their profit margins were often small, requiring yeoman women to provide labor in the fields. While plantation owners concentrated on cash crops such as tobacco and cotton, most yeomen raised produce and farm animals not only for their own consumption but also for sale to planters. To make such potentially lucrative sales, yeoman wives had to participate in what was considered a traditionally male duty. In addition to their household responsibilities of cooking, cleaning, laundering, storing food, serving as midwives, and rearing children, yeomen wives toiled in the fields alongside their husbands. Although the wives of yeomen fulfilled their gendered duties of domesticity, field toil, according to the era's ideals of republican motherhood and true womanhood, rendered them lesser women (McCurry 1995).

Native American Women

Native American women represented a unique threat to the era's ideals because they were hardly controlled or defined by their men. Cherokee women, for example, derived power and authority from agricultural production, which was their most vital responsibility. According to Cherokee beliefs, women were givers of life who were also responsible for sustaining life. Throughout the year, Cherokee women grew and harvested corn and also gathered nuts and root vegetables to provide for their families. In the same vein, Choctaw women were also farmers and controlled the distribution of food within the tribe, placing them in a position of power. While Cherokee and Choctaw women occupied a specific gendered sphere, their position was the antithesis to the ideals of true womanhood. As a result, white Americans frequently misread Indian society and concluded that Indian men were lazy and Indian women were slaves. Bernard Romans, on his travels through the South in the 1770s, observed that "a savage has the most determined resolution against labouring or tilling the ground, the slave his wife must do that" (Romans 1962, 41). Louis-Philippe similarly remarked, "the Indians have all the work done by the women. They are assigned not only household tasks, even the corn, peas, and beans and potatoes are planted, tended, and preserved by the women. The man smokes peacefully while the woman grinds corn in the mortar" (Louis-Philippe 1977, 73). While Romans and Louis-Philippe rendered disapproving observations, for the Cherokees these functions fell within their traditional gendered customs that structured family and society.

During the early republic, the gendered norms of Indian society faced many challenges from the outside. Much of these threats came from the trading networks that brought various European goods into Indian communities. Throughout eastern America, Natives traded deer, beaver, and other animal skins, tobacco, and baskets (made by women) for manufactured European goods such as guns, ammunition, and alcohol. They also traded

Sarah J. Hale (1788–1879)

Sarah Josepha Hale is an inspiring figure. Born shortly after the American Revolution, she helped to shape the new vision of the American woman. Hale was born to the Buell family of New Hampshire in 1788. Subject to the traditional principals of gendered spheres, she was educated in the fundamentals of home and child care by her mother.

Formal education was not available to young girls. However, her brother Horatio shared his knowledge and education gained from Dartmouth with his sister and encouraged her self-study. She cultivated an acute knowledge of literature and a talent for writing, which would later serve her as a means of survival.

In 1813, Sarah wed lawyer David Hale. Unlike most men of his time, David encouraged his wife to write and to continue her self-taught education. Unfortunately, after nine years of marriage and five children, David suc-cumbed to a sudden bout of pneumonia and died in 1822, leaving his wife with little savings and a family to support. With the help of her sister-in-law and her husband's Masonic associates, Sarah published a book of poems titled *The Genius of Oblivion: and Other Original Poems*. Shortly thereafter, she produced a second publication titled *Northwood* that addressed the controversial topic of slavery. These two successful publications led to an unexpected and life-altering opportunity, one that would influence a generation of American women.

In 1827, Sarah accepted the position of editor of the *Ladies Magazine and Literary Gazette*, later renamed *American Ladies Magazine*. In 1836, the magazine was bought out and renamed *Godey's Lady's Book*. Sarah used the magazine as a platform to advocate the development of women's minds through formal education—the same offered to men. Equality of

for metal utensils and tools, iron tools, brass containers, and European clothing. Although many of these goods lessened the burden of daily toil for both men and women, Native Americans became increasingly dependent on them. These novel wares quickly replaced those that were traditionally made by tribal women. Rather than crafting their cookware and utensils, agricultural tools, and clothing, many Native women became dependent on their men to obtain the necessary European goods. This change in roles threatened the autonomy and economic independence of Native women. Native women no longer independently produced many of the goods for the tribe but became dependent on their men to obtain what they needed to perform their chores of farming, cooking, sewing, and crafting. Rather than crafting wares from the bounty of their environment, tribes had to pay for their necessities.

The Second Great Awakening

The role of women in the new republic was tied to religious changes that transformed the young nation. Between 1795 and 1830, America experi-

Sarah Josepha Hale, novelist, editor of the influential *Godey's Ladies Book,* and promoter of a national Thanksgiving Day holiday (1788–1879). (*Library of Congress*)

education was a radical notion in the 19th century, but Sarah remained a fierce activist. Throughout her periodical, Sarah included works by the most popular and formidable literary minds of the time, such as Edgar Allan Poe, Ralph Waldo Emerson, and Henry Wadsworth Longfellow, so that her readers could benefit from their prose. She also provided reports on the latest openings of women's educational facilities and was a strong supporter of Vassar College. Sarah advocated not only the education of women but the employment of women as teachers and doctors. After all, she maintained that mothers were the best and most natural teachers and caregivers. Sarah remained the editor of *Godey's Lady's Book* until 1877, when once again the publication was sold. Throughout her tenure, Sarah greatly influenced countless women's lives through encouragement and her tireless dedication to the condition of women.

enced a revival in evangelical Christianity, a movement widely known as the Second Great Awakening. This movement had a tremendous impact on the nation's women. It facilitated the break from the popular stereotype of women as evil temptresses like the biblical Eve, and the religious fervor transformed the woman into a gentile, pious, moral being whose job was to moralize her family, cementing the desired image of the republican mother and later the true woman.

For many women, religion served as a socially acceptable gateway to becoming active in society. Women used religious-inspired reforms as a way to wield influence and power, both socially and politically. These reforms— from temperance to abolition—frequently began as offshoots of church organizations. Working according to religious tenets, women were allowed to fulfill their obligations as pious and moral protectors of the home. Even calls for the advancement of women adhered to the era's ideological expectations. For instance, Sarah J. Hale's promotion of female education and enlightenment was constrained by the ideology of true womanhood and the will of God. In an 1828 essay published in *Ladies Magazine*, Hale declared that the biblical statement that "'he shall rule over thee,' was in reference to the social condition of man and woman to be the punishment of Eve's transgression;

but remember it is not said he shall have more *mind* or more *knowledge* than his helpmate" (Hale, September 1828, 422–23).

The egalitarian tenets of evangelical Christianity also appealed greatly to the enslaved population. Bondwomen such as Old Elizabeth clung to Christianity as a means to survive their plight. When separated from her mother, she turned to God and prayed the Lord's Prayer to free her from her sorrow and to be saved. During her emotional plea, Elizabeth experienced the moment of salvation; she was 13 years old. Shortly after her moment of enlightenment, Elizabeth lost her zeal. However, once her freedom was granted, she was free to explore, to seek religious guidance, and once again to become a believer.

For some Native American women, Christianity also occasionally served as a means of becoming assimilated into the American norm. In the early republic, countless missionaries set up formal and informal schools in an effort to train Native girls and women in the appropriate functions of housewifery and other domestic work in an effort to civilize the perceived heathens. Many Native women used these innovative skills to maintain their centrality in their villages and to support their families in traditional ways. Other Native American women, like those among the Cherokees and Choctaws, became increasingly dependent on these new skills and as a result grew marginalized in their communities.

Breaking the Bonds of Womanhood

Although women during this period were restricted by rigid social boundaries, they began to make small strides of progress, especially in the realm of female education. Traditional female education consisted of supervised training in housewifery taught by mothers to their daughters. Girls from privileged families occasionally attended private female academies or boarding schools, where they received primary and secondary education with a strong concentration in religion. Eliza Ann Mulford attended a girls school in Litchfield, Connecticut, and in 1814 cited in her notebook that students were required to pray morning and evening and to attend church every Sabbath. Eliza also indicated that the girls were questioned every day as to whether they had read their assigned Scriptures and said their prayers. Just as importantly, they were schooled in the ornamental arts. They learned skills that allowed them to engage in polite society and to appear to be the prized possessions of their husbands. Their educations emphasized painting, music, dancing, fashion, needlework, and perhaps a foreign language. However, formal education remained unattainable for girls without means, and advanced education remained elusive to all young women.

An early activist for the cause of female education was the author of the *Female Advocate*, a women's magazine founded in 1801. This anonymous female writer bemoaned the inequality faced by women. Given the same quality of education as men, the author explained, women would be just as successful, and they would be enabled to perform in professional occupations just as aptly. She spoke of education as a preventative measure against the victimization of women. She deemed that women armed with knowledge would have the ability to thwart reckless seducers who would otherwise prey on feminine naïveté. She also asserted that through education and knowledge women could reform the would-be seducers and instill in them respect for women: This would be "the mean of enabling us [women] to possess some command over ourselves" (Cott 1978, 232). This champion went further to illustrate the advantage of knowledge for widowed women. If an uneducated woman were widowed and left in a disagreeable financial state, she would most likely become a burden on her family or the state. However, if a widow were educated, she could draw on her knowledge to support herself and her family without consequence.

Sarah J. Hale exemplified the educated widow spoken about in the *Female Advocate*. Hale's husband David unexpectedly passed away in 1822, and Sarah was faced with raising four young children on her own. Luckily, Sara's family, including her husband, had encouraged her continued education. She successfully published three novels and was subsequently offered the position of editor of a popular woman's reader titled *Ladies Magazine*, later known as *Godey's Lady's Book*. Sarah served as a staunch advocate for the advancement of women in the area of education and dedicated her publication to the cause. Hale encouraged women to become educated within their proper sphere, as the caretakers and pious conveyers of morality. She advocated the development of the woman's intellectual mind, supported the employment of female physicians and female foreign missionaries, but did not endorse women to enter the political arena. In the first issue of the magazine, Hale included an introduction regarding the purpose and intent of her publication:

> [I]n this age of innovation, perhaps no experiment will have an influence more important on the character and happiness of our society than the granting to females the advantages of a systematic and thorough education. The honor of this triumph, in favor of intellect over long established prejudices, belongs to the men of America.

Hale depicted female education as an honor to men because, once women acquired intellectual depth, they would be worthy companions for their husbands. Sarah further buttressed her stance by arguing that female education allowed women to be better mothers; "then the sons of the republic will become polished pillars in the temple of our national glory, and the daughters bright gems to adorn it." Hale insisted on female education for the betterment of a woman in her role as wife and mother, not to enhance her role outside the home or to compete with her husband in the social or political sphere. Sensitive to the threat that may have been perceived by her rhetoric, Hale worked within the realm of domesticity to influence the acceptance of her plea. She appealed to gentlemen that the patronage of her periodical would not inhibit women and that a subscription to the magazine would be "a memento of his affection" (Hale, January 1828, 1–4).

Conclusion

As the early republic came to an end, the lives of women had been in many ways transformed. The American Revolution brought forth the birth of a new nation and new beginnings. For the women of America, a new definition of woman commenced as well, with the republican mother, followed by true womanhood. Change continued to abound as the 18th century gave way to the 19th century, which ushered in a period of unprecedented growth for America. This growth initiated a large-scale transformation in American society—economically and ideologically. As new cities and towns emerged, as immigration increased, and as cotton spread across the South, American women struggled to live up to the expectations placed upon them. Many were no longer willing to accept the limitations that defined a woman of America's early republic. The progress of the new era applied not only to commerce and expansion but also to the state of women. Women garnered influence and authority through their virtuous piety as wives and mothers. As the market economy expanded, women were able to apply their traditional home production skills to the emergent centralized wage labor industries. Their participation in the market allowed many to gain a modicum of independence. Not all women benefited from this evolution, however. Black women remained enslaved and subject to the whims of their masters. Native women lost their once beloved, admirable, and influential status within their tribes. Their land was measured, parceled, and fenced, as was their spirit. For women of color, liberation and independence remained elusive for many years to come. However, under the guise of religious tenets and obligation, advocacy and reform allowed many women to obtain more education, which in turn facilitated independence. As the 19th century progressed, change became the promise of a new day. Advocacy and reform gained momentum and would become the staple of women's activity in the coming years, eventually benefiting all women.

References and Further Reading

Boydston, Jeanne. *Home and Work: Housework, Wages, and the Ideology of Labor in the Early Republic*. New York: Oxford University Press, 1990

Branson, Susan. "Women and the Family Economy in the Early Republic: The Case of Elizabeth Meredith." *Journal of the Early Republic* 16 (Spring 1996): 47–71

Chambers-Scheller, Virgina Lee. *Liberty a Better Husband: Single Women in America: The Generations of 1780–1840*. New Haven, CT: Yale University Press, 1984

Cott, Nancy. *The Bonds of Womanhood: "Woman's Sphere" in New England, 1780–1835*, 2nd ed. New Haven, CT: Yale University Press, 1997

Cott, Nancy. "Passionlessness: An Interpretation of Victorian Sexual Ideology, 1790–1850." *Signs: Journal of Women in Culture and Society* 4, no. 2 (1978): 219–36

Cott, Nancy. "Young Women in the Second Great Awakening in New England." *Feminist Studies* 3 (Fall 1975): 15–29

Duane, William, ed. *Extracts from the Diary of Christopher Marshall 1774–1781.* Albany: New York Times, 1877

Goodfriend, Joyce D., and Claudia M. Christie, eds. *Lives of American Women: A History with Documents*. Boston: Little, Brown and Company, 1981

Gutman, Herbert. *The Black Family in Slavery and Freedom, 1750–1925*. New York: Pantheon, 1976

Hill, Sarah H. *Weaving New Worlds: Southeastern Cherokee Women and Their Basketry*. Chapel Hill: University of North Carolina Press, 1997

Hale, Sarah J. "Education." *Ladies Magazine* 1 (September 1828): 422–23

Hale, Sarah J. "Introduction." *Ladies Magazine* 1 (January 1828): 1–4

Jabour, Anya. *Marriage in the Early Republic: Elizabeth and William Wirt and the Companionate Ideal*. Baltimore, MD: Johns Hopkins University Press, 1998.

Kerber, Linda. "The Republican Mother: Women and the Enlightenment—An American Perspective." *American Quarterly* 28 (Summer 1976): 187–205

Kidwell, Clara Sue. "Choctaw Women and Cultural Persistence in Mississippi." In Nancy Shoemaker, ed. *Negotiators of Change: Historical Perspectives on Native American Women*, 115–34. New York: Routledge, 1995

Kierner, Cynthia A. *Beyond the Household: Women's Place in the Early South 1700–1835*. Ithaca, NY: Cornell University Press, 1998

Lewis, Jan. "The Republican Wife: Virtue and Seduction in the Early Republic." *William and Mary Quarterly* 3rd ser. 44 (October 1987): 689–710

Louis-Philippe. *Diary of My Travels in America*. Translation by Stephen Becker. New York: Delacorte Press, 1977

Mason, Mary. *The Young Housewife's Counsellor and Friend: Containing Directions in Every Department of Housekeeping, Including the Duties of Wife and Mother*. New York: E. J. Hale & Son, 1875

McCurry, Stephanie. *Masters of Small Worlds: Yeoman Households, Gender Relations, and the Political Culture of the Antebellum South Carolina Low Country*. New York: Oxford University Press, 1995

McMillen, Sally G. *Southern Women: Black and White in the Old South*, 2nd ed. Wheeling, IL: Harlan Davidson, 2002

Memoire of Old Elizabeth, a Coloured Woman. Philadelphia, PA: Collins Printer, 1863

Perdue, Theda. *Cherokee Women: Gender and Culture Change, 1700–1835.* Lincoln: University of Nebraska Press, 1998

Roberts, Mary Louise. "*True Womanhood* Revisited." *Journal of Women's History* 14, 1 (2002): 150–55

Romans, Bernard. *A Concise Natural History of East and West Florida.* Gainesville: University of Florida Press, 1962 (Orig. pub. 1775)

Ruether, Rosemary Radford, and Rosemary Skinner Keller, eds. *Women and Religion in America, Volume 1: The Nineteenth Century: A Documentary History.* Cambridge, MA: Harper & Row, 1981

Schloesser, Pauline E. *The Fair Sex: White Women and Racial Patriarchy in the Early American Republic.* New York: New York University Press, 2002

Sedgwick, Catharine M. "Diary Entry, May 18, 1828." In Nancy Woloch, ed. *Early American Women: A Documentary History 1600–1900,* 2nd ed. 163–165. Belmont, CA: Wadsworth, 1997

Stansell, Christine. *City of Women: Sex and Class in New York 1789–1860.* Urbana: University of Illinois Press, 1982

Ulrich, Laurel Thatcher, ed. *A Midwife's Tale: The Life of Martha Ballard, Based on Her Diary, 1785–1812.* New York: Vintage, 1990

Welter, Barbara. "The Cult of True Womanhood: 1820–1860." *American Quarterly* 18 (Summer 1966): 151–74

White, Deborah. "Female Slaves: Sex Roles and Status in the Antebellum Plantation South." In Catherine Clinton, ed. *Half Sister of History: Southern Women and the American Past,* 56–75. Durham, NC: Duke University Press, 1994

Zagarri, Rosemarie. *Revolutionary Backlash: Women and Politics in the Early American Republic.* Philadelphia: University of Pennsylvania Press, 2007

States of Liberty, States of Bondage: African Americans in the Early Republic | 5

Jennifer Hull Dorsey

Introduction

In 1799, the agriculturalist John Beale Bordley confidently declared that slavery was "done with in America" (Bordley 1801, 389). Bordley's declaration was certainly premature, but it was neither outrageous nor controversial, and many readers, especially in the Mid-Atlantic and Northeastern states, would have nodded their heads in agreement. In 1799, one-sixth of the African Americans in Bordley's home state of Maryland were free, and more free African Americans lived in Virginia than in the so-called free state of Pennsylvania. If these steps toward a general African American emancipation seemed small and incremental, they were nevertheless impressive, and they gave legitimacy to Bordley's claim.

Of course, Bordley was wrong: In 1799 slavery was not done with in America. In fact, over the next 50 years American slavery continued to grow, spread, and change. In 1790, fewer than 700,000 enslaved African Americans lived in the United States, but by 1840 the enslaved population had increased to 2.5 million. Slavery was done with in some parts of America, but it was quite alive and prospering in other parts. This simultaneous and seemingly contradictory spread of African American freedom and slavery shaped and defined the African American experience in the early republic.

The African American Experience

How did African Americans experience life in the early republic? For free African Americans, life was about testing the limits of their new freedom, making choices about where to work and live, deciding on marriage and

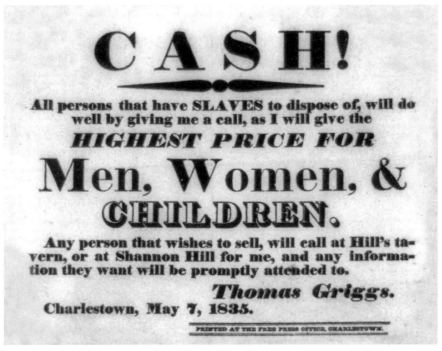

Advertisement for the purchase of slaves, 1835. (*Library of Congress*)

child rearing, and defining themselves in an overtly racist society. For enslaved African Americans, life in the early republic meant adapting to new work routines, resisting exploitation and violence at the hands of slaveholders, experiencing forced migration, and suffering from extended separations from extended family. For all African Americans, the era was a time for building family and cultural traditions as well as social institutions that provided a foundation for a nascent African American nationalism.

The Centrality of Work

More than anything else, work defined the lives of African Americans in the early republic. In an age that celebrated the self-sufficient yeomen farmer, in 1790 the nation's 700,000 African American slaves and 60,000 free African Americans could hardly be called small farmers. Instead, they toiled as day laborers, working long hours for little or no pay and performing their roles in a broad range of industries that were key to the young republic's economic growth and expansion. Agriculture especially depended on African American laborers, and all across the United States slaves and free people of color plowed, planted, hoed, and harvested the corn, wheat, cotton, tobacco,

Slaves preparing tobacco in Virginia, 1790. (*Art Resource*)

hemp, rice, and sugar that created prosperity for the era's farmers and plantation owners. In the 1780s, the seasonal rhythm of tobacco farming directed
the lives of most slaves from North Carolina to Delaware. In his memoir
Slavery in the United States, Charles Ball, a Maryland-born slave, described his
work routine on a tobacco plantation:

> From the period when the tobacco plants are set in the field, there is no resting
> time until it is housed; but it is planted out about the first of May, and must be
> cut and taken out of the field before the frost comes. After it is hung and dried,
> the labour of stripping and preparing it for the hogshead in leaf, or of manufac-
> turing it into twist, is comparatively a work of leisure and ease. Besides, on
> almost every plantation the hands are able to complete the work of preparing
> the tobacco by January, and sometimes earlier; so that the winter months form
> some sort of respite from the toils of the year. (Ball 1837, 57–58)

As Ball and others recalled, tobacco cultivation required what seemed to be
an endless list of tasks that dominated the daily lives of many slaves.

Although the winter months offered respite from tobacco work, slaves
continued to perform other important and arduous tasks. Ball remembered
that, when the slaves were not in the tobacco fields, they were sent to work
"cutting wood for the house, making rails and repairing fences, and in clearing new land, to raise the tobacco plants for the next year" (Ball 1837, 57).

Other slaves worked in the winter making barrels, fixing tools, tending to animals, repairing housing structures, or doing one of the many other agricultural tasks. Masters rarely were content to allow their slaves to enjoy months of nonproductivity. Their labor was simply reallocated.

Cotton Culture

Since the 17th century, generations of slaves had performed the tobacco-related work described by Charles Ball, but by the end of the early republic, cotton had replaced tobacco as the crop that defined the lives of America's slaves. In 1790, only a few planters in Georgia and South Carolina grew cotton. The invention of the cotton gin, along with its ability to make cotton a commodity rather than a luxury item, transformed this reality. By 1820, most planters, from South Carolina to Louisiana, almost exclusively grew cotton, and the nation's new staple crop accounted for more than 32 percent of value of the nation's exports. To grow cotton, planters transported thousands of experienced tobacco-growing African American slaves from the Upper South to the developing Old Southwest. Cotton, however, was not tobacco, and it required a much more rigorous set of backbreaking tasks. As a result, Maryland-born Charles Ball, who was among those sold to a South Carolina cotton plantation, offered mostly positive memories of his tobacco work routine when he compared it with his experiences laboring on a cotton plantation. In South Carolina, he recalled, "the life of a black man was no more regarded than that of an ox" (Ball 1837, 83).

Ball remembered that on tobacco plantations slaves worked hard and year-round at a variety of assignments, but in South Carolina, "This business of picking cotton, constitutes about half the labour of the year." The issue, however, was not about the number of days that he worked. Instead, Ball emphasized the nature of the work itself.

> The manner of doing the work is this. The cotton being planted in hills, in straight rows, from four to five feet apart, each hand or picker, provided with a bag, made of cotton bagging, holding a bushel or more, hung around the neck, with cords, proceeds from one side of the field to the other, between two of these rows, picking all the cotton from the open burs, on the right and left, as he goes. It is the business of the picker to take all the cotton, from each of the rows, as far as the lines of the rows or hill. . . . A day's work is not estimated by the number of hills, or rows, that are picked in the day, but by the number of pounds of cotton in the seed, that the picker brings into the cotton house, at night. (Ball 1837, 211–12)

Cotton picking was hard and unfamiliar work for Ball, who had difficulty meeting the weight quota assigned by the plantation overseer. Much to his own surprise, Ball initially picked less cotton than the women and children who worked alongside him.

Cotton cultivation mandated that slaves work hard and long days, but the worst was yet to come for slaves who could not meet the cotton weight quotas set by their masters or overseers. Solomon Northup, a free African American who was kidnapped and sold to a Louisiana cotton planter, remembered that slaves who failed to make their quotas faced daily whippings during the cotton picking season. At the end of a 12-hour day, any enslaved man "whose weight had fallen short, was taken out, stripped, made to lie upon the ground, face downwards, where he received a punishment proportioned to his offence. . . . The crack of the lash, and the shrieking of the slaves, can be heard from dark till bed time" (Northup 1853, 179). In the early republic, the whip and the fear of the whip permeated the African American experience.

Beyond Cotton

African American men, women, and children worked side by side on farms and plantations, but work routines for enslaved men and women varied by crop and location. Solomon Northup was surprised to discover that, on Louisiana sugar and cotton plantations, men and women worked at the same tasks, and slave women were "in all respects, doing the field and stable work, precisely as do the ploughboys of the North" (Northup 1853, 163–64). By comparison, Maryland and Virginia slaves were often assigned gender- and age-appropriate tasks. On wheat plantations, for example, only men plowed and scythed, and women and children bound and stacked the ripe wheat. Enslaved children went to work for the slaveholder by the time they had reached age 7 or 8. Some, like John Brown, worked in the fields alongside their mothers, "picking off tobacco-worms from the leaves" (Brown 1855, 12). Other slaves performed domestic chores. Escaped slave James Williams remembered that, as a 10-year-old, one of his first jobs was "to stand at the table and brush off the flies while the guests were dining" (Williams 1873, 13). Others cooked and served food, cleaned clothes, swept and dusted houses, tended to children, or performed any imaginable task that the household required.

In addition to their work on America's plantations and farms, African Americans provided crucial labor in Atlantic seaports and Mississippi River towns. Before 1776 only a small fraction of America's slaves lived in urban areas. But the emancipation of nearly 50,000 slaves during the First Emancipation (1776–1804) precipitated a mass migration of African Americans to the country's commercial centers. Between 1790 and 1800, Philadelphia's black population increased by 176 percent. Baltimore's black population increased by 70 percent, and Charleston's black population tripled. In 1795, a Massachusetts man noticed that, since the state had abolished slavery in 1783, African Americans had "generally, but not wholly left the country, and resorted to the maritime towns" ("Queries" 1795, 206). In the Atlantic seaports, free people of color and enslaved men often worked as stevedores and draymen, loading the corn, wheat, cotton, tobacco, hemp, rice, and sugar harvested by slaves and free black day laborers onto commercial vessels bound for the Caribbean and Europe. In St. Louis, Memphis, Vicksburg, New Orleans, and Mobile, African American men served as deckhands on steamboats that carried crops, freight, and passengers toward the Gulf of Mexico.

Some free African Americans opened new avenues of economic opportunities for themselves, working as barbers and chimney sweeps, seamstresses and laundresses, musicians and performers, cooks and peddlers. In 1820, for example, Philadelphia's streets were crowded with free African American peddlers, including a few women who set up a small bakery near the Pennsylvania legislature. According to one city resident, they sold "apple & cranberry tarts & beautiful pastry [that] exceeds any thing now to be met with" (Nash 1988, 151). African Americans were also among the early republic's first industrial workers. Slaves and free people of color labored in coal, salt, and gold mines, in iron manufactories, in shipyards, in sawmills, and in a few Southern textile mills. In Baltimore, the Maryland Chemical Works hired slave and free black workers to manufacture chemicals, pigments, and medicines in the 1820s and 1830s.

Family Life

Work defined African Americans' lives, but it was the duties of family life that gave their lives meaning. African American men and women who worked for slaveholders and miserly employers during the day came home to their cabins and shanties after dark and took up the responsibilities of being the providers and protectors of their spouses, children, and elderly loved ones. Having completed 12 hours of drudgery in the fields, enslaved parents used evenings to catch up with their children about the day's events, to teach important life lessons, and to attend to their own household chores. Enslaved fathers and their sons gathered wood to start cooking fires, and mothers and daughters prepared their families' meals. Although many slaveholders in the early republic provided their slaves with weekly allowances of corn and fatty pork, slave parents worked hard in their own gardens to supplement these meager rations with fresh vegetables, dairy products, and other kinds of meat proteins. Many slave women kept gardens and raised hens, and the men of the plantation hunted game, fished, and caught crayfish and oysters. In addition, there was no shortage of cabin work to be done each night, but many slaves considered these tasks to be labors of love. Looking back on his childhood in slavery, Isaac Williams of North Carolina remembered watching his young mother

> spinning by the light-wood fire, that she might have yarn for kitting socks, wherewith to purchase a jacket or a hat or a pair of shoes for his Sunday wear, or sewing industriously to make or mend some needful garment, when so

fatigued with the day's labor that she nodded between the stitches, and at last sat down in heavy slumber over her work. (Williams 1858, 10)

Between plantation work and cabin work, slave parents had little free time for their children, and so every moment of interaction was an opportunity to instruct children not only in practical life skills, but in skills that would foster African American children's self-worth. Girls, for example, learned quilting and sewing skills, and boys learned how to make animal traps and canoes from logs or felled trees. Children listened to folktales and stories, and some learned the storytelling skills that kept alive their family's history and customs. Charles Ball remembered listening to his father "relating such stories as he had learned from his companions, or in singing the rude songs common amongst the slaves" (Ball 1837, 19). Such teaching moments not only reinforced African American parents' roles as providers and protectors of their children, but also allowed parents to pass on to their children an awareness of their distinct heritage, culture, and values. Through the telling of stories and the singing of songs, parents taught their children everything from their cultural heritage to survival techniques.

In testimonies, memoirs, and autobiographies, African Americans routinely celebrated their relationships with their parents, siblings, and extended family, and they emphasized the lengths their parents and grandparents went to in order to keep their families whole. Renowned abolitionist Frederick Douglass remembered that his mother walked 12 miles one way to visit with him and that, even at a tender age, he understood "the pains she took, and the toil she endured, to see me" (Douglass 1855, 53). Although John Brown met his paternal grandfather, a native African, only once, he nevertheless maintained "a distinct recollection of him" and their single visit with one another (Brown 1855, 1–2). Charles Ball similarly remembered that, when his father visited him on Saturday nights, he regularly brought "some little present, such as the means of a poor slave would allow—apples, melons, sweet potatoes, or, if he could procure nothing else, a little parched corn, which tasted better in our cabin, because he had brought it" (Ball 1837, 18). Greensbury Washington Offley, a slave from Maryland for 27 years before his emancipation, remembered that when slaveholders offered to "hire" him from his parents, his newly freed mother angrily responded that "she had two hands, and she could work and take care of her children without their help" (Offley 1859, 5).

Divided Families

The informal yet widespread practice of sanctioning marriage created ties that were frequently broken or strained by the realities of slavery and freedom. After the American Revolution a significant number of slaveholders legally freed thousands of African American slaves, including Offley's own mother. One remarkable consequence of these manumissions was a rise in the number of African American families with both enslaved and free family members. Offley's own family included his freed mother, his freed African American father, three older siblings who were born in slavery but "willed free at the age of twenty-five," an older brother and grandmother who were purchased from slavery by Offley's father, and younger siblings who were "free born" (Offley 1859, 3–5). Unheard of in the colonial era, these blended African American families were commonplace in Maryland, Delaware, Virginia, and North Carolina. Divided by the distinctions of freedom and slavery, African American families also struggled with the divisions created by distance. In the Upper South, large slaveholders often leased some of their slaves to distant planters when their own labor need diminished, and these lease arrangements created special burdens for African American families. Such was the case for Frederick Douglass's mother, who was separated from her son when she was leased to another planter.

Sold Down the River

Leasing slaves to neighboring planters made African American family life more difficult, but the threat of being hired out locally paled in comparison to the threat of being moved or sold to the American Southwest. As thousands of farmers and planters left their struggling farms in Virginia, Maryland, Delaware, and North Carolina to start afresh in the comparatively undeveloped lands of Kentucky, Tennessee, Alabama, Mississippi, and Louisiana, African American families were systematically divided and broken. Before 1800, white planters transported approximately 100,000 slaves to the Lower South. After the federal government banned the importation of additional African slaves in 1808, the pace of this migration picked up. The farmers who settled the Old Southwest necessarily purchased their slaves from the existing American supply of slaves, most of whom were concentrated in the Upper South. Historians estimate that, between 1820 and 1830, the height of this transcontinental slave trade, Upper South slaveholders sold as many as 250,000 African American men, women, and children to the Lower South. These slaves were typically not Africans, but often American-born people of African descent, living in established slave communities comprised of extended families that included grandparents, parents, and children. Not surprisingly, the transcontinental slave trade fractured and broke many of these communities. Although entire families were frequently sold, the nature of the interstate trade resulted in the routine breakup of families as they often were literally sold down the river.

Slaveholders offered many justifications for selling slaves on the domestic market. Slaveholders insisted that they sold only "bad" or troublesome slaves, or they sold slaves only out of economic desperation, in which case it was in the slave's best interest to find a better home. These excuses meant little to African Americans who lost loved ones to the trade and who often

Charles Ball (1781–d.?)

Charles Ball's memoir, *Slavery in the United States: A Narrative of the Life and Adventures of Charles Ball* (1837), explains in heart-wrenching detail how the domestic slave trade devastated African American families. Born on a Maryland tobacco plantation, Charles Ball was only 4 years old when his mother and siblings were sold on the domestic slave market. Charles's father never recovered from the shock of losing his wife, but, fearing his own sale, he fled to Pennsylvania and never returned. Charles grew up in the care of his elderly grandfather, a native African named Old Ben, and as a young adult he married Judah, a slave on a neighboring plantation, with whom he had three children.

One otherwise ordinary morning, as Charles finished his breakfast and left for work, a slave trader's agents seized him. Charles instantly thought of his family and pleaded for the opportunity to say good-bye to Judah and his children. But the slave trader refused his request, answering that Charles could "get another wife in Georgia" (Ball 1837, 36). Charles was one of 51 enslaved men, women, and children, bound together with ropes and chains, headed for the Lower South. At the beginning of the month-long journey to South Carolina, dreams of his mourning wife and children tortured Charles. He envisioned his son begging him not to go and his wife "weeping and lamenting my calamity" (Ball 1837, 39). But by the time he reached North Carolina, Charles knew "I had now no hope of ever again seeing my wife and children" (Ball 1837, 69). Over the next few years, he labored on cotton plantations in South Carolina and Georgia before successfully escaping and returning to Maryland in 1809.

Charles was reunited with his family, but he was now a fugitive. He accepted work as a mariner, and then in 1820 he bought a small plot of land, where he raised vegetables to sell in Baltimore's markets. Charles Ball lived like a free man, but he remained a fugitive slave. One day in 1830, while working his land, slave catchers seized him and returned him to Georgia. Charles escaped, but, when he returned to Maryland, his wife and children were gone, abducted and sold on the domestic slave market that had already claimed his mother, his siblings, and the better part of his own life.

considered the sale of a loved one as akin to murder. Isaac Williams, for example, remembered that, when his mother's first husband was sold away, "the sale was truly like death, for she never saw or heard from Abram again." For six months after Abram's sale, Williams's mother "could not think of her husband without tears, and her health suffered from the shock she had received" (Williams 1858, 81).

Slaves in the early republic lived in constant fear that slaveholders would sell their loved ones on the domestic slave market. John Brown remembered that, in anticipation of the division and sale of his whole family, his mother "took to kissing us a good deal oftener" (Brown 1855, 6). Well aware of their slaves' fears, slaveholders used the threat of sale to frighten their slaves into submission. Former slave James Williams remembered that as a boy his slaveholder warned him that, if he ran away and was caught, he would be sold to "Georgia, where they will bore holes in your ears and plow you like a horse" (Williams 1873, 13). Such threats suggested to Williams that his own behavior determined whether he would be sold, but Williams and all slaves knew that slaveholders sold slaves not because they were good or bad, but because they were valuable. Like stocks or bonds, slaves were an investment, to be cashed out when it suited the slaveholder's financial needs. No narrative better illustrates this fact than John Brown's memory that his Virginia slaveholder "used to call us children up to the big house every morning, and give us a dose of garlic and rue to keep us 'wholesome,' and make us 'grow likely for market'" (Brown 1855, 3).

So fearful were slaves of being sold to the Southwest that many of them attempted to escape slavery altogether rather than face an unknown fate in a distant and foreign land. Benedict Duncan fled when he learned his "master's business was going down hill," and he suspected that he would be sold to pay outstanding debts (Drew 1856, 110). When Robert Belt heard a rumor that "there was a notion of selling me," he escaped with his wife to Canada (Drew 1856, 112). In the 17th and 18th centuries, few slaves successfully escaped from slavery. But after the American Revolution, as more Northeastern slave states became free states, slaves planned their escapes with greater optimism. Access to free states meant that slaves did not just run *away* from violent and oppressive slaveholders but that they ran *toward* the possibility of freedom. Such was the thinking of Alexander Hemsley, who, in planning his own escape from slavery, set his sights on the free state of New Jersey, "where, I had been told, people were free, and nobody would disturb me" (Drew 1856, 34). Although many slaves either failed to reach their destinations or were distraught over the racial codes in the North, the possibilities for freedom encouraged many to risk their lives.

Gradual Emancipation

After the Revolution, one at a time, the Northern states increasingly distanced themselves from slavery. A few states immediately abolished slavery. Most, however, did so through a process of gradual emancipation. In 1780, Pennsylvania became the first state to pursue this option. In the preamble to An Act for the Gradual Abolition of Slavery, the Pennsylvania General Assembly declared the emancipation to be the last unfinished work of the American Revolution, "removing as much as possible the Sorrows of those, who have lived in undeserved Bondage, and from which by the assumed Authority of the Kings of Britain, no effectual legal Relief could be obtained." Antislavery activists throughout the Atlantic World celebrated Pennsylvania's scheme for gradual emancipation, and the act provided a model for legal emancipation that was duplicated by lawmakers in Rhode Island (1784), Connecticut (1784), New York (1799), and New Jersey (1804), as well as the British Parliament (1824).

Notwithstanding the law's influence and historical significance, Pennsylvania's Act for the Gradual Abolition of Slavery did not, in fact, free any slaves in 1780. Emancipation applied only to future generations of unborn African American children, not existing slaves who remained slaves. In other words, African American children born after 1780 were identified as freeborn even though their parents remained slaves for life. Moreover, the gradual emancipation acts adopted by Northeastern states during the early republic consistently put slaveholders' financial interests above former slaves' claims to liberty and citizenship. From Pennsylvania to Connecticut, state legislators included provisions in their emancipation acts that effectively compensated slaveholders for their lost labor. Typically this was accomplished by requiring freeborn African Americans to serve their parents' masters as unpaid, indentured servants. Like Irish or German indentured servants, these freeborn African Americans could be bought or sold, moved within the state, and disciplined by their masters. But unlike foreign-born indentured servants, who typically served between four and seven years, emancipated African Americans spent a significant portion of their adult lives as unpaid laborers. Pennsylvania, for example, required freeborn African American children to serve their parents' masters until they reached 28 years of age. In Connecticut, freeborn African Americans served to age 25; in New York, African American men served to age 28 and women served to age 25. In effect, these gradual, compensated emancipation schemes made freedom not a birthright but rather something that free people of color earned with 20 or more years of hard, unpaid labor.

The Fugitive Slave Law

Limited freedom in Pennsylvania, New Jersey, or New York was significantly more appealing than slavery in Kentucky, Maryland, or Georgia, and so slaves planned their escapes with an eye toward reestablishing their lives in the free states. Slaveholders in the early republic understood that Pennsylvania and other free states offered a haven to their escaped slaves and sought to eliminate this threat to their livelihoods. Slaveholders took their concerns to the U.S. Congress, and, with the rhetoric of protecting property rights, it responded with the 1793 Fugitive Slave Law. This law required the state and county officials of the free states to return escaped slaves to their masters. With the force of federal law behind them, slaveholders hired professional slave catchers to hunt through the free states in search of escaped slaves, paying handsome bounties for every slave successfully captured and returned.

Testimonies given by former slaves suggest that, if the Fugitive Slave Law did not always work, it did make escape more difficult, requiring fugitive slaves to run farther to get out of the slave catchers' reach. Such was the case for Thomas Cooper, who in 1800 successfully escaped to Philadelphia, took up work as a free man in a lumberyard, married, fathered children, and even bought his own property, only to be betrayed to his master. In the presence of his wife and children, Cooper was handcuffed and marched to Washington,

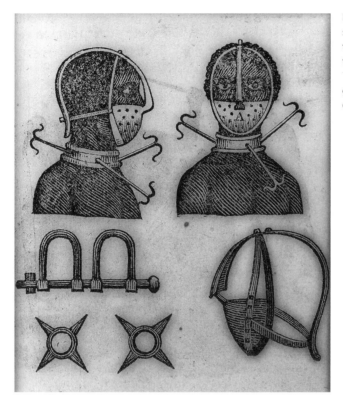

Iron mask, collar, leg shackles, and spurs used to restrict slaves. Illustrated in *The Penitential Tyrant* by Thomas Branagan, 1807. (*Library of Congress*)

D.C., where his master attempted to sell him "to Georgia, or some other market." He escaped again "to the woods; but in a few hours, he was pursued by his avaricious master, with a company he had collected to assist him" (Hopper 1832, 7, 11). Cooper eventually found his way back to Pennsylvania, but, fearing another capture, he moved on to New Jersey, then to Boston, and on to London, before ultimately settling in Sierra Leone, Africa.

Although the Fugitive Slave Law targeted escaped slaves, it actually put free African Americans at risk of seizure and sale. Slave catchers terrorized free African Americans, who usually had no way to defend themselves against the threat of illegal abduction. The law presumed the accused runaway's guilt, and so slave catchers were not required to present evidence that their captives were in fact runaway slaves. Moreover, accused fugitives, brought to the court by bounty hunters, could not call their own witnesses to testify to their status as free people of color. Although free people of color could apply to their local county courts for freedom papers that identified them as free members of their community, these papers hardly guaranteed their safety. A piece of paper would not always deter a kidnapper who stood to make considerable profits selling free people of color into slavery. Moreover, kidnappers generally targeted free black children, who rarely carried freedom certificates, because they were easier to manipulate and restrain than adults. Such was the case for Peter and Levin Still, brothers who were less than 8 years old when a stranger coaxed them away from their New Jersey home with "gentle words and timely gifts" and "cakes of marvelous sweetness" and then sold them to a Kentucky slaveholder. Peter later recalled that, when the slaveholder realized that he had purchased kidnapped children, he responded by saying, "I bought these boys, and paid for them, and I'll stop their talk about being free, or I'll break their black necks" (Pickard 1856, 28, 30).

The Antislavery Movement

Kidnappings and the domestic slave trade were two of the issues that brought African Americans into common cause with a small but vocal population of antislavery whites. Free states and some slave states, including Delaware, Virginia, and Maryland, passed antikidnapping laws and prosecuted those who kidnapped free African Americans and sold them illegally as slaves. In Maryland, as was common throughout the Mid-Atlantic and Northern states, few white people supported abolition. Yet this did not deter many residents from publicly supporting efforts to stop the illicit trade in freedmen. The Maryland Abolition Society, for example, petitioned the state's general assembly for more stringent antikidnapping laws in 1790, 1815, and 1816, and white Baltimoreans organized the Protection Society of Maryland in 1816 to lobby both the General Assembly and the U.S. Congress for more protective legislation. In 1818, the *Niles Weekly Standard*, a Maryland newspaper with a national distribution, publicized and celebrated these efforts, noting that "the Protection Society of Maryland had lately had the glory to release a number of kidnapped black people, and to restore them to freedom and their families. May heaven prosper their work!" Not surprisingly, Baltimore's free African Americans also supported the Protection Society in their work by taking up monetary collections and by organizing patrols to guard their neighborhoods from kidnappers (*Niles Weekly Standard*, May 9, 1818).

New Freedoms for African Americans

The 1793 Fugitive Slave Act chipped away at free African Americans' already limited legal rights and represented a turning point in the history of race relations in the early republic. The American Revolution did not abolish slavery, but it had raised white Americans' consciousness about the condition of African Americans, and it created conditions that increasingly favored African American freedom. In the 1780s, many white Americans, including national heroes like Benjamin Franklin, successfully urged state and federal authorities to extend the revolutionary principles of equality, liberty, and self-determination to the nation's African Americans. These advocates for African

American freedom achieved some noteworthy goals, including the abolition of slavery in every state from Vermont to Pennsylvania. Even the U.S. Congress had sanctioned the spread of African American freedom with the 1787 passage of the Northwest Ordinance, which expressly prohibited slavery in the future states of Ohio (1803), Indiana (1816), and Illinois (1818), and with the constitutional ban on the transatlantic slave trade (1808).

Throughout the 1780s, free states extended rights and privileges to free African Americans, including the rights to own property, to vote in local and state elections, to serve in militia units, and to move freely from state to state. Even white Americans' attitudes toward interracial sex, or at least its legal approach, changed in the 1780s. Before the American Revolution, states strictly forbade marriages between whites and blacks. Maryland law, similar to that of several other states, authorized county courts to sell white mothers of mixed-race children into indentured servitude for a term of seven years. Mixed-race children could be sold as servants until they reached 31 years of age. In the early republic, Maryland and Virginia law still allowed communities to prosecute and even fine white women who had relationships with African American men, but both discontinued the practice of selling white mothers and their mixed-race children as servants. In fact, the increase in the number of African Americans identified as mulatto (mixed European and African ancestry) suggests that early Americans often turned a blind eye to interracial relationships among the working and poorer classes. One example of white Americans' indifference to interracial relationships comes from eastern Maryland, where in 1822, a 28-year-old mulatto woman named Margaret Johns appeared before the county court to register for freedom papers. When the court clerk asked her to present evidence of her freedom, Margaret brought a white neighbor, who testified that Margaret Johns was the daughter of Ann Ayers, a white woman, and Hercules Johns, a slave, and that "during all the time this deponent knew her, [Margaret's mother] cohabited with a Negro man slave named Hercules who called himself Hercules Johns" (Whitman 1997).

Racial Integration

If interracial families were uncommon or even taboo in the early republic, it was not because black and white Americans lived in separate or segregated communities. Segregation, as it was practiced in the late 19th and early 20th centuries, was not the law during the nation's first few decades. In fact, racial integration was the norm in late 18th- and early 19th-century worship communities. In the colonial era, Christianity, like skin color, was an important characteristic that separated slaveholders from slaves, and so colonial slaveholders frequently prohibited their African-born slaves from converting to Christianity. This changed after the Revolution. Early republic slaveholders frequently encouraged their slaves to convert to some branch of Christianity, often inviting itinerant preachers to evangelize among their slaves. Masters also worshipped with their slaves and read the Bible to them. G. W. Offley, for example, learned about Christianity and the Bible from his parents, but his mother learned elements of Christianity from her former master, who "used to read the Bible to his slaves" (Offley 1859, 12). Alexander Hemsley similarly remembered that his "master used to catechize us, and tell us if we were good honest boys, and obedient to our master, we should enjoy the life that now is, and that which is to come" (Drew 1856, 33).

Slaveholders encouraged Christian conversion, anticipating that Christian slaves would be more obedient, more disciplined, and more contented with their lot in life. They would, in essence, learn to turn the other cheek and accept their subservient position. But beginning in the 1770s, thousands of African Americans embraced Christianity, not because of its emphasis on obedience but because they saw variations of their history and experience in the Bible. African Americans identified with the Old Testament heroes, especially Moses and Aaron, who led the enslaved Israelites out of Egypt and into a promised land of liberty. They also identified with Jesus Christ, a friend and champion of the poor and the oppressed. By 1800, large numbers of African Americans worshipped in Roman Catholic, Presbyterian, Episcopalian, and Quaker churches, but the vast majority of black Christians were either Baptist or Methodist. By 1815, for example, half of Baltimore's 6,600 Methodists were African Americans.

Christianity played a vital role in shaping African Americans' identity, culture, and relations with the larger white community. Church meetings, prayer groups, and religious revivals offered white and black Americans a unique opportunity to interact with one another not as master and slave, but as fellow Christians. Whether African American Methodists worshipped in the so-called African congregations or in the racially mixed congregations, they enjoyed access to a unique training ground for leadership available only to church members. African American preachers like the Methodist preacher Harry Hosier gained a following with both white and black audiences in Delaware, Maryland, and Virginia. A white minister who traveled with Hosier in 1784 remembered that "Harry will preach to the blacks; but the whites always stay to hear him. . . . I really believe he is one of the best preachers in the world, there is such an amazing power attends his preaching" (Williams 1984, 143–44).

African American Churches

African American preachers were among the most identifiable black leaders in the early republic. Men like Absalom Jones and Richard Allen, freed slaves and Methodist lay preachers, applied their preaching and leadership skills to build distinctly African American institutions. In 1787, after years of preaching before African American Methodists, Jones and Allen organized

Richard Allen (1760–1831), founder and first bishop of the African Methodist Episcopal Church. *(Payne, Daniel Alexander.* History of the African Methodist Episcopal Church, *1891)*

the Free African Society (FAS), a mutual aid society that served Philadelphia's growing African American population. Jones, Allen, and the other FAS members were proudly Christian and proudly African. They consciously included the term "African" in the title and in the society's incorporation papers, and Jones and Allen thoughtfully described themselves as "two men of the African race." By the 1790s blacks had publicly embraced their African identity, organizing schools, mutual aid societies, and worship communities that included "Africa" or "African" in their names. The Free African Society, the Free African Union Society (Newport, Rhode Island), the Bethel Free African Society (Baltimore), and dozens of other such institutions gave voice to the nation's free African American communities.

From the 1770s to the 1790s, Christianity, especially Methodism, had inspired and informed African Americans, leading them to construct what would be the most significant and lasting African American institution of the early republic: the African Methodist Episcopal Church. As the population of African American Methodists grew all through the 1780s and 1790s, the Methodist Episcopal Church encouraged Richard Allen and other African

American deacons and lay preachers to organize separate African congregations for their black worshippers. In Philadelphia, Allen organized the Bethel Church (1795), in Baltimore, Daniel Coker organized the Sharp Street Methodist Episcopal Church (1800), and in Wilmington, Delaware, free people of color organized the Ezion Methodist Church (1805). Although technically separate entities, these congregations were not completely autonomous because the Methodist Church refused to ordain African American deacons. For 25 years, Richard Allen led his mostly black congregation in Sunday worship, but he turned his pulpit over to a white minister for weddings, funerals, and communion. By 1812, the Bethel, Sharp Street, and Ezion congregations were frustrated with their subordinate status within the Methodist Church. After a bitter argument in which the Ezion congregation insisted on their right to reject white pastors that they found unsuitable, Peter Spencer, a freedman and senior member of the church, left Ezion to build Delaware's first truly independent African Methodist church. Established in 1813, the founders of the African Union Methodist Church (Old Union) asserted in their charter that this was an African Methodists' church, by and for "Africans and the descendants of the African Race" (Essah 1996, 149). Three years later on April 9, 1816, Richard Allen, Daniel Coker, Peter Spencer, and 13 other African Methodists representing five churches across the Mid-Atlantic organized a new denomination, the African Methodist Episcopal (AME) Church.

The organization of the AME Church in 1816 anticipated a new era, in which free African Americans would no longer seek equality with whites through integrated institutions. During the early republic, African Americans had learned from their experience with the Methodist Episcopal Church that separate African American institutions—not integrated institutions—provided the best platform for achieving and advancing their social and political interests. This lesson made a lasting impression on the next generation of African Americans, who in the 1820s and 1830s experienced a surge in white prejudice and race-related violence in the nation's seaports. Thousands of European immigrants, who settled in New York, Philadelphia, Baltimore, and Charleston, resented having to compete with the native African American population for housing and employment. White laborers not only bullied, insulted, and threatened individual African Americans, but they also attacked African American communities and targeted their institutions. In 1822, for example, an angry mob destroyed Charleston, South Carolina's AME Church, and sent the church's minister, Morris Brown, fleeing for his life. In Philadelphia, a white mob attacked a black neighborhood over three days in August 1834, destroying a black church and fatally injuring at least one free African American. In Baltimore, white carters organized themselves and submitted a petition to the Maryland General Assembly in 1828, urging the legislature to prohibit free blacks and slaves from working as draymen. Ten years later, a white mob attacked Baltimore's oldest black church, the Sharp Street Methodist Episcopal Church.

Zilpha Elaw (1790–1845?)

Zilpha Elaw's self-published *Memoirs of the Life, Religious Experience, Ministerial Travels, and Labours of Mrs. Zilpha Elaw, an American Female of Colour* (1846) offers an incomparable account of how one early republic African American woman was transformed and empowered by her experiences as a member of the Methodist Episcopal Church. Zilpha was an orphaned adolescent, working as a domestic servant in Philadelphia, when she started attending Methodist prayer meetings. In 1808, she joined the Methodist Episcopal Church, uniting herself "with the fellowship of the saints with the militant church of Jesus on earth" (Elaw 1986, 57). Two years later Zilpha married Joseph Elaw, with whom she moved to Burlington, New Jersey, where she gave birth to their only daughter. Zilpha was not happily married. Joseph's fondness for music, dancing, and other "merriments of the world" alienated her from her husband and heightened her devotion to her spiritual life (Elaw 1986, 63). In 1817 Zilpha attended her first Methodist camp revival, a weeklong event in which hundreds of white and black Americans gathered to pray, sing, worship, and hear testimonies from Christian converts. At this camp meeting, Zilpha stepped forth and gave her first public sermon, and at that moment she found her calling to minister. She began her ministry in New Jersey and Pennsylvania, and she even opened a school for African American children in Burlington that received much positive attention and support from the local community.

After her husband's death in 1823, Zilpha devoted the remainder of her life to a traveling ministry, preaching and testifying before racially integrated congregations in every state from Virginia to Maine before heading to England in 1840. In her 30-year ministry Zilpha encountered prejudice in America and sexism in England, where men "reprobated female preaching as unscriptual" (Elaw 1986, 147), and she struggled daily to balance her responsibilities as mother and provider with her passion and commitment to her work. Notwithstanding these challenges, Zilpha Elaw urged young women to "imagine themselves as their own mistresses" (Elaw 1986, 61) and offered in her *Memoirs* a powerful example of African American womanhood.

Later Organizations

During the early republic, African churches gave the nation's African Americans a forum where they could meet separately from the white majority to discuss and address their community concerns. In the subsequent antebellum years, African Americans would organize other forums, including national conventions and newspapers, where free blacks would meet to devise and discuss strategies for advancing abolition and civil rights. In 1830, free African Americans gathered together at the first National Negro Convention in Philadelphia. Forty African Americans attended the first convention, but hundreds more would participate in conventions hosted in Albany, Rochester, Cincinnati, Buffalo, and Cleveland over the next 20 years. African American newspapers, including *The Colored American* (1839), the *Weekly Advocate* (1837), and Frederick Douglass's *The North Star* (1847), would provide yet another forum where African Americans could discuss their hopes, dreams, and concerns, and where they could reaffirm their commitment to African American solidarity.

Slave Rebellions

African Americans who joined the African Methodist Episcopal Church, attended Negro Conventions, or read *The North Star* believed that they could end slavery and win civil rights through discussion, debate, education, and peaceful protest. Other African Americans, however, knew that American slavery would not end without violence. In 1800, Gabriel Prosser, an enslaved blacksmith, recruited hundreds of slaves and free African Americans to lead an attack on the state's capitol at Richmond, Virginia. Gabriel intended to seize the legislature and the governor's mansion and to hold Governor James Monroe prisoner. The group further planned to carry banners that read "death or liberty," a motto that thoughtfully linked African American liberty to the American Revolution and to the well-publicized slave revolt on the French island of Saint-Domingue: a revolt that eventually abolished slavery in the French Empire and created the Republic of Haiti (1804). But Gabriel Prosser's much anticipated revolution never happened. Torrential rains stalled the army on the day of attack (August 30, 1800), giving white Virginians time to organize and respond with force. In 1822, Denmark Vesey, a freed slave in Charleston, South Carolina, may have organized a second revolt to end American slavery, but, like Gabriel's Rebellion, Vesey's revolt was uncovered before it even started. When the white community learned the details of the plot, Charleston authorities rounded up Vesey and dozens of other African Americans, tried the conspirators, and then executed 35 defendants and exiled 42 others.

Rebellions in the early republic failed to end slavery through violence, but Nat Turner's Rebellion represented a grave threat to the institution. Turner was a Christian, and, had he been a free man, he would have likely become a leader in one of the many Christian reform movements that gained popularity in the North in the 1820s and 1830s. As an enslaved Christian in Virginia, however, Turner knew there was no hope in reforming slavery, and so he resolved to destroy it. Convinced that God had directed him to "slay my enemies with their own weapons" (Turner 1831, 11), Turner and seven companions set out in August 1831 to kill every white person in their path. As Turner and his men moved through Southampton County, Virginia, at least 30 other men spontaneously joined them, and in less than two days Turner's army had killed nearly 60 white people. Virginia mobilized its militia, captured most of the rebels, and, after a two-month search, caught Turner and brought him to trial. While awaiting trial, Turner

Newspaper cartoon depicts the violent slave uprising led by Nat Turner that began on August 22, 1831, when Turner killed his master and his master's family. The revolt only lasted about a week but Turner eluded capture until October of that year. He was later tried and hanged for the crime. (*Library of Congress*)

made a confession to his court-appointed attorney in which he likened himself to Jesus Christ, and, when asked at his trial how he pleaded, Turner responded "*not guilty*: saying to his counsel, that he did not feel so" (Turner 1831, 20). The relative success of Nat Turner's Revolt, combined with his lack of remorse, so terrified Virginians that the state legislature fiercely debated a proposal to abolish slavery. Yet, in spite of the recent bloodshed and the overall atmosphere of fear and anxiety, the Virginia legislature failed to adopt an emancipation act before the Civil War.

Conclusion

While they offered conflicting models for how to end American slavery and advance African American civil rights, the lives and experiences of early republic African Americans like Nat Turner, Absalom Jones, Richard Allen, and Charles Ball made a lasting impression on the generation of African Americans who followed them. African Americans passed on a tradition of resistance to slavery and a commitment to personal, familial, and cultural integrity. In a nation divided between slavery and freedom, African Americans never lost sight of the fact that the futures of slaves and of free people of color were inextricably linked. Frederick Douglass, a child of the early republic who grew up to become the foremost African American civil rights leader of the 19th century, clearly and passionately articulated this legacy of resistance and integrity in a dedication entitled "To Our Oppressed Countrymen." In 1847, he assured America's 2.5 million slaves that "what you suffer we suffer; what you endure, we endure" and in the same breath reminded America's 400,000 free people of color that "we are one" with our enslaved brethren and that "we must help each other, if, we would succeed" (Douglass 1847, 1–2).

References and Further Reading

Ball, Charles. *Slavery in the United States: A Narrative of the Life and Adventures of Charles Ball, a Black Man, Who Lived Forty Years in Maryland, South Carolina and Georgia, as a Slave under Various Masters, and was One Year in the Navy with Commodore Barney, During the Late War*. Lewistown, PA: J. W. Shugert, 1837

Bordley, John B. *Essays and Notes on Husbandry and Rural Affairs*, 2nd ed. Philadelphia: Thomas Dobson, 1801

Brown, John. *Slave Life in Georgia: A Narrative of the Life, Sufferings, and Escape of John Brown, a Fugitive Slave, Now in England*. London: M. W. Watts, 1855

Douglass, Frederick. *My Bondage and My Freedom*. New York: Miller, Orton & Mulligan, 1855

Douglass, Frederick. "To Our Oppressed Countrymen." January 2, 1848. Typescript. The Frederick Douglass Papers. Library of Congress, Washington, DC

Drew, Benjamin. *A North-Side View of Slavery. The Refugee: or the Narratives of Fugitive Slaves in Canada. Related by Themselves, with an Account of the History and Condition of the Colored Population of Upper Canada*. Boston: J. P. Jewett and Co., 1856

Elaw, Zilpha. *Memoirs of the Life, Religious experience, Ministerial Travels and Labors of Mrs. Zilpha Elaw. Sisters of the Spirit*. Edited by William L. Andrews. Bloomington: Indiana University Press, 1986 (Orig. pub. 1846)

Essah, Patience. *A House Divided: Slavery and Emancipation in Delaware, 1638–1865*. Charlottesville: University of Virginia Press, 1996

Frey, Sylvia, and Betty Wood. *Come Shouting to Zion: African American Protestantism in the American South and British Caribbean to 1830*. Chapel Hill: University of North Carolina Press, 1998

Hopper, Isaac T. *Narrative of the Life of Thomas Cooper*. New York: I. T. Hopper, 1832

Nash, Gary. *Forging Freedom: The Formation of Philadelphia's Black Community, 1720–1840*. Cambridge, MA: Harvard University Press, 1988

Northup, Solomon. *Twelve Years a Slave: Narrative of Solomon Northup, a Citizen of New York, Kidnapped in Washington City in 1841, and Rescued in 1853*. Cincinnati, OH: Henry W. Derby, 1853

Offley, G. W. *A Narrative of the Life and Labors of the Rev. G.W. Offley, a Colored Man, Local Preacher and Missionary; Who Lived Twenty-Seven Years at the South and Twenty-Three at the North; Who Never Went to School a Day in His Life, and Only Commenced to Learn His Letters When Nineteen Years and Eight Months Old; The Emancipation of His Mother and Her Three Children; How He Learned to Read While Living in a Slave State, and Supported Himself from the Time He Was Nine Years Old Until He Was Twenty-One*. Hartfot, CT: [s.n.], 1859

Pickard, Kate E. R. *The Kidnapped and the Ransomed. Being the Personal Recollections of Peter Still and his Wife "Vina," after Forty Years of Slavery*. Syracuse, NY: W. T. Hamilton, 1856

Phillips, Christopher. *Freedom's Port: The African American Community of Baltimore, 1790–1860*. Urbana: University of Illinois Press, 1997

"Queries Respecting the Slavery and Emancipation of Negroes in Massachusetts, Proposed by the Hon. Judge Tucker of Virginia, and Answered by the Rev. Dr. Belknap. Williamsburg, Virginia, January 24, 1795." In *Collections of the Massachusetts Historical Society, for the year M, DCC, XCV*, 4: 191–211. Boston, MA: Samuel Hall, 1795

Turner, Nat. *The Confessions of Nat Turner, the Leader of the Late Insurrection, in Southampton VA*. Baltimore, MD: Thomas R. Gray, 1831

White, Shane. *Somewhat More Independent: The End of Slavery in New York City, 1770–1810*. Athens: University of Georgia Press, 1991

Williams, Isaac. *Aunt Sally: or, The Cross the Way of Freedom. A Narrative of the Slave-life and Purchase of the Mother of Rev. Isaac Williams of Detroit, Michigan*. Cincinnati, OH: American Reform Tract and Book Society, 1858

Williams, James. *Life and Adventures of James Williams, a Fugitive Slave, with a Full Description of the Underground Railroad*. San Francisco, CA: Women's Union Print, 1873

Williams, William H. *The Garden of American Methodism: The Delmarva Peninsula, 1769–1820*. Wilmington, DE: Scholarly Resources, 1984

Wilson, Carol. *Freedom at Risk: The Kidnapping of Free Blacks in America, 1780–1865*. Lexington: University Press of Kentucky, 1994

Whitman, T. Stephen. *The Price of Freedom: Slavery and Manumission in Baltimore and Early National Maryland*. Lexington: University Press of Kentucky, 1997

Colonizing the "Western World": Western Settlers (1780–1830)

6

David Nichols

Introduction

In 1780, the boundary between white American and Native American settlement extended along the western slope of the Appalachian Mountains. By 1830, it had moved 600 miles to the west, across the Mississippi River and into the valleys of the Missouri and Arkansas rivers. During the intervening half-century, the 600,000-square-mile frontier region between these two lines experienced a dramatic social transformation. At the start of the period, the Trans-Appalachian West was a lightly settled expanse of woodland and prairie, inhabited by about 150,000 Indians and 40,000 white traders and farmers. Inhabitants of the Atlantic states called the region the western world and viewed it as remote and exotic. Indeed, one frontier resident, Northwest Territory Governor Arthur St. Clair, described himself in a letter as "a poor devil banished to another planet" (St. Clair to Alexander Hamilton, August 9, 1793, St. Clair Papers, 4: 170). By 1830, however, the western world was fast becoming the United States' center of gravity, with a population of more than four million (one-third of the national total), exports valued in the millions of dollars, growing cities, and 65 representatives and senators in the U.S. Congress, not to mention a native son, Andrew Jackson, in the White House.

The Migrants

The agents of this transformation were the hundreds of thousands of Easterners, white and black, male and female, young and old, who migrated to or within the Trans-Appalachian West after the American Revolution. They

Flatboat loaded with men and animals on the Ohio River. (*Library of Congress*)

came by wagon through the Cumberland Gap, by flatboat down the Ohio and Mississippi rivers, or by sail or steamship along the Gulf Coast, bringing with them their household goods, their tools and livestock, and their plans for the future. They comprised three distinct migratory waves, each associated with a particular region of settlement. The first wave (1780–1795), settled primarily in the Kentucky Bluegrass region and the Tennessee Valley, increasing the non-Indian population of those future states from 10,000 to 250,000. The second wave (1795–1810), drawn to the frontier by the end of the Northwest Indian War and the opening of the Mississippi River to American navigation, colonized the future state of Ohio and the lower Mississippi Valley, increasing the total Trans-Appalachian population to about 1 million people by 1810. A third migration (1815–1830) poured into the lower Ohio Valley, the Southern cotton belt, and the Missouri and Arkansas territories after the War of 1812, quadrupling the Western United States' population and helping start a national market revolution.

The first two waves of settlers came from rural New England, Pennsylvania, the Carolina uplands, and especially Virginia, the birthplace of over 425,000 future settlers of the Ohio and Tennessee Valleys. Half of them were native-born Americans of English or Welsh descent, but another 30 percent claimed Scottish, Irish, or German parentage, and they distinguished themselves from Anglo-Americans by their diet, accents, and religious denominations. In the territories south of the Ohio River where human slavery was legal, at least 15 percent of the migrants were African American slaves, unwillingly separated from their old homes (and in many cases their family members) in the South Atlantic states.

Indeed, many if not most, of the frontier migrants left their old homes involuntarily, at the command of the adult white men who legally controlled their persons. This was true for slaves, for children, and for the wives and dependent female relatives of male settlers. For women, emigration often meant leaving behind the dense social networks of family and friends who had sustained them in the East and adjusting to a difficult new life of toil and isolation. The English traveler Frances Trollope noted the toll that migration took on frontier women when she observed, during an excursion in rural Ohio, that "it is rare to see a woman in this station who has reached the age of thirty without losing every trace of youth and beauty" (Trollope 1997, 92). As we will see, however, Western women began to rebuild their networks of family and friends from the moment they reached their new homes.

The motives of the white men who led their spouses, slaves, and other dependents to the Trans-Appalachian West were similar to the motives of trans-Atlantic immigrants. They sought to escape the overcrowded seaboard states, where a rapidly growing population and a limited supply of arable land restricted the opportunities available to the young and the poor. Many saw emigration as an alternative to becoming a tenant farmer or working for wages—in either case, living as a dependent of the landlord or employer. Indeed, some received bequests of Western land or money for moving expenses from parents who wanted to ensure that their sons became self-sufficient farmers.

Male migrants were also responding to the lure of fertile Western land and to the glowing appraisals of the region's climate and productivity written by relatives or land companies. The North American Land Company, a syndicate established in 1795 by Robert Morris and other Eastern merchants, published a brochure that described Kentucky as "abound[ing] with almost every thing that man can desire: fruits of all kind, grain, roots, and herbage" (Harper 1796, 46–47). (The partners owned 400,000 acres in Kentucky; so one might doubt their objectivity.) Twenty years later Morris Birkbeck, an English developer living in Illinois, informed potential settlers that "for about half of the capital that is required for the mere cultivation of our worn-out soils in England, a man may establish himself as a proprietor here, with every comfort belonging to a plain and reasonable mode of living, and with a certainty of establishing his children as well or better than himself" (Birkbeck 1818a, 18).

Land Speculation

Land speculators had an obvious interest in attracting settlers to the frontier; they sought to make money by selling or leasing parcels of real estate there. Many speculators were well-connected merchants or lawyers who

Settlement of Batavia in western New York, 1801–1846. Three-and-a-half million acres were purchased by the Holland Land Company in 1802, which extended from western New York to Pennsylvania, Lake Ontario, and Lake Erie. (*Library of Congress*)

had procured large tracts on the cheap from pliant legislatures—like the North Carolinians who bought 2.5 million acres of Tennessee land from their state assembly (1783) or the land company partners who bribed the Georgia legislature into selling most of present-day Alabama and Mississippi for 1.4 cents per acre (1795). Other speculators, however, had more limited means, if not equal ambition. These were early emigrants or land company agents who surveyed the land, selected choice parcels of real estate, and claimed them under liberal state land laws. Daniel Boone, for instance, claimed over 20,000 acres of Kentucky land under Virginia's 1779 preemption law, not for his own cultivation but for sale to future settlers.

Emigrating farmers often resented the claims of Eastern speculators and developers, believing that land properly belonged to the white Americans who settled on it and farmed it—"improved" it, to use the contemporary phrase. Some expressed their disapproval by tearing down absentee proprietors' fences, killing their cattle, or illegally occupying their land. Some migratory families repeatedly squatted on other men's lands, made a little money from the sale of crops or livestock, then moved on to other pastures. A few protestors, primarily concentrated in the Northeastern backcountry (Maine, New York, and Pennsylvania), even ambushed surveyors or state officials sent to uphold landlords' property claims.

In most cases, though, the number of potential settlers willing to buy or rent speculators' land exceeded the number of squatters or insurgents who contested their claims. Speculator developers, after all, had to offer migrants considerable incentives to settle on their tracts because speculators were in competition with one another for customers. They also competed with the federal government, which between 1800 and 1820 dropped the price of public land from $2.00/acre (with a minimum purchase of 320 acres) to $1.25/acre (with a minimum purchase of 80 acres). Some private speculators thus built roads, warehouses, and mills for the benefit of their customers; some offered to swap emigrants' worn-out lands in the East for new land in the West; and some allowed tenants to occupy their land rent-free if they agreed to break ground for crops and build fences and cabins within a set period of time. These incentives made it easier for Eastern farmers of limited means to move to the frontier.

Families and Communities

Land companies were not the only groups who actively encouraged settlers to emigrate. Frontiersmen themselves asked or encouraged family members and former neighbors to join them. In a phenomenon called chain migration, extended families, church congregations, even entire communities uprooted themselves and moved to new homes on the frontier. The adult sons of heads of household frequently went ahead of their fathers to find the best land, stake claims, fell trees, and break ground for the first corn crop. Their parents, spouses, and siblings followed, both to build their homes and farms and to claim undeveloped tracts of land that they could sell to the relatives and neighbors who followed them.

Chain migration helped enrich the first migrants, but more importantly it allowed settlers to pool their resources and risks and to recreate familiar social institutions with familiar people. Among the first social institutions that frontiersmen created in new settlements were social exchange networks, patterns of labor sharing and resource sharing that helped newcomers establish themselves and that built a sense of community (Faragher 1986, 133). Neighbors freely shared food and tools with new arrivals and gathered to build cabins and raise barns for them. Men assembled to hunt wolves and snakes or to display their masculine prowess in wrestling and log-rolling contests. Women met to husk corn, to hold sewing and quilting bees, and to attend the births of one another's children. Both sexes also met for weddings, dances, and other celebrations. At most of these gatherings, including the workday ones, men played music and consumed large quantities of alcohol, which may explain why men in the Northwest called them frolics. They served many functions other than frolicking, though: They reaffirmed traditional gender roles and family structures, bound private farmsteads together into communities, and offset the loneliness of settlers'—especially women's—lives. (During a sojourn in Pittsburgh, Elizabeth Trist noted that without occasional dances and other "recreations I should certainly have been very miserable" (Trist 1990, 214).

Anna Symmes Harrison (1775–1864)

The daughter of Anna Tuthill Symmes and John Cleves Symmes, Anna Harrison was born in Flatbrook, New Jersey. Following the early death of her mother, Anna lived with her maternal grandparents on Long Island. She attended private academies in Easthampton and New York City, and in 1794 she left the Northeast to join her father, a territorial judge and land speculator, in Cincinnati.

While visiting her sister, Maria Short, in Lexington, Kentucky, Anna met her future husband, William Henry Harrison, a U.S. Army lieutenant and a member of a distinguished Virginia family. In 1795 Lieutenant Harrison moved to Cincinnati and courted Anna Symmes, who despite her father's explicit instructions not to marry the penniless officer agreed to elope with William. The two married in November.

Anna Symmes Harrison gave birth to her first child, Elizabeth Bassett, in September 1796. For the next two decades she was almost

Anna Symmes Harrison, wife of William Henry Harrison and early frontier resident. (*Library of Congress*)

Barn raisings, bees, frolics, and the social exchange networks that they defined and strengthened were familiar Eastern social institutions. Another was the church congregation, which provided frontier settlers with both a spiritual center and an ad hoc law enforcement agency. Elite European and Eastern travelers commonly assumed that frontiersmen had no religious beliefs or described their practices as emotional and outré. For Western settlers, however, the church was the vital core of the community, a place of conversation, song, celebration, and hope. (This was particularly true of marginalized sects like the Shakers or Quakers, who moved to the frontier to establish religious sanctuaries.) Frontier white families supplemented their churchgoing with annual outdoor revival meetings, to which they would travel dozens of miles by wagon. There they would encamp and spend several days singing and listening to the fiery sermons of itinerant ministers. Whether in their churches or at camp meetings, frontier settlers preferred unlettered preachers with powerful speaking and storytelling skills to college-educated ministers, and they sought direct emotional communion with the Holy Spirit to the chaste ritualism of established Eastern churches.

constantly pregnant or nursing, giving birth to three more daughters [Lucy (1800), Mary (1809), and Anna Tuthill (1813)] and six sons [John Cleves (1798), William Henry Jr. (1802), John Scott (1804), Benjamin (1806), Carter (1811), and Findlay (1814)]. Only one of these children, the last, died in infancy, but the unhappy event devastated Anna, and she still recalled the heartbreak 20 years later.

In addition to her child-rearing responsibilities, Anna took charge of the Harrisons' household economy: cooking, cleaning, sewing, gardening, and entertaining. Her domestic burdens were not lightened by the family's frequent moves. In 1796 the Harrisons moved from Cincinnati to North Bend (present-day Ohio); in 1800 Anna accompanied her husband to Richmond, Virginia; and in 1801 the family moved to Vincennes. There William, the new territorial governor of Indiana, built a Georgian-style brick mansion called Grouseland. In the course of these moves, Mrs. Harrison developed a network of friends and correspondents throughout the Ohio Valley with whom she regularly exchanged visits: the wives of her husband's friends, her stepmother Susan Livingston Symmes, her sister Maria Short, and (after her sister's death) her brother-in-law's second wife Jane.

In 1812 the outbreak of war with Britain caused William Harrison to send his wife and children to North Bend, where Anna remained most of the rest of her life. In the 1820s and 1830s she provided advice and assistance to her children as they went off to school, married, and had their own families. Her husband returned to his career as a public servant, becoming a senator, a diplomat, and ultimately president. Anna Harrison was packing to move to Washington when she received news of her husband's death in April 1841. Thereafter she lived with her son John Scott Harrison, helping to raise her grandchildren, until her death in 1864.

Frontier Religion

Frontier communities in Kentucky, Tennessee, Ohio, and western New York were fertile ground for the evangelical revivalists who led the Second Great Awakening (1800–1840), and their inhabitants soon built makeshift community meeting houses for ministers from nonmainstream denominations: Baptists, Methodists, Presbyterians, and Disciples of Christ. These churches were not merely community centers; their lay members also enforced community norms, often more effectively than local sheriffs and courts could do. Church tribunals arbitrated disputes between fellow congregants, and they censured or expelled members for blasphemy, drunkenness, assault, and other interpersonal crimes.

Sometimes frontier churches were also the only sources of local education; some congregations, following the lead of Eastern Sunday school societies, began in the 1810s and 1820s to hold Sunday school classes wherein local children could learn to read the Bible. Frontier education was otherwise a haphazard affair, usually conducted in private homes by itinerant male schoolteachers who taught reading, writing, and basic math several months out of the year and who took their pay in cash (usually $5–10 per pupil) or kind (food, firewood, lodging). Some of the old Southwestern towns, like New Orleans, supported private academies for the sons and daughters of wealthy planters; some Ohio communities settled by New Englanders had taxpayer-supported public schools; and some states, like Illinois and Alabama, passed common school laws in the 1820s, though no one would enforce them for several decades. In general, Daniel Drake's memory of the state of education in late 18th-century Kentucky could apply to most of the Trans-Appalachian West before 1830: "Our preachers and teachers were . . . almost as destitute as the people at large, many of whom could neither read nor write" (Rohrbough 1990b, 43).

Militias

Another social institution that white settlers brought to the West was the militia company, which in the Eastern states was partly a military and police reserve and partly a male social club. In many frontier districts, however, militia companies became active paramilitary defense forces, because the land occupied by white pioneers was usually already claimed or exposed to attack by neighboring Indian nations. Of course, there were long periods in the first half century of white settlement in the Trans-Appalachian West when Native American townsmen and white American frontiersmen lived in peace with one another. Indians and whites swapped food and furs for salt, liquor, and homespun cloth; consulted one another's healers when they were sick; and even attended one another's funerals and weddings. However, the frontier was just as frequently a seat of war, as Cherokee, Creek, Miami, and Shawnee warriors seeking to protect their lands and to preserve a separate Indian identity clashed with white Americans seeking personal economic independence. The latter often found little distinction between combatants and civilians on the early Trans-Appalachian frontier; every man, no matter what his profession, was also a warrior.

Fighting between settlers and Indians inflamed the Ohio and Tennessee Valleys from the closing years of the War for American Independence until 1794, when Anthony Wayne's Legion of the United States, along with Kentucky and Tennessee volunteers, defeated the Northwest Indian Confederacy and their Creek and Chickamauga allies. Frontier militias also battled Tecumseh's Indian confederacy in the Northwest and the Seminoles and Red Stick Creeks in the Lower South between 1811 and 1818. During these conflicts, Woodland Indian warriors raided white farmsteads, scalped travelers, and plundered flatboats, and white militiamen retaliated by destroying the fields and houses of nearby Indian communities—as often as not occupied by friendly or neutral Indians—while their families huddled in crowded wooden blockhouses. Frontier militia attacks often failed to stop Indian raids and indeed tended to drive formerly neutral Native Americans into the arms of pan-Indian militants. However, they also obliged Native militants to concentrate their supply and operations bases in limited areas, like the town complex at The Glaize or the Red Stick Creek communities in the Coosa-Tallapoosa region, which federal troops and state volunteers could then assault and destroy.

Moreover, militia attacks on Indian communities served useful psychological purposes for white settlers. They allowed frontier men to prove their manliness and military prowess, and they allowed Western whites to draw a clear racial boundary line between their culture and that of neighboring Native Americans. By destroying Indians' fields and towns and killing them without regard for age, gender, or behavior, settlers asserted that they were different from and superior to their Indian neighbors, no matter how much the two cultures might resemble one another.

Natives and Neighbors

For a while the first white settlers in the Trans-Appalachian West often regarded Indians as enemies, at the same time adopting economic and social customs similar to those of their adversaries. For instance, many of the first white American migrants, like Daniel Boone in Kentucky and David Crockett in Tennessee, made their living the same way as Woodland Indian men: as commercial hunters. Other white men who came west to farm actually spent much of their time hunting and trapping to kill pests or to put meat on the table. Using firearms, traps, hunting dogs, and torches (which made animals freeze and illuminated their eyes), white hunters killed millions of wild animals every year: rattlesnakes, rabbits, squirrels, wild turkeys, partridges, deer, bears, and bison. (In the 1820s small hunting parties in Kentucky and Ohio could each kill up to 19,000 squirrels per week.) The killing became another source of tension between whites and Native Americans because both groups hunted the same limited game animal population and some larger species consequently became scarce or extinct. Buffalo, for instance, died out east of the Mississippi River by 1830.

There were other noticeable similarities between the early settlers and the Indians they displaced. The two peoples cultivated or gathered the same plant foods: maize, beans, pumpkins, hickory nuts, and maple sugar. White male backcountry settlers often wore the same clothing as Woodland Indian men—hunting shirts, leggings, breechcloths, and moccasins—because such clothes were more practical when hunting or traveling and because buckskin was easier to replace than cloth. Both groups also practiced free-range stock raising, which the Delawares, Cherokees, and other Woodland Indians had begun to adopt in the mid-18th century and which Eastern gentleman farmers considered a crude and slovenly form of husbandry.

Elite white observers often derided Western settlers as "white savages," a term that Benjamin Franklin had coined. Hector St. Jean de Crevecoeur

George Champlin Sibley (1782–1863)

The son of John and Elizabeth Hopkins Sibley, George Sibley was born in Great Barrington, Massachusetts, and grew up in Fayetteville, North Carolina. In 1803 his father departed for Natchitoches, Louisiana, where he became an Indian agent. Two years later, George also applied for a position in the Indian service as assistant factor at the U.S. Indian trading house in Natchitoches.

The trading house was one of nine so-called factories run by the War Department, where public traders, or factors, bought Native Americans' furs at market prices and sold them inexpensive manufactured goods. The factories' primary function was to increase the government's influence in Indian communities. A less commonly admitted goal was to lure prominent Indian leaders into debt, then trade the debts for land.

Lacking a position for him at Natchitoches, the War Department instead gave him the job of assistant factor at the Bellefontaine factory, near Saint Louis. The assignment was not a fulfilling one. The factory did little business, because it was too distant from the Plains Indians' settlements, and Sibley's ill-tempered supervisor Rudolph Tillier fired him after a bookkeeping dispute. In 1808, however, the secretary of war took Sibley's side. He fired Tillier and hired Sibley as factor of the trading house at Fort Osage, Missouri.

George Sibley's tenure at Fort Osage proved successful. The post did ample business with the Missouri Valley Indians, earning a cumulative profit of $10,000 by 1811. Sibley also served as a diplomat to the southern Plains Indians; in 1810–1811 he visited the towns of the Kansas, Osages, and Pawnees and secured their neutrality during the forthcoming war with Britain.

In 1812 Sibley returned to Saint Louis where he married Mary Easton. In 1817 the couple moved to Fort Osage, and George resumed working at the U.S. Indian factory until an economizing Congress (influenced by fur trading magnate John Astor) voted to close down the federal trading houses in 1822. In the meantime, Sibley had profited from the growing Missouri settler population. In the 1810s he made about $10,000 on a land deal, established a mercantile business in Saint Louis, and opened a hog farm and gristmill at Fort Osage.

Profits fell off after the Panic of 1819, and in 1825 Sibley returned to federal service, accepting a commission to survey a road to Santa Fe and to obtain right-of-way permits from the Osages and Mexican officials. He ran afoul of officials in Santa Fe by refusing to pay petty fees or submit to local regulations, but, despite Sibley's undiplomatic conduct, his mission succeeded, and the Santa Fe Trail became a profitable American trade route.

Sibley returned home to find that a business partner had defaulted on a loan that he had cosigned, leaving him penniless except for 280 acres of land in Saint Charles. George and Mary moved there in 1827 and devoted their lives to philanthropy, founding schools for girls and for African-American children.

characterized the most isolated frontiersmen as "no better than carnivorous animals of superior rank" (Nobles 1997, 105). In 1803 New Englander Thaddeus Harris described Kentuckians as "rough and savage . . . full of sloth and indolence" (Harris 1805, 56), and ten years later Andrew Jackson, ostensibly a champion of frontier egalitarianism, described cypress cutters in the lower Mississippi Valley in similar language: "They raise nothing from the earth for subsistence, and have to depend on the uncertainty of chance for a living . . . [They] have all the wildness of look and countenances displaying the same ferocity as their savage neighbors" (Jackson 1926–1935, 1: 267).

Westerners knew quite well that Eastern elites viewed them as indolent and outlandish. Some, as noted, tried to differentiate themselves from Indians through warfare, whereas most others tried to emulate Easterners by working to achieve a comfortable and respectable living standard—a "plain and reasonable mode of living," in Morris Birkbeck's words. Frontier farmers pursued comfort and respectability by practicing what historian Richard Bushman has called composite agriculture: the simultaneous production of goods for household consumption and for market (Bushman 1998). After their first year or two in a new settlement, male farmers, though they continued to spend much of their time raising corn and meat for their families, also began producing marketable goods that they could barter with their neighbors or sell for cash. These might be surplus food or lumber, or they might be commodities for which there was no local household demand, like furs or tobacco. Meanwhile, women produced a variety of basic foodstuffs—raising chickens, making butter and cheese, growing vegetables—and made much of their families' clothing from the flax, wool, or cotton that their husbands or male relatives grew. Many produced a surplus of homespun, eggs, or dairy products that they could barter or sell locally. On Southern farms, African American slaves had their own domestic economy because masters encouraged their bondsmen to grow gardens, raise chickens, and catch fish to stretch their rations; some produced a modest surplus that they could sell or trade.

The Frontier Economy

Frontier inhabitants of both genders (and all races) traded their surpluses with one another whenever they could. However, they could not develop a genuine market economy until they found an inexpensive means to ship their produce to distant markets. Many early settlements were connected to the outside world only by rutted, muddy, poorly marked wagon trails; so the cost of shipping goods to market towns exceeded any profit that frontiersmen could make from their sale.

Western farmers did have a few ways of earning cash. Some produced and sold durable commodities that had a high value in proportion to their weight, like whiskey, maple sugar, potash, and barrel staves. The lightness of these goods meant that their shipping costs were low, but they required a great deal of labor (and often expensive equipment) to produce. Others relied on the sale of surplus livestock, which could move to market towns under their own power. Around 1800 farmers in the Ohio Valley began driving hogs and cattle to Cincinnati and Baltimore, where they sold for 5¢ to 13¢ per pound. By the 1820s Kentuckians were driving over 100,000 swine across the Appalachians each year. However, hog and cattle drives were also time-consuming and not profitable for farmers who raised only a few ani-mals for home consumption.

The most reliable way of earning cash was by selling bulk produce to European markets, and the cheapest way for Western farmers to transport their flour, tobacco, or cotton to those markets was by loading it onto river-boats and floating it down the Ohio, Tennessee, or Missouri Rivers to the Mississippi River and thence to New Orleans. The most common type of riverboat between 1790 and 1820 was a flat-bottomed wooden raft, about 45 by 15 feet with 6-foot-high sides (and a partial roof to shelter cargo and passengers). Settlers referred to these craft as Kentucky boats, New Orleans boats, arks, or flatboats. Carpenters and sawmill operators in Pittsburgh and Wheeling manufactured and sold flatboats to emigrating farmers, who used them to transport their families to their new farmsteads and then dismantled the rafts to reuse the timbers to build houses.

Thousands of other settlers used flatboats to float cargo to market—all kinds of cargo. One traveler on the Ohio River observed Kentucky boats car-rying "horses, pigs, poultry, apples, flour, corn, peach brandy, cider, whiskey, bar-iron and castings, tin and copper wares, glass, cabinet work, chairs, mill-stones, grindstones [and] nails" to New Orleans (Blane 1824, 101–102). Reg-ular American trade through this Spanish-controlled port proved difficult in the 1780s, when Spain imposed heavy restrictions and duties on American shippers. However, after 1795, when the Treaty of San Lorenzo (Pinckney's Treaty) guaranteed U.S. access to the river and the city, New Orleans grew into the Western United States' principal commercial outlet. By 1807, four years after the Louisiana Purchase incorporated the city into the United States, Trans-Appalachian American farmers were sending over 1,800 flat-boats a year to New Orleans, carrying $5.3 million of produce. By 1819 West-ern exports through New Orleans had tripled in value to $16.7 million.

Since flatboats were unpowered vessels, they were strictly one-way freight carriers. After selling their produce and boat timbers at New Orleans and buying manufactured goods, early Western travelers could either hire a keelboat—a 40- to 80-foot craft with a crew of oarsmen—for the return trip, or they could load their purchases onto mules and return by road. Those selecting the road option commonly journeyed along the Natchez Trace, a 444-mile trail between Natchez, Mississippi, and Nashville, Tennessee, which American boatmen began using in 1785.

Increasingly after the War of 1812, a new form of river transport eclipsed both the flatboat and the keelboat. This was the steamboat, first patented by Robert Fulton in 1807. In addition to being expensive to build, steamboats were dangerous to operate because captains overpressurized their boilers to increase their speed, thereby increasing the risk of malfunc-tions and explosions. However, the new vessels could carry more cargo and passengers than flatboats and could operate in equally shallow waters, thanks to their tall superstructures, shallow drafts, and surface-churning paddle wheels. (One boat reportedly carried 80 passengers and 80,000

Boats on the Ohio River in 1835, drawing by Carl Bodmer. (*Hart, Albert Bushnell,* The Mentor, The Ohio River, *vol. 8, no. 12, August 2, 1920*)

pounds of freight through 2 feet of water.) More importantly, they were fast, able to travel from Louisville to New Orleans in a week (compared to three months for flatboats), and return in a week and a half. Due to their size and speed, steamboats cut shipping costs on the Mississippi and its tributaries by more than 75 percent. As investors realized the profitability of steamboats, the numbers of these craft in the Mississippi Valley grew from one vessel in 1811 to several hundred by 1830.

At the same time, state and federal governments sponsored a number of public transportation improvements. In 1806 the U.S. government began surveying a National Road from Maryland to Illinois, sending out teams to pull stumps and build bridges. Meanwhile, the new state governments of the Old Northwest marked state roads and, following the success of New York's Erie Canal in 1825, appropriated funds for canals linking the Great Lakes and the Ohio River. Most of these roads remained uncompleted by 1830, however, and the Ohio, Indiana, and Illinois canals were not finished until the late 1830s—and even then saw relatively light traffic. In the Southern states and territories, roads remained in poor condition and canals nonexistent throughout the antebellum period. More than any other innovation, it was the privately owned steamboat that tied the Trans-Appalachian West to the national market economy and that commercialized the white settlements there.

As Western settlers sold their growing agricultural surpluses for cash, storekeepers shipped an increasing quantity of imported and manufactured goods into frontier districts to sell to them. As early as 1792 Lexington, Kentucky, had over 20 retail stores, selling cloth, hose, gloves, china, glassware, razors, and books. Other Western market towns—like Cincinnati, Louisville, Knoxville, and Natchez—grew into equally important commercial emporia after 1800, and itinerant peddlers brought fancy merchandise into more remote frontier districts. Prosperous settlers increasingly replaced their buckskin and homespun clothing with broadcloth, left their cabins for frame or brick houses, and supplemented their diets with store-bought wine, coffee, and sugar.

More prosperous Westerners invested their cash profits in land speculation, which reached a fever pitch in the late 1810s (federal land sales grew from 500,000 acres in 1813 to 4 million in 1818), and in a variety of local industries. Kentuckians built linen manufactories, whiskey distilleries, and rope walks, where free and enslaved workers wound hemp into rope. Pittsburgh became a center of flatboat and steamboat manufacture, and local businessmen also invested in iron foundries and glassworks; by 1815 the city produced nearly $1 million worth of iron and glassware. Settlers in southeastern Ohio and in the future state of West Virginia built saltworks and dug coal to sell to farmers downriver, while early Illinois settlers mined for lead. Grist- and sawmills became common in virtually every growing frontier community, using draft animals or waterpower to grind grain and to saw lumber into boards. Merchants exported some of these products but sold most of them to the Trans-Appalachian region's growing population.

Inequality

As the Trans-Appalachian West become more commercial and more economically diversified, socioeconomic inequality grew. Prosperous farmers and shopkeepers could purchase additional lands, hire a large free workforce or (in slave states) buy African American slaves, and invest in mercantile ventures, mines, and light industries, thereby increasing their wealth and chances for success. Poorer settlers found themselves squeezed by economic hard times, like the depression that followed the Panic of 1819, and vulnerable to lawsuits brought by wealthier neighbors with competing claims to their land.

Economic historian Lee Soltow has discovered that, although Kentucky's overall economic output grew at an annual rate of 2.4 percent from 1800 to 1840, economic inequality in the state grew to levels comparable to present-day Brazil or sub-Saharan Africa. The new grandees of the Bluegrass state—slave-owning planters and lawyers—displayed their wealth and distanced themselves from poor Kentuckians by building palatial estates, organizing fox hunts and cotillion dances, and raising thoroughbred race horses (over 90,000 of them as early as 1800). Meanwhile, thousands of poor whites left Kentucky and the older sections of Tennessee for newer, better surveyed lands in Ohio, Indiana, and Illinois.

Many of these new emigrants were fleeing the domination of South-western society by slave owners, but high inequality was not a characteristic solely of slave states. By the 1820s fewer than half of all adult men in Ohio owned land, and the top 12 landowners in the state collectively owned nearly 500 square miles of real property. In Sugar Creek, Illinois, the amount of acreage owned by the poorest fifth of families fell from 10 percent in 1838 to 5 percent by 1858. Two-fifths of families there owned no land at all.

Conclusion

By 1830, large sections of the western world had become indistinguishable from the East. American settlers had transformed forests into farmland, hunting trails into roads, log cabins into frame houses, and fortified outposts into commercial cities with their own newspapers and musical societies. Perhaps the most significant change is that a minority of lucky or wealthy or well-connected Western whites had been able to monopolize the land and resources of the older frontier districts: central Kentucky, the Tennessee Valley, and much of Ohio. They compelled poorer or less fortunate settlers either to work for them as tenants and wage laborers or to look for better opportunities in new borderlands, which tens of thousands chose to do. That a large part of the Trans-Appalachian West had become a significant source of *emigration* to other parts of the United States was perhaps the clearest sign that the region's status as an undeveloped borderland—its frontier phase of development—was coming to an end.

References and Further Reading

Abernethy, T. Perkins. *From Frontier to Plantation in Tennessee.* Chapel Hill: University of North Carolina Press, 1932

Abernethy, T. Perkins. *The South in the New Nation, 1789–1819.* Baton Rouge: Louisiana State University Press, 1961

Aron, Stephen. *How the West Was Lost: The Transformation of Kentucky from Daniel Boone to Henry Clay.* Baltimore, MD: Johns Hopkins University Press, 1996

Bates, Frederick. *The Life and Papers of Frederick Bates.* Edited by Thomas Marshall. 2 vols. St. Louis: Missouri Historical Society, 1926

Belue, Ted Franklin. *The Long Hunt: Death of the Buffalo East of the Mississippi.* Mechanicsburg, PA: Stackpole Books, 1996

Billington, Ray Allen. *America's Frontier Heritage.* New York: Holt, Rinehart, and Winston, 1966

Birkbeck, Morris. *Letters from Illinois*. London: Taylor and Hessey, 1818a

Birkbeck, Morris. *Notes on a Journey in America*. London: Severn and Co., 1818b

Blane, William. *An Excursion Through the United States and Canada in the Years 1822 and 1823*. London: Baldwin, Craddock, and Joy, 1824

Bradbury, John. "Travels in the Interior of America, 1809–1811." In *Early Western Travels, 1748–1846*, Volume 5. Edited by Reuben Gold Thwaites. 31 vols. Cleveland, OH: A. H. Clark, 1904

Bushman, Richard. "Markets and Composite Farms in Early America." *William and Mary Quarterly* 3rd ser. 55 (July 1998): 351–74

Calloway, Colin. *New Worlds for All: Indians, Europeans, and the Remaking of Early America*. Baltimore, MD: Johns Hopkins University Press, 1997

Carson, W. Wallace. "Transportation and Traffic on the Ohio and Mississippi Before the Steamboat." *Mississippi Valley Historical Review* 7 (June 1920): 26–38

Cashin, Joan. *A Family Venture: Men and Women on the Southern Frontier*. New York: Oxford University Press, 1991

Cayton, Andrew R. L. *Frontier Indiana*. Bloomington: Indiana University Press, 1996

Cayton, Andrew R. L., and Fredrika Teute, eds. *Contact Points: American Frontiers from the Mohawk Valley to the Mississippi, 1750–1830*. Chapel Hill: University of North Carolina Press, 1998

Cleaves, Freeman. *Old Tippecanoe: William Henry Harrison and His Time*. New York: Charles Scribner's Sons, 1939

Davidson, Victor. *History of Wilkinson County, Georgia*. Macon, GA: J. W. Burke Co., 1930.

Davis, James. *Frontier Illinois*. Bloomington: Indiana University Press, 1998

Dowd, Gregory Evans. *A Spirited Resistance: The North American Indian Struggle for Unity, 1745–1815*. Baltimore, MD: Johns Hopkins University Press, 1992

Etchison, Nicole. *The Emerging Midwest: Upland Southerners and the Political Culture of the Old Northwest, 1787–1861*. Bloomington: Indiana University Press, 1996

Faragher, John Mack. *Sugar Creek: Life on the Illinois Prairie*. New Haven, CT: Yale University Press, 1986

Friend, Craig, ed. *The Buzzel about Kentuck: Settling the Promised Land*. Lexington: University Press of Kentucky, 1999

Gruenwald, Kim. *River of Enterprise: The Commercial Origins of Regional Identity in the Ohio Valley, 1790–1850*. Bloomington: Indiana University Press, 2002

Harper, Robert Goodloe. *Observations on the North American Land Company*. London: H. L. Gallabin, 1796

Harris, Thaddeus. *Journal of a Tour into the Territory Northwest of the Allegheny Mountains*. Boston: Manning and Loring, 1805

Henretta, James. "Families and Farms: Mentalité in Pre-Industrial America." *William and Mary Quarterly* 3rd ser. 35 (January 1978): 3–32

Hinderaker, Eric. *Elusive Empires: Constructing Colonialism in the Ohio Valley, 1673–1800*. New York: Cambridge University Press, 1997

Hurt, R. Douglas. *The Ohio Frontier: Crucible of the Old Northwest, 1720–1830*. Bloomington: Indiana University Press, 1996

Isenberg, Andrew. "The Market Revolution in the Borderlands: George Champlin Sibley in Missouri and New Mexico, 1808–1826." *Journal of the Early Republic* 21 (Fall 2001): 445–65

Jackson, Andrew. *Correspondence of Andrew Jackson*. Edited by John Spencer Bassett. 7 vols. Washington, DC: Carnegie Institution of Washington, 1926–1935

Knouff, Gregory. "Soldiers and Violence on the Pennsylvania Frontier." In John Frantz and William Pencak, eds. *Beyond Philadelphia: The American Revolution in the Pennsylvania Hinterland*, 171–93, 243–51. University Park: Pennsylvania State University Press, 1998

Kukla, Jon. *A Wilderness So Immense: The Louisiana Purchase and the Destiny of America*. New York: Alfred A. Knopf, 2003

Kulikoff, Allan. *The Agrarian Origins of American Capitalism*. Charlottesville: University of Virginia Press, 1992

Lockridge, Kenneth. "Land, Population, and the Evolution of New England Society, 1630–1790." *Past and Present* 39 (April 1968): 62–80

Nobles, Gregory. *American Frontiers: Cultural Encounters and Continental Conquest*. New York: Hill and Wang, 1997

Owsley, Frank. *Plain Folk of the Old South*. New York: Quadrangle Books, 1965 (originally published 1949)

Rohrbough, Malcolm. *The Land Office Business: The Settlement and Administration of American Public Lands, 1789–1837*. Belmont, CA: Wadsworth, 1990a

Rohrbough, Malcolm. *The Trans-Appalachian Frontier: People, Societies, and Institutions, 1775–1850*. Belmont, CA: Wadsworth, 1990b

Rothman, Adam. *Slave Country: American Expansion and the Origins of the Deep South*. Cambridge, MA: Harvard University Press, 2005

Sellers, Charles. *The Market Revolution*. New York: Oxford University Press, 1991

Sibley, George Champlin. *The Road to Santa Fe: The Journal and Diaries of George Champlin Sibley*. Edited by Kate L. Gregg. Albuquerque: University of New Mexico Press, 1995

Silver, Timothy. *A New Face on the Countryside: Indians, Colonists, and Slaves in the South Atlantic Forests, 1500–1800*. Cambridge: Cambridge University Press, 1990

Soltow, Lee. "Inequality Amidst Abundance: Land Ownership in Early Nineteenth Century Ohio." *Ohio History* 88 (Spring 1979): 133–51

Soltow, Lee. "Kentucky Wealth at the End of the Eighteenth Century." *Journal of Economic History* 43 (September 1983): 617–33

St. Clair, Arthur. Arthur St. Clair Papers, 1746 through 1882. Microfilm. 8 rolls. Columbus: Ohio Historical Society, 1976

Taylor, Alan. "Agrarian Independence: Northern Land Rioters After the Revolution." In Alfred Young, ed. *Beyond the American Revolution: Further Explorations in the History of American Radicalism*, 221–45. Dekalb: Northern Illinois University Press, 1993

Taylor, Alan. *William Cooper's Town: Power and Persuasion on the Frontier of the Early American Republic*. New York: Alfred A. Knopf, 1995

Toulmin, Harry. *Collection of All the Public and Private Acts of the General Assembly of Kentucky*. Frankfort, KY: William Hunter, 1802

Trist, Elizabeth. "The Diary of Elizabeth House Trist." Edited by Elizabeth Kolody. In William Andrews et al., eds. *Journeys in New Worlds: Early American Women's Narratives*, 181–232. Madison: University of Wisconsin Press, 1990

Trollope, Frances. *Domestic Manners of the Americans*. New York: Penguin, 1997

Vickers, Daniel. "Competency and Competition: Economic Culture in Early America." *William and Mary Quarterly* 3rd ser. 47 (January 1990): 3–29

Wade, Richard. *The Urban Frontier: The Rise of Western Cities, 1790–1830*. Cambridge, MA: Harvard University Press, 1959

Wyckoff, William. *The Developer's Frontier: The Making of the Western New York Landscape*. New Haven, CT: Yale University Press, 1988

"My Joy Has Ebbed and Flowed, with the Complexion of the Times": Immigrants and Migrants in the Early Republic | 7

Dawn Hutchins

Introduction

In the post-Revolutionary decades, thousands of European immigrants came to the United States with the hope of escaping their impoverished pasts and enjoying the promise of the young republic. Many of these immigrants left their homelands and sometimes their families, only to find that American cities did not meet their expectations. Employment in the nation's first factories or at the docks was often difficult to find and poorly paid. As the market revolution transformed the nation's economy, many immigrants fled to the recently opened lands of the backcountry to enjoy the independence that drew them to the United States. In this manner, immigrants became migrants, and the migrants increasingly became Americanized. Their experiences of arriving in the United States and then uprooting again to the backcountry provide tremendous insight into an ordinary citizen's view of the early republic. Similarly, their daily experiences—their family life, religion, and political inclinations—reveal an American experience that contrasts sharply with those of the so-called great men of the era. These immigrants and backcountry settlers carved out a new path for their families and communities, and contributed to the ever expanding United States. They also faced a tremendous nativist (anti-immigrant) movement that typified the early republic.

Most immigrants who came to the United States during the early republic underwent a massive change—one that is often called Americanization. Since many immigrants in the era were desperate to escape economic and political problems in their homelands, many of the newcomers came under the legal burdens of servitude. They were part of what historian Aaron

Excerpt from a broadside by Redern & Compagnie, a French land company, announcing the availability of stock in 100 acres of land in Virginia and Kentucky, 1820. (*Reuben T. Durrett Collection on Kentucky and the Ohio River Valley, Special Collections Research Center, University of Chicago Library*)

Fogelman describes as "a complex world of the free and the unfree, occupying different conditions of liberty and bondage, some tied to masters for brief periods, others viewed as criminal outcasts rightly condemned to forced labor, and many more branded by race and doomed to servitude for life, with no rights of their own" (Fogleman 1998, 43). This connection between servitude and immigration survived the Revolution, albeit in a significantly weakened and different form. Even though many Americans came to believe that holding people in bondage as indentured servants or as slaves opposed the core meaning of the Revolution, many immigrants continued to come to America in bondage.

An Open and Then Shut Case

During the early republic, the United States alternated between opening the doors to citizenship and closing the doors to foreigners. As a result, at least in comparison to other American eras, European immigrants may have had their smallest effect in the early republic. George Washington epitomized those who thought that the United States should be a haven. "The bosom of America," he wrote in 1783, "is open to receive not only the Opulent and respected Stranger, but the oppresed and persecuted of all Nations and Religions." This attitude resulted in widespread immigration in the nation's earliest years. The U.S. Constitution contained a means for newcomers to become citizens, and in 1790 Congress had approved a naturalization act for white men. These legal conditions encouraged many disaffected Europeans to pick up and move. Many, but not all, found themselves in the nation's relatively few large cities. In 1791 alone, for example, at least 3,000 Irish immigrants made their home in Philadelphia.

Washington was clearly not alone in his desire to see America grow through immigration. Others saw welcoming immigrants into the United States as part of a peculiarly virtuous national purpose. In 1802, for example, a Pennsylvania newspaper reminded its readers of the obligations they had when "the fairest portions of Europe have, for nearly twenty years, been desolated by war, depopulated by famine and their inhabitants drinking deep of the cup of misery, while, within these United States, we have enjoyed the countless blessings of peace and plenty" (Dooley 2004, 109, 119). This proimmigrant sentiment, in large part, helps explain the decision in 1792 to restrict participation in the militia to "each and every free ablebodied white male citizen of the respective states" (Jacobson 1998, 25).

The open door policy for white newcomers did not last for the entire era. Fearful of the presumed ideological and political leanings of many immigrants, Congress repeatedly placed restrictions on immigration in the early republic. In 1795 and 1796, for example, Congress extended the time it took immigrants to become citizens, which increased from 2 years, to 5 years, to 14 years. Perhaps most importantly, the 1798 Alien Act authorized the president to deport foreigners who were deemed "dangerous to the peace and safety of the United States." This angered many Americans, who thought that it "[w]as inhospitable, unjust, unconstitutional, and oppressive; and intended to aid the British government in its endeavors to prevent the miserably subjects of it extortion and inhumanity from seeking an asylum on our free and comparatively, happy shores" (Dooley 2004, 120).

The German Experience

With the exception of African slaves, most immigrants during the early republic came from Europe. Germans formed the largest group of European immigrants in the nation's first few decades. In 1790, about 300,000 Germans lived in the newly formed United States. This comprised about 10 percent of the nation's white population. Most of the Germans concentrated in Pennsylvania, where they constituted about one-third of the population. Although the number of immigrants declined in the early republic, new Germans continued to arrive. Between 1819 (when Congress first mandated keeping statistics on immigrants) and 1840, about 155,000 Germans came to the country. Most of these Germans came to smaller towns like Reading, Pennsylvania, or Frederick, Maryland, if not even smaller villages like the Pennsylvania towns of Berks, York, Schuylkill, or Mancaster.

Impoverished Germans typically came to the United States under the control of an owner and suffered tremendous difficulties in their new endeavors.

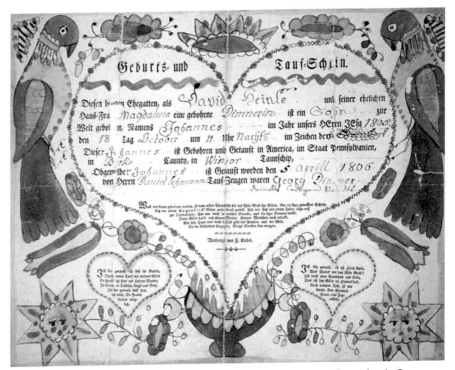

Illuminated birth certificate for Johannes Heinle, born 1805, in Berks County, Pennsylvania. Germans formed the largest group of immigrants in the early republic, most migrating to smaller towns in Pennsylvania. Poor Germans came to the U.S. as indentured servants, contracted to work for years before having the opportunity to buy land and start families of their own. (*Library of Congress*)

Called redemptioners, these immigrants suffered many misfortunes and injustices on the transatlantic journey to America, and they were often subjected to "unspeakable brutality." Children tended to suffer the most on the journeys, with one observer commenting how "the cry of the children for bread was, I am informed, so great that it would be impossible for man to describe it." Another man who went on board a recently arrived vessel found that the ship was a "revolting scene of want and misery. The eye involuntarily turned for some relief from the horrible picture of human suffering" (Mesick 1922, 45). In addition to the routine mistreatment by ship captains and crews, these German immigrants normally arrived malnourished, exhausted, and without an American owner. Instead, the German immigrants signed multiyear labor contracts (called indentures) with the ship captains, who, upon arrival to the United States, sold the indentures (and thus the immigrant's labor) to the highest bidder. Most of these contracts were purchased by farmers in the Pennsylvania region.

German immigrants suffered the trauma of the journey with the hope of someday enjoying the fruits of their labor. German immigrants, like other newcomers, hoped that they could survive their indentures and then partake of the opportunities of the young nation. One immigrant, for example, commented that "the moment I set my foot on the shore, I embraced it for my own . . . my joy has ebbed and flowed, with the complexion of the times" (Mesick 1922, 3). For many Germans, opportunities often came slowly. After seemingly endless years of toil, many German servants outlived their bondage only to find themselves impoverished again. They were free, but they could still not afford to buy their own land. Many of these redemptioners worked and persevered until they finally purchased supplies and land with the hope of attaining a better existence.

The Irish Immigrants

Irish immigrants had fundamentally similar experiences in the young republic. Irish immigrants, like their German counterparts, also came to America with the hope for a better livelihood. These immigrants predominantly came from Northern Ireland, especially the Ulster region. In the 1790s, over 60,000 Irish immigrants came to the United States; about 80 percent of them were Ulster Presbyterians and only 20 percent were Catholic. By the end of the early republic, the religious imbalance began to even out as the numbers of Irish immigrants rapidly increased. Between 1819 and 1840, approximately 335,000 Irish immigrants came to the United States. By the 1820s, Irish newcomers were the largest group of European immigrants. These mostly Presbyterian Protestants struggled to feed their families in Ireland, even before the dreadful potato blight occurred, and then faced the double indignity of religious and political persecution.

Upon their arrival, many of these rural immigrants rapidly left the eastern shore for inland opportunities. They traveled as families, often as members of an extended clan, and within a generation they dominated the backcountry—a region that began the era along the western slope of the Appalachian Mountains and that ended the era in the valleys of the Missouri and Arkansas Rivers. This region, which was recently and sometimes currently Indian land, offered newcomers the opportunity to make their own luck, to achieve economic stability with their own hard labor of clearing and planting fields and herding livestock. During the era, Irish and Scots-Irish immigrants made up approximately 15 percent of the region's population.

In the backcountry, Irish families typically lived the same subsistence-level lifestyle that they had experienced in their homeland. They built and lived in crude log homes, they herded hogs, and they planted corn and other crops. Many landed members of their communities disparaged the Irish way of life. A prominent early 19th-century doctor, for example, remarked how "a most important step in the course of improvement among the poor Irish, is the formation of a habit of economy" (Carey 1838, 322). Americans, like the doctor, frequently chastised the Irish for not embracing

American culture, especially when they pursued paths that often conflicted with the staple crop orientations of their neighbors or that lacked the refinement treasured in the East. Anti-Irish sentiments also resulted in thousands of Irish immigrants being arrested for various felonies and with the common belief that Irishmen were "white Negroes" (Ignatiev 1995, 47). Other Irish immigrants found employment in the Northeastern towns, often in the new factories. There, too, they often faced equally hostile neighbors. In 1798, for example, Massachusetts Congressman Harrison Gray Otis warned Americans that "hoards of wild Irishmen" had invaded the country. "This mass of vicious and disorganizing characters who can not live peaceably at home, and who, after unfurling the standard of rebellion in their own countries, may come hither to revolutionize ours" (Dooley 2004, 109). Not surprisingly, then, many Irish immigrants left the urban centers for a life in the backcountry.

Because of linguistic differences, Irish and Germans did not have identical experiences in the workforce. A language barrier prevented German immigrants from entering the emerging workforce. The Ulster Irish, however, spoke English, albeit with a distinct dialect, and as a result many Irish immigrants obtained better jobs, and their children were schooled in much the same way as other children in their communities. "Thus their everyday lives were little different from those of other European Americans. Children attended the same schools as other children, wives performed the same domestic chores as other wives, and husbands engaged in the same types of work as other men, both in rural and urban settings" (Heidler 2004, 164). These Irish families typically looked favorably on their decision to emigrate to the United States.

French Immigrants

In the early republic, many French immigrants came to the United States as a result of the political turmoil of the era. Many of these French newcomers came during and after the Haitian Revolution in the 1790s. This bloody revolution, which overthrew the slaveholding French colony of Saint-Domingue and killed thousands of French residents, created a diaspora of French slaveholders and officials. Approximately 20,000 refugees, mostly merchants and plantation owners, came to the United States. Some eventually decided to leave the United States and return to France. However, many stayed in the Philadelphia area. Their continued presence caused tremendous anger when they inadvertently transmitted yellow fever, a highly contagious and deadly disease, to the city's residents. This particular outbreak of yellow fever was particularly dreadful and tested the faith of many residents. As one widely distributed account of the fever expressed:

> On this occasion general attendance was given at the several churches, and the throne of God was solemnly addressed in behalf of our brethren at Philadel-

phia, who experience yellow fever, and to avert so great an evil from falling on this populous city, and other exposed places. ("Monthly Register" 1793, 574)

Other French immigrants came during the years following the Napoleonic Wars in an attempt to evade political persecution. Still others traveled to America in search of the grandly idealized American experiment—what many called the United States' democratic form of government.

In later years, thousands of French political refugees, many of them anxious after the exile of Napoleon, came to the United States. Many of these newcomers settled in what would be southwestern Alabama. The most famous of these immigrants was Joseph Bonaparte, the brother of Napoleon Bonaparte. After Napoleon's defeat at Waterloo, the two brothers took flight. Whereas Napoleon "thr[e]w himself on the mercy of the English," Joseph headed to New York (Dawson 1944, 92). Joseph Bonaparte, along with other French exiles in Philadelphia, then relocated to the South, where they established Demopolis in an effort to farm olives and wine. Within a few decades, their colony failed and many returned to France. Others simply relocated to more favorable locations in the United States. One family, the Fourniers, still reside in the New Orleans region, and other descendants are scattered throughout the Gulf Coast region.

French immigrants, perhaps more so than any other European group, shaped the general character of American society. Many Americans associated the French with a certain level of sophistication, and Americans who wanted to demonstrate their refined culture increasingly emulated this style. Recipes often reflected French influence, and newspapers promoted French cuisine. French clothing and hairstyles also became popular throughout the early republic. Older men still wore the traditional wigs, but younger men adopted the shorter hairstyle. Women also emulated French hairstyles, choosing to forego the colonial braided look in lieu of simpler styles. In terms of clothing, men started wearing French breeches and coats, and women fashioned their clothing in the Empire style (so named for Napoleon's empire). For Americans in the early republic, societal changes were inevitable. Many citizens in the republic were bound to emulate incoming immigrants, even if they did not desire to do so.

Even as many Americans purchased French products and ate French food, hostility to French immigrants was common in early America. This was especially true in the 1790s and early 1800s, when many Americans worried that an expansionist France had thoughts of invading the young United States.

> Look at your houses, your parents, your wives, and your children. Are you prepared to see your dwellings in flames, hoary hairs bathed in blood, female chastity violated, or children writhing on the pike and the halberd? If not, prepare for the task of protecting your Government. Look at every leading Jacobin, as a ravening wolf, preparing to enter your peaceful fold. (Dooley 2004, 111–12)

FRENCH ACADEMY,

NO. 33 BEAVER-STREET,

NEW-YORK.

TERMS—BOARD AND TUITION, $300 PER ANNUM—HALF IN ADVANCE.

LADIES AND GENTLEMEN,

Of this Metropolis, of the United States of America, of South America, and the various countries of Europe, are respectfully informed, that

L' Academie Française,

on an improved system of "Nature Displayed," in her mode of teaching Language to Man, is now open for the reception of pupils in the English, French, Spanish, Italian, German, Greek, and Latin languages.

Reading, Penmanship, Stenography, English Grammar, Arithmetic, Book-keeping, Geography, (with the use of Maps and Globes,) Painting and Drawing, History, Algebra, Geometry, Plain and Spherical Trigonometry, Mensuration, Surveying, Navigation, the Practice and Theory of Lunars, with the Use of Chronometers, Astronomy, Natural and Moral Philosophy, Botany, Chymistry, Logic, Rhetoric, and Criticism, will be taught by experienced Instructers, on the most reasonable terms.

The course of theoretical instruction will also comprise the practical illustration of the most useful branches, from Manuscript Lectures of distinguished Professors, European and American.

I have the honour,
Ladies and Gentlemen,
To be very respectfully,

Will. L. Hart P. M. L.

Mr Jefferson

N. B. Apply to either of the American or European Consulates.

Circular advertising a "French Academy," in New York. (*Library of Congress*)

Not all Americans shared this belief, but its expression certainly helped convince French immigrants of the efficacy of living in ethnic enclaves. Other Americans feared that the antislavery ideology and racial egalitarianism of the Haitian Revolution would spill over into the United States. White Southerners, in particular, feared the words of one South Carolina congressmen: "Liberty and Equality has been infused into the minds of the negroes." Thomas Jefferson similarly feared the specter of Haiti. "The West Indies," he worried "appears to have given considerable impulse to the minds of the slaves . . . in the United States" (Johnson 2006, 104–105.)

From City to Backcountry

Many immigrants initially moved to the nation's urban areas, where the prospects of employment were presumed to be greater than elsewhere. Normally, these immigrants formed ethnic enclaves, not always by choice. As a result, they continued to live among people with similar languages, religions, and interests. Some immigrant families, such as the Fourniers of Demopolis for example, chose to stay in the same general area. Many of these ethnic communities failed, however, often leaving immigrants with few choices but to uproot their families again. Many of these frustrated urbanites were attracted by the great lure of the frontier or backcountry, those lands on the edge of so-called settlement. During the early republic, the Southern backcountry extended westward from parts of Virginia, Georgia, the Carolinas, Tennessee, and Kentucky. The Northern backcountry extended into the Ohio Territory and seemed to be expanding on a daily basis. The backcountry, the "waste lands . . . across the mountains," held much promise for vast numbers of immigrant settlers (Aron 1992, 181). These areas seemed to guarantee great possibility for land speculators and ordinary folk just trying to make a living. While many immigrants moved to these Western lands, their stories are often difficult to locate. One has to rely on the occasional diary or travel narrative to glean a feel for the day.

The Kindness of Neighbors

Many immigrants, whether as families or as lone settlers, fled the Eastern cities for the American frontier. As the United States expanded its western borders, especially with the Louisiana Purchase, the frontier increasingly became associated with opportunity. It was not, however, a sure thing. As much as immigrants relied on the wider communities as they traveled from Europe or first settled in the United States, migrants to the frontier depended greatly on the benevolence and assistance of other families in the area. William Calk, a frontier settler in Kentucky, traveled without a dependent

Daniel Boone (1734–1820)

Daniel Boone, although not a firsthand immigrant to the United States, perhaps best fits the description of immigrants and those of recently immigrated parents to the fledgling United States of America. Boone's entrepreneurial spirit, like that of so many immigrants, led him continually to test the boundaries of settlement.

Boone was born on October 22, 1734, to Squire Boone, who had emigrated from England in 1713, and Sarah Morgan Boone. Raised in the backcountry of Pennsylvania, Boone quickly discovered his passion for hunting and exploring new lands. Even after the family relocated to North Carolina, Boone retained and refined his passion for hunting, particularly the long hunt. During these exploits, Boone familiarized himself with Native American hunting techniques and quickly became successful in the hunting business.

A dependable network or family life was particularly important to many immigrants and backcountry settlers, and the Boone clan was no exception. Boone, one of 11 children, eventually married Rebecca Bryan, and they had 10 children together. The close network between the Boone and Bryan families helped them in making their new settlements, especially when Boone was away on long hunts. Daniel and Rebecca Boone managed to relocate repeatedly and depended on kin and neighbor for assistance in doing so.

Boone eventually blazed a trail through to the Bluegrass, or what is now Kentucky, in 1775 (Hinderaker and Mancall 2003, 161). Boone, along with several other families, eventually founded the town of Boonesborough in April 1775. During the Revolutionary War, local Shawnee Indians and Bluegrass settlers engaged in multiple confrontations. In 1778, the Shawnees captured Boone, but he escaped and retrieved his family from North Carolina and returned them to Boonesborough the fol-

family, yet he realized the necessity for joining a larger group. Calk left his family behind in Virginia so that he could prospect for land in Kentucky. His diary depicts the difficulty that was the frontier. One Saturday, Calk remarked how "we Start Early. travel over Some more very Bad mountains . . . and there we Staid till Thursday morning. on Tuesday night & Wednesday morning it Snowed Very hard and was very colad & we hunted a good deal there while we Staid in Rough mountains & Kild three Deer & one turkey" (Eslinger 2004, 70). Calk's experience in the backcountry exemplified a typical day in the life of a prospective frontiersman. Life revolved around the search for land, game, and overall survival.

For immigrant groups traveling to the backcountry, life was fraught with difficulty and hardship. For many, traveling to the backcountry proved to be a difficult endeavor. In 1783, settlers, such as Englishman James Smith, traveled to the backcountry of Kentucky to satisfy his natural curiosity in regard to the West, as well as to ascertain whether living on the frontier was an option for him. He left Virginia in 1783 with his brother, George Rapin Smith, and a slave, Manuel. He eventually chose to settle in Ohio, not Kentucky, but his diary concerning his travels in the backcountry is laden with

lowing year. After being court-martialed and later acquitted for suspicion of questionable loyalties during the war, Boone endeavored to regain his integrity and began to serve in various political offices in the Kentucky area, such as a representative in the Virginia General Assembly. After several failed business attempts, Boone and many of his family members moved in 1799 to the Missouri territory. Boone spent the remainder of his life in Missouri and died in September of 1820. Boone's legacy typifies the entrepreneurial immigrant spirit of early America and remains one of adventure and the daring to move on to better pastures.

Daniel Boone was a pioneer who forged a route through the Appalachians and helped establish Kentucky's first white settlement. His battles with Native Americans are legendary. (*Library of Congress*)

details of the traveling life of pioneers. His experience on the road was full of sickness and bad weather. He describes one instance as being

> still cloudy and raw, and I was also still very unwell after one of the most disagreeable night's lodging that I ever had in my life, for the ground being wet, all our bedding wet, the wind all night blowing exceeding hard and either rain or snow frequently beating in upon us was the cause of my being seized with a shivering ague, which continued till the middle of the day. (Eslinger 2004, 107)

Many other immigrant families experienced the same type of circumstances in pursuit of a better life. Joel Watkins, born in Virginia to recent English immigrants, traveled down the Wilderness Road to find a place for settlement. Not satisfied with Kentucky, he eventually returned home to Virginia. Others delighted in Kentucky and found that it held much promise for a better life. Mary Coburn Dewees was one of those settlers. Dewees and her family left Philadelphia for Kentucky in 1788, choosing to travel alongside relatives, with the intention of meeting up with family already in Kentucky. Dewees kept a diary of the entire journey, a strange endeavor for a woman responsible for children and domestic tasks. "Despite her refined

James Harrod (ca. 1746–d.?)

James Harrod was born in Bedford County, Pennsylvania, around 1746 to recently immigrated parents, John Harrod and Sarah Moore. The Harrod clan, from Bedfordshire, England, had already suffered greatly in their new lands. John Harrod was previously married with two sons, Thomas and John. While John was away on a hunting expedition, his young wife was killed by local Native Americans. Harrod relocated to the town of Joppa and married his second wife, Sarah. They eventually had 12 children together.

James, the third-born son to John and Sarah, spent much of his youth and early adulthood helping his widowed mother relocate to new homes. In 1755, the Harrod family fled their Great Cove home because of impending attacks by King Shingas of the Delaware tribe. James and his brothers relocated their family to Fort Littleton, Pennsylvania. Along with a few of his brothers, James entered into military service soon thereafter and ultimately fought under John Forbes during the French and Indian War.

During the 1760s and 1770s, James, along with his brother Sam, ventured to Western lands, embarking on the fur trade business. After their enlistments, both brothers traveled throughout the Illinois territory and struck up business with French traders. James eventually learned French, and the two brothers built a fur trading business, which often took them along the Mississippi River to New Orleans and later into Kentucky and Tennessee. Here they met other traders and frontiersmen, such as Daniel Boone and George Michael Holsteiner.

On June 16, 1774, after surveying lands in Kentucky, James and approximately 48 others established the first settlement in what is now known as Kentucky. Just after arriving, Lord Dunmore summoned them back to fight against

background, Dewees's adventurous spirit and good humor carried her over a number of unpleasant experiences. One of the distinctive qualities of her account is the frequent appreciation for wild beauty" (Eslinger 2004, 130). Dewees's experience in the backcountry typified the general circumstances of women while traveling. Her fresh insight and descriptive prose relay myriad details of life along the trail. "Tho but a few days since my friends concluded I could not reach Kentucky, will you believe me when I tell you I am sitting on the Bank of the Susquehanah, and can take my bit of ham and Biscuit with any of them." Eventually, the Dewees family settled about 9 miles from Lexington. Dewees remarked, "I can assure you I have enjoyed more happiness the few days I have been here than I have experienced these four or five years past. I have my little family together. And [I] am in full expectations of seeing better days" (Eslinger 2004, 145).

Conclusion

Just as in other periods in American history, immigrants in the early republic came to the United States to escape political and economic problems and otherwise to pursue a better life for themselves. In the nation's first decades,

Native Americans in Lord Dunmore's War. Never seeing battle, Harrod returned to his new settlement. Harrod's Town, a land that was "delightful beyond conception," originally consisted of about 30 houses, but soon the settlers expanded their boundaries with additional buildings and plantation areas (Mason 1951, 48). During this time, Harrod and others met with the Boones at Boonesborough to initiate the first legal claims to the area.

Family life was important to recent immigrants and backcountry settlers, and James Harrod fits this description well. After years of taking care of his widowed mother and siblings, James Harrod eventually married Ann Coburn McDonald in 1778 and later had one daughter, Margaret, in 1785. During Harrod's latter years, he initiated campaigns to establish colonization not only of his settlement but of Kentucky County and later to further the cause

of Kentucky's statehood. Harrod was elected to the Virginia House of Delegates in 1779 and continued to be involved in several military expeditions.

Harrod died sometime during the winter of 1792–1793 on a hunting and trapping trip. The circumstances of his death remain debated, with multiple causes offered for speculation. Some claimed that a fellow hunter killed him, but Harrod's body was never found. Others claimed that Harrod did not die while hunting and either went to live with a previous wife or with Native Americans. There is no official basis for these accounts, and most scholars accept that Harrod most likely died at the hands of a man named Bridges, with whom Harrod was disputing land ownership. Regardless of how he died, Harrod remains known as "beloved—honorable—no seeker after fame; he served his country & race" (Mason 1951, 236).

the nation struggled to decide whether to embrace European immigrants or to shut the door to them entirely. Despite these challenges, thousands of Irish, German, French, and other immigrants made the United States their new homes. Some came free, others came with indentures. Some stayed in their Eastern seaboard communities, and others uprooted their lives for the lure of Western lands. For most of these immigrants, the early republic simply meant an opportunity to further their own interests, with many choosing to capitalize on their newfound chance to obtain land and economic opportunities. The story of immigrants, their transatlantic travels, their initial Eastern settlements, their daily struggles, and their eventual move to the backcountry proves just how dynamic and opportunistic the people of the fledgling United States were. These settlers were not the first to cross the sea and the mountains, nor would they be the last.

References and Further Reading

Aron, Stephen. *How the West Was Lost: The Transformation of Kentucky from Daniel Boone to Henry Clay.* Baltimore, MD: Johns Hopkins University Press, 1996

Aron, Stephen. "Pioneers and Profiteers: Land Speculation and the Home-stead Ethic in Frontier Kentucky." *Western Historical Quarterly* 23 (May 1992): 179–98

Baseler, Marilyn C. *"Asylum for Mankind": America, 1607–1800*. Ithaca, NY: Cornell University Press, 1998

Baylor, Ronald H. *Race and Ethnicity in America: A Concise History*. New York: Columbia University Press, 2003

Calloway, Colin G. "Neither White nor Red: White Renegades on the American Indian Frontier." *Western Historical Quarterly* 17 (January 1986): 43–66

Carey, Henry Charles. *The Credit System in France, Great Britain, and the United States*. Philadelphia: Carey, Lea, & Blanchard, 1838

Crass, David Colin, Steven D. Smith, Martha A. Zierden, and Richard D. Brooks, eds. *The Southern Colonial Backcountry: Interdisciplinary Perspectives on Frontier Communities*. Knoxville: University of Tennessee Press, 1998

Crozier, Alan. "The Scotch-Irish Influence on American English." *American Speech* 59 (Winter 1984): 310–31

Daniels, Roger. *Coming to America: A History of Immigration and Ethnicity in American Life*. New York: HarperCollins, 1990

Dawson, John Charles. "The French in Alabama: The Vine and Olive Colony." *French Review* 18 (December 1944): 92–95

Dinnerstein, Leonard, and David M. Reimers. *Ethnic Americans: A History of Immigration and Assimilation*. New York: Dodd, Mead and Company, 1975

Dooley, Patricia L. *The Early Republic: Primary Documents on Events from 1799 to 1820*. Westport, CT: Greenwood Press, 2004

Dublin, Thomas. *Immigrant Voices: New Lives in America, 1773–1986*. Urbana: University of Illinois Press, 1993

Erickson, Charlotte. *Invisible Immigrants: The Adaptation of English and Scottish Immigrants in Nineteenth-Century America*. Coral Gables, FL: University of Miami Press, 1972

Eslinger, Ellen, ed. *Running Mad for Kentucky: Frontier Travel Accounts*. Lexington: University Press of Kentucky, 2004

Faragher, John Mack. *Daniel Boone: The Life and Legend of an American Pioneer*. New York: Henry Holt and Company, 1992

Fogleman, Aaron S. "From Slaves, Convicts, and Servants to Free Passengers: The Transformation of Immigration in the Era of the American Revolution." *Journal of American History* 85 (June 1998): 43–76

Friend, Craig T. "Merchants and Markethouses: Reflections on Moral Economy in Early Kentucky." *Journal of the Early Republic* 17 (Winter 1997): 553–74

Gemery, Henry A. "Disarray in the Historical Record: Estimates of Immigration to the United States, 1700–1860." Symposium on the Demographic History of the Philadelphia Region, 1600–1860. *Proceedings of the American Philosophical Society* 133, no. 2 (June 1989): 123–27

Grabbe, Hans-Jurgen. "European Immigration to the United States in the Early National Period, 1783–1820." Symposium on the Demographic History of the Philadelphia Region, 1600–1860. *Proceedings of the American Philosophical Society* 133, no. 2 (June 1989): 190–214

Grubb, Farley. "The End of European Immigrant Servitude in the United States: An Economic Analysis of Market Collapse, 1772–1835." *Journal of Economic History* 54 (December 1994): 794–824

Hammon, Neal O., ed. *My Father Daniel Boone: The Draper Interviews with Nathan Boone.* Lexington: University Press of Kentucky, 1999

Heidler, David Stephen. *Daily Life in the Early American Republic, 1790–1820.* Westport, CT: Greenwood Press, 2004

Henderson, Archibald. "The Creative Forces in Westward Expansion: Henderson and Boone." *American Historical Review* 20 (October 1914): 86–107

Herman, Daniel J. "The Other Daniel Boone: The Nascence of a Middle-Class Hunter Hero, 1784–1860." *Journal of the Early Republic* 18 (Autumn 1998): 429–57

Hinderaker, Eric, and Peter C. Mancall. *At the Edge of Empire: The Backcountry in British North America.* Baltimore, MD: Johns Hopkins University Press, 2003

Ignatiev, Noel. *How the Irish Became White.* New York: Routledge, 1995

Jacobson, Matthew Frye. *Whiteness of a Different Color: European Immigrants and the Alchemy of Race.* Cambridge, MA: Harvard University Press, 1998

Johnson, Paul E. *The Early American Republic, 1789–1829.* New York: Oxford University Press, 2006

Kenny, Kevin. *The American Irish: A History.* New York: Longmans, 2000

Mason, Kathryn Harrod. *James Harrod of Kentucky.* Baton Rouge: Louisiana State University Press, 1951

McClure, David. *Diary of David McClure, Doctor of Divinity 1748–1820.* New York: Knickerbocker Press, 1899

Mesick, Jane Louise. *The English Traveller in America, 1785–1835.* New York: Columbia University Press, 1922

"Monthly Register." *The New York Magazine, or Literary Repository* 4 (September 1793): 574

Nolt, Steven M. *Foreigners in Their Own Land: Pennsylvania Germans in the Early Republic.* University Park: Pennsylvania State University Press, 2002

O'Brien, Michael Joseph, ed. *The Irish in America: Immigration, Land, Probate, Administrations, Birth, Marriage and Burial Records of the Irish in America in and about the Eighteenth Century.* Baltimore, MD: Genealogical Publishing Company, 1965

Rischin, Moses, ed. *Immigration and the American Tradition.* Indianapolis, IN: Bobbs-Merrill Company, 1976

Taylor, Alan. *The Divided Ground: Indians, Settlers, and the Northern Borderland of the American Revolution.* New York: Vintage, 2006

Trommler, Frank, and Elliott Shore. *The German-American Encounter: Conflict and Cooperation Between Two Cultures, 1800–2000.* New York: Berghahn Books, 2001

Ward, Matthew C. *Breaking the Backcountry: The Seven Years' War in Virginia and Pennsylvania, 1754–1765.* Pittsburgh, PA: University of Pittsburgh Press, 2003

Wharton, Mary E., and Roger W. Barbour. *Bluegrass Land & Life: Land Character, Plants and Animals of the Inner Bluegrass Region of Kentucky, Past, Present, and Future.* Lexington: University Press of Kentucky, 1991

White, Richard. *The Middle Ground: Indians, Empires, and Republics in the Great Lakes Region, 1650–1815.* New York: Cambridge University Press, 1991

Wilson, David A. *United Irishmen, United States: Immigrant Radicals in the Early Republic.* Ithaca, NY: Cornell University Press, 1998

Wright, Franklin W. "The Haitian Revolution." *American Historical Review* 105 (February 2000): 103–15

Moving and Removing, Adapting and Adopting to the New Nation: Native Americans Respond to American Expansion

8

Andrew K. Frank

Introduction

In 1830, as the prospect of forced removal became a reality for the south-eastern Indians, Cherokee leader Speckled Snake reflected on the nature of Cherokee-American relations in the early republic. The "great father," the term reserved for the U.S. president,

> loved his red children; but said, "You must move a little farther, lest I should, by accident, tread on you." With one foot he pushed the red man over the Oconee [River], and with the other he trampled down the graves of his fathers . . . . He said much; but it all meant nothing, but "move a little farther; you are too near me." I head a great many talks from our great father, and they all began and ended the same. (Moquin 1973, 149–50)

According to Speckled Snake, two recurring themes characterized the early republic. First, the federal government made promises of peace and yet accommodated the wishes of land-hungry backcountry settlers. Second, Native American communities ineffectively resisted the waves of invading settlers and placed too much trust in the federal government to help preserve the peace.

Speckled Snake's characterization intentionally oversimplified the history of Indian-American relations because he was protesting the most recent demands for the Cherokees to leave lands recently set aside for them by the United States. Yet at the same time he voiced a widespread frustration that the daily lives of many Native Americans had deteriorated because of decisions made by the recently formed republic. Speckled Snake astutely understood that the formation of the United States and its victory over Great

Native Americans travel through a snowstorm in a forced migration to land set aside by the Indian Removal Act of 1830. (*North Wind Picture Archives*)

Britain ushered in a tumultuous era for Native Americans. This era began with the American victory over the British and the Peace of Paris in 1783, and it culminated with the 1830 Indian Removal Act, federal legislation that redefined Native life once again. During this era, Native Americans underwent tremendous cultural and social changes, fought devastating wars with the United States and with neighboring Indians, increasingly participated in a market economy, and faced land-hungry settlers. Each tribal nation faced these issues separately, making separate economic and cultural decisions and enjoying a tremendous range of successes and failures in their endeavors. In some cases, their successes came at the expense of other Indians, and in other cases they occurred as a result of pan-Indian alliances. Yet all Native Americans faced a series of external pressures that largely culminated during the era and resulted in one of the most critical periods in their histories. By the end of the era, though, much of their eastern lands had been ceded or would soon be ceded to the United States, and Indian societies had been irrevocably transformed. Native Americans began the era as independent nations, and, when the era ended, most of them were members of what the Supreme Court would call conquered "domestic, dependent nations" (Perdue and Green 2007, 82).

The Postwar Reality

Many of the issues faced by Native Americans in the early republic were creations of the Revolutionary War and peculiar to postwar society. With the eradication of British rule, Native Americans had to adjust to a series of new realities. The United States and many individual states arranged and enforced treaties that relinquished Indian lands as payment for prewar and postwar debts or as punishments for their hostility during the American Revolution. Furthermore, American citizens were no longer constrained by the Proclamation Line of 1763, which had largely prevented the expansion of colonial society onto many Indian lands. Americans, eager to occupy and transform Indian lands into corn and cotton fields, pressured their newly formed democratic governments to satisfy their economic desires, and the public demands for Indian removal mounted. The expansion of the American economy also created new pressures for Native Americans. As cotton agriculture expanded in the American South and industrial growth transformed the North, the value of deerskins, beaver furs, and other Native merchandise plummeted. In short, Native American lands were increasingly coveted, while their labor and their produces were not.

Although Speckled Snake confined his anger to the Great Father and the policies of the United States, he and other Native Americans recognized that many of their predicaments predated the Revolution. At the top of most lists of grievances were those concerning what seemed to be a continuous stream of squatters, herders, and farmers who coveted Indian lands. As much as European governments had frequently kept this flood of intruders at bay, Natives understood that the flow of migrants never receded. In addition to settlers, Native American communities filled with scores of missionaries, both religious and cultural, who sought to convince them to embrace modern farming techniques, Christianity, animal husbandry, capitalist values, and patriarchal gender roles. Finally, Indian villages were similarly filled with American traders, who hawked every imaginable product in return for furs, skins, and hides. Many Indian hunters and families fell into debt with the traders, leaving land as the only collateral for their losses. Many of these missionaries and traders were invited guests, remaining under the control of village chiefs and providing for the needs of chiefs and families. Others were either tolerated guests or intruders—mostly men who were allowed to remain only because of the diplomatic and economic needs of the village. Together, these newcomers encouraged and helped Natives become more dependent on the marketplace for their daily survival.

The American victory in the War of Independence, particularly the Peace of Paris in 1783, altered diplomatic relationships for Native Americans. In this treaty, Great Britain relinquished to the United States their claim to lands east of the Mississippi River that extended from Florida's northern border to the Great Lakes. Much of these lands were Indian territory, and as a result many tribal leaders felt betrayed by their British allies.

Mohawk leader Joseph Brant, for example, pleaded with the British governor in Quebec, reminding him that the Mohawks were "friend and allies,
joining you from time to time against your enemies, sacrificing numbers of
our people and leaving their bones scattered in your enemies country" (Calloway 1994, 167). Brant simply could not believe that the British had
ignored the Mohawks, their long friendship, and, perhaps most importantly,
their sovereignty. Brant was not alone; the postwar peace typically had
equally devastating effects for those who fought against or with the British
during the Revolution.

Other British allies found the terms of the postwar peace equally frustrat-
ing and difficult. Alexander McGillivray, a leader of the Creek Indians in Georgia, complained that Great Britain signed away lands to the United States that
technically belonged to the Creeks and otherwise ignored promises and obligations to its Indian allies. Yet McGillivray's protest pointed directly to the
American rationale for their treatment. Great Britain did not have the "power
of giving our property away, unless fighting by the side of his soldiers in the
day of battle and Spilling our best blood in the Service of his Nation can be
deemed so" (Caughey 1938, 91–92). In the postwar settlement, the United
States did not distinguish between British allies and British subjects.

The evacuation of the British from the eastern shore also angered many
of its Indian allies, tribal nations who were often left to create new relationships with their new Spanish and American neighbors. Frequently, this
meant the arrival of new traders and the introduction of new regulations.
The law of supply and demand and the rigid expectations of the financial
ledger replaced the personal relationships that had earlier characterized the
trade. New American traders brought to an end generations of reciprocal gift
giving and of mutually earned trust. In many cases, American negotiators
introduced and insisted on more aggressive negotiation techniques. Without
the ability to pit the Europeans against one another to obtain gifts and fair
trading practices, Native Americans increasingly could not effectively
respond to U.S. belligerence. Perhaps most importantly, American politicians listened to Western settlers, who demanded the destruction or removal
of Indian communities.

The Diplomatic World

In the years that followed the Treaty of Paris, American diplomacy continued to marginalize Native American concerns and otherwise diminish
Native sovereignty. In the Ohio Valley, for example, the Iroquois, Shawnee,
Delaware, Wyandot, and Ojibwa were all coerced into ceding territory as
part of the postwar settlement between Britain and the United States. This
treaty was comparable to treaties signed in the East. In each case, Native
Americans protested that their lands were ceded by tribesmen without the
authority to do so or by Indians from different nations. Other Native Amer-

icans complained that the United States created boundaries between Native and white settlements that ignored generations of practice and the economic needs of the Indians. After the 1795 Treaty of Greenville, for example, Little Turtle of the Miami Indians, proclaimed that the United States drew a boundary that "takes in the greater and best part of your brothers' hunting ground. Therefore, your younger brothers are of the opinion you take too much of their lands away and confine the hunting of our young men within the limits too contracted" (Vanderworth 1971, 56–59).

The Arrival of Settlers

The expansion of American settlements compounded the new diplomatic reality for Native Americans. Unlike the British prior to the Revolution, who restrained westward expansion, the Americans increasingly sanctioned it. Buttressed by a belief that westward growth was preordained, American settlers pushed onto Native lands and pressured their local and federal governments to secure their titles. The pace of American expansion brought new frustrations to many Indian communities, especially when boundaries were drawn and then redrawn to take more Indian lands and to allow American settlements to expand. Only four years after the Treaty of Paris, Corn Tassel, a Cherokee man, observed that "in every Treaty we Have had that a bound[ary] is fixt, but we always find that your people settle much faster after a Treaty than Before. It is well known that you have taken almost all our Country from us without our consent. . . . Truth is, if we had no Land we should have Fewer Enemies" (Calloway 1994, 170). In 1830, Corn Tassel fatally learned that the United States would do more than claim Cherokee lands; it would attempt to destroy the Cherokee's ability to control their own internal affairs. As the early republic came to an end and Indian removal had become a reality, Corn Tassel was sentenced to death by a Georgia court for killing an Indian on Cherokee lands. Corn Tassel declared that this was an issue for the Cherokees to determine, and, when the Supreme Court and Justice John Marshall ruled in his favor, the Georgia legislature met in a special session to ensure his hanging.

In many cases, squatters and herders claimed the lands before treaties and negotiations officially turned them into American territory. Native hunting parties repeatedly confronted the newly arrived Americans, and American herds trampled on cornfields and otherwise scared away the game on which Natives relied. Natives responded to these incursions in various ways. In the Ohio Valley, Indian warriors repeatedly attacked travelers who passed through their territory, and they raided settlements on confiscated lands. Americans launched raids of their own, and warfare engulfed the region. In the summer of 1784, for example, 240 Indians—including Iroquois, Shawnee, Cherokee, Chickasaw, and Choctaw—voiced their concerns to the Spanish governor of Saint Louis.

Maj. Stephen H. Long and members of his expedition meet with a Pawnee council, 1823. (*Library of Congress*)

> The Americans, a great deal more ambitious and numerous than the English, put us out of our lands, forming therein great settlements, extending themselves like a plague of locusts in the territories of the Ohio River which we inhabit. They treat us as their cruelest enemies are treated, so that today hunger and the impetuous torrent of war which they impose upon us with other terrible calamities, have brought our villages to a struggle with death. (Calloway 1995, 281)

By 1787, many Mingos, Miamis, Delawares, Wyandots, and Shawnees felt equally aggrieved, and they too joined in raiding settlements on the Kentucky and western Virginia frontier. Almost immediately upon his inauguration, George Washington authorized a militia to attack the Indians, and a full-scale war erupted. Although this war initially resulted in military victories for the Native Americans, it typified the military story elsewhere. In the end, it resulted in devastating losses for Indian tribes and the further dispossession of their lands.

The Louisiana Purchase in 1803 complicated matters even more. Just as Great Britain ceded lands to the United States in 1783 that belonged to their Indian allies, France sold thousands of square miles of land that belonged to the Osages and other Indians of the American interior. Once again, the sovereignty of Indians was ignored in the diplomatic negotiations of non-Natives. As a result, the Osages were forced to defend their lands from speculators and surveyors, who foresaw the land's value as agricultural fields and hunting grounds. After trying to intimidate and manipulate the newcomers to the region, whether Indian or American, the Osage were ultimately forced into a land cession in 1808. The Osage had little choice but to acquiesce, and yet they continued to hope that the land cession would lead to a diplomatic alliance with the Americans that could ensure their future protection from enemy Indians. This did not occur. Instead, they found themselves overwhelmed by the Cherokee Indian migrants who acted with the sanction of the United States.

The Indian Trade

While Native Americans struggled to find diplomatic and military solutions to the assaults on their territorial claims, changes in the deerskin and fur trades brought new disruptions to daily life in Indian communities. In the colonial era, Great Britain regulated the Indian trade with varying degrees of success as part of a larger diplomatic effort to create military alliances. The United States largely abandoned these principles, and, when regulation occurred, the new republic used monopolies to prevent abuses and to prevent states from interfering with the trade. These regulations typically went unenforced, and hundreds of traders invaded virtually every Indian village east of the Mississippi River. Some stayed for days or weeks, others remained for years, and they carried with them every imaginable European product, from mirrors to woven cotton, to guns, ammunition, knives, beads, and alcohol. In return for these products, Native Americans provided an equally wide range of goods, especially animal pelts. Although Natives sold woven baskets, oils, nuts, and a variety of other products, deerskins dominated the Southern trade, and beaver furs characterized trade in the North.

Long accustomed to many European material goods, few Native Americans sought to eliminate the trade in its entirety. Instead, most village leaders welcomed white traders into their villages in an attempt to control the trade. Many Native communities used marriages with traders to regulate their behavior and otherwise evicted traders who repeatedly committed egregious acts. For example, in 1798 a few Creek chiefs banished six white traders who "meddle in public affairs, are constantly circulating reports injurious to our peace, that they have information that mischief is brewing, the American troops are coming on our land and such like stories" (Frank 2005, 34). Despite these attempts, an illicit trade continued, and even regulated traders often became increasingly more brazen in their disregard for local customs and American laws. At the start of the 19th century, an increasing number of traders acted without the sanction of village leaders, illicitly trading goods with Indian warriors on the outskirts of Indian society. These actions frustrated both Indian and American leaders, especially because they resulted in countless acts of violence. The traders plied the trade with alcohol, used false weights, and extended extensive credit to individual warriors. As a result, trade, which was once the source of mutually beneficial relationships, increasingly became a source of Indian-American tensions.

Europeans began to trade with Natives almost immediately after they arrived in the New World, but many of its ramifications did not become

William McIntosh (ca. 1775–1825)

Born to a Scottish father and a Creek Indian woman, William McIntosh became a controversial Creek Indian leader during the early republic. He used his knowledge of white and Indian society to accumulate wealth and power and ultimately betrayed his nation with the signing of the 1825 Treaty of Indian Springs.

As a teenager and young adult, he forged and used connections to Indian agents, U.S. military officers, and deerskin traders to obtain enough trade goods to become a powerful leader. Indeed, McIntosh amassed a tremendous personal estate. He owned slaves, ran an inn, built plantations, and otherwise personified many of the hopes for the civilization plan. Despite these cross-cultural tendencies, McIntosh was a member of a Creek clan, lived largely according to Creek rules, and, by virtue of the Creek's matrilineal understanding of kinship and identity, was accepted as a Creek.

For most of the early 19th century, McIntosh helped negotiate treaties with the United States on behalf of the Creek Indians. His loyalty to or dependence on the United States became very clear in the War of 1812, when McIntosh fought against the Red Stick Creeks and allied himself with General Andrew Jackson. This relationship continued in the First Seminole War, when in 1818, McIntosh and other Creek warriors helped Jackson raid Seminole villages.

McIntosh's position as a chief came to an abrupt end in 1825 when he signed the Treaty of Indian Springs that February. In this treaty, McIntosh and 51 other Creeks ceded almost all of the Creek lands in Georgia to the United States. McIntosh was able to get only a handful

evident until much later. At first, Native Americans traded their skins and furs for rare prestige goods, metal goods, as well as guns and ammunition. The extension of credit to Indian warriors frequently created ties of dependence between Native hunters and American traders. To pay back increasing debts, many war parties hunted for longer periods and traveled with women who could clean and otherwise prepare the skins for sale. This development left less time for women to cultivate their farms or otherwise provide for the basic necessities of their communities. As a result, many Indian communities became dependent on American traders for their basic necessities, and in time these changes left many Indian communities destitute. In the early 19th century, for example, many Native Americans struggled to provide for their basic needs.

Trade also shaped the political world inside many Indian communities. Native Americans who were able to secure and control trade obtained access to rare prestige goods, and as a result they frequently secured new forms of authority in their communities. Several Indian chiefs obtained and maintained their authority because of their ability to distribute trade goods and otherwise address issues of hunger and poverty. Such was the case for William McIntosh, a Creek chief who used his connections to the marketplace and American government officials to emerge as one of the most powerful chiefs in the region. These leaders, however, were often beholden to

of headmen to sign the treaty because most of the nation vehemently opposed it. Soon after, the Creek National Council called on the Law Menders, a centralized police force that McIntosh helped create, to enforce a law against ceding lands—a law that McIntosh helped write and that made ceding land a capital crime.

On April 30, 1825, the Law Menders set McIntosh's house on fire and fatally shot him as he tried to escape. After an investigation, the U.S. Senate confirmed the treaty.

Portrait of William McIntosh, a Creek chief, by 19th-century American painter Charles Bird King, from *The Indian Tribes of North America*. (McKenney, Thomas L. and James Hall. The Indian Tribes of North America, 1836–1844)

American officials and other individuals who provided this kind of support. In 1825, under pressure from the United States, an overly confident McIntosh illegally ceded thousands of acres of Creek lands in Georgia to the United States. His subsequent execution by the Creek tribe, ironically on the basis of a law McIntosh himself introduced, did little to alter the land cession. The so-called Treaty of Indian Springs was ratified, and the terms of the agreement were enforced (Frank 2005).

Civilization Plans

As many backcountry settlers demanded Indian lands and moved west with or without governmental sanction, many Americans struggled to define a place for Native Americans. Many politicians, most notably Thomas Jefferson and Henry Knox, believed that Native Americans could be eventually civilized and brought into the American nation as citizens. Taking a cue from how trading relationships had transformed many Native communities, the United States stepped up its efforts to transform Native Americans for its own desires. Hungry to convert hunting grounds into privately owned wheat and cotton fields, Thomas Jefferson and many other Americans worked to convince Indians that they should abandon communal fields for smaller, privately controlled family plots. If Indians could become private landowners, herders, cotton spinners and weavers, and even slave owners, then the communal grasp on hunting grounds could be broken. This, the Jeffersonian logic concluded, would benefit both the Americans and the Indians. Native Americans could escape their "savagery" and become "civilized Indians," and, perhaps most importantly, thousands of square miles of Indian lands would be opened for American expansion and settlement. The result would be "expansion with honor" (Green 1996, 489).

To assist with the so-called civilization plan, the United States hired several agents to live among the Indians, provide them with the basic tools of agrarian life, and otherwise encourage the transition. Jefferson, in an 1803 letter to Benjamin Hawkins, explained what the civilization plan could do.

> In truth, the ultimate point of rest & happiness for them is to let our settlements and theirs meet and blend together, to intermix, and become one people. Incorporating themselves with us as citizens of the U.S., this is what the natural progress of things will of course bring on, and it will be better to promote than to retard it. Surely it will be better for them to be identified with us, and preserved in the occupation of their lands, than be exposed to the many casualties which may endanger them while a separate people. (Ford 1892–1899, 7: 214)

With these lofty ambitions, Hawkins lived among the Creeks from 1796 to 1816, attempting to transform the daily lives and social norms of Creek society.

Through trade and the civilization plans, many attributes typically associated with American society and formerly nonexistent among Indians became increasingly commonplace in Indian villages. Some Native Americans grew cotton, owned slaves, built fences, herded cattle, spoke English, and practiced Christianity. David Folsom, a Choctaw Indian, integrated many of these ideas when he stated in 1820 that the "Choctaws know and are sensible that our white brethren ways are good, and we know that we Choctaws must turn our gun into a plow, and work like as our white brothers do" (Carson 1999, 70). Several Indian nations replaced or augmented oral traditions with written laws and constitutions. Sequoya, a Cherokee Indian, created a syllabary for the Cherokee language to become a written form of communication. Soon after, the Cherokees created a newspaper (the *Cherokee Phoenix*) that had both Cherokee and English content. Transformations in the Cherokee Nation made it known as the most civilized Indian nation. In 1825, the Cherokees had 33 gristmills, 13 sawmills, 69 blacksmith shops, 762 looms, 2,486 spinning wheels, 172 wagons, 2,923 plows, 7,683 horses, 22,531 head of cattle, 46,732 pigs, and 2,566 sheep. By 1830, it also had a written constitution, a slaveholding planter elite, a newspaper, a written language, Christian churches, and many intermarriages with white society. Some Cherokees built fences, herded cattle and hogs, grew cotton and corn, and otherwise embraced the elements of American culture. In some

The *Cherokee Phoenix,* first published in 1828, was the first Native American newspaper. (*Library of Congress*)

respects, the Cherokee nation became what historian Mary Young called the "Mirror of the Republic" (Young 1981).

Despite the relatively long list of innovations within many Indian communities, most Native Americans adapted the new technologies and ideas for their indigenous needs. Also, they traded for certain material goods and rejected others. They carefully selected and rejected the teachings of the agents and missionaries who came to their territories. Although the missionaries had some successes, these agents frequently discovered that Indians carefully integrated new technologies and ideas with traditional ones. For example, many southeastern Indians turned to cattle herding when their ability to hunt deer was curtailed. Yet their cultural need for the hunt and the coming-of-age rituals associated with it led many Indians to literally stalk their branded cattle for weeks before shooting it. Other communities struggled in their attempts to become American farmers. In 1789, some Mohegan Indians appealed to the Connecticut state assembly because "all our hunting and fowling and fishing is [sic] entirely gone. And we have begun to work out land, keep horses and cattle and hogs; and we build houses and fence in lots. And now we plainly see that one dish and one fire will not do any longer for us" (Calloway 1994, 178).

Many Indians linked the cultural innovations within Indian society with the era's diplomatic difficulties. This was the case for Handsome Lake, a Seneca Indian who suffered from alcohol abuse at the end of the 18th century. The Seneca Indians were members of the Iroquois Confederacy, a political entity that once controlled the northeastern part of what became the United States. During the early republic, its members lived in exile in Canada or on relatively small parcels of lands reserved for them on their ancestral lands. In 1799, the Seneca, one of the six members of the confederacy, occupied only about 200,000 of the more than 4 million acres they once controlled. Rather than blame his troubles on his American neighbors, that year Handsome Lake had a religious vision that led him to renounce his use of alcohol and otherwise preach a new Iroquois path. The Longhouse Religion, as it came to be called, emphasized the importance of education, horticulture, and American gender norms, and it incorporated elements of the traditional Iroquois cosmology with ceremonies and beliefs from Christianity.

Other Native Americans linked cultural change, diplomatic frustrations, and religion differently. A few years after Handsome Lake had a religious vision, Tenskwatawa received a different message. In his 1805 vision, the Master of Life led him to avoid Americans and their cultural influences. Like Handsome Lake, Tenskwatawa, or The Prophet, preached against the use of alcohol. The rest of the message, though, was quite different. Rather than coexistence, he led his followers away from Christian teachings, intermarriage, manufactured and metal tools, American styles of dress, domesticated animals, and private property. Instead, he called for a revitalization of

Shawnee traditions. They were to eat traditional foods like corn and beans, wear traditional clothing, and reembrace the communal ownership of property. Tenskwatawa established Prophetstown on the Tippecanoe River in Indiana for his followers, and their numbers grew after he predicted the solar eclipse of 1806. Although most of his followers were Shawnee, he also attracted many Delaware, Potawatomi, Kickapoo, Ottawa, and other neighboring Indians (Dowd 1992).

Tenskwatawa and Tecumseh

As Tenskwatawa continued to call for the rejection of parts of American culture, especially the elements that resulted in a loss of self-determination, and for the revitalization of Indian traditions, new grievances emerged among the Shawnees and other Indian communities. In 1809, at the so-called Whisky Treaty at Fort Wayne, a handful of Shawnee chiefs sold three million acres of land without the consent of the entire nation. This outraged Tecumseh, a twin brother of Tenskwatawa. The "white people," he explained are "never contented, but always encroaching," and they find Indians willing to help their designs. The solution for Tecumseh was simple.

> The way, and the only way to check and stop this evil, is, for the red men to unite in claiming a common and equal right in the land, . . . That no part has a right to sell, even to each other, much less to strangers . . . . They may sell, but all must join. Any sale not made by all is not valid. . . . It requires all to make a bargain for all. (Drake 1837, 5: 21–22)

For Tecumseh, this treaty further confirmed Tenskwatawa's teachings and convinced him to find a new solution to the American problem.

Tecumseh's solution to the American land grab led him to travel south on a diplomatic mission to Native Americans throughout the Mississippi Valley. He met with Indians as far south as Florida, appealing for their support in an anti-American alliance. Most of his calls fell on deaf ears because the majority of the southeastern Indians refused to sever their ties with the United States and otherwise reject Euro-American material goods and culture. When he spoke to the Creeks in the fall, many prominent leaders confronted Tecumseh and warned of the dangers he would bring upon the continent. A large group of Creeks, though, listened closely to Tecumseh and began to purge, symbolically and literally, their society of many outside influences. Led by prophets of their own, these so-called Red Stick Creeks also waited for a continentwide assault against American settlements. Over the next two months, they daily broke one of a bundle of red sticks that Tecumseh had left for them to mark the time before the coordinated attack. Tecumseh had left similar bundles elsewhere on his travels, and he told them that,

Tenskwatawa (ca. 1775–1836)

Widely known as The Prophet, Tenskwatawa was a spiritual leader among the Shawnee Indians in the Ohio territory. Along with his brother Tecumseh, he helped lead a nativist pan-Indian movement during the early 19th century.

As a young child, the future prophet was called Lalawthika. Born to a Creek Indian mother and Shawnee Indian father, the boy was raised by one of his older sisters after his father was killed in the 1775 Battle of Point Pleasant and his mother left Shawnee society a few years later.

Tenskawatawa became a community shaman in 1804. The following year, he experienced a series of visions that revealed the paths to heaven and away from hell, and he began to call himself Tenskwatawa (The Open Door). He urged other Indians to reject Christianity, alcohol, and other European intrusions in their midst. If his followers heeded his teaching, he explained, the population of wild animals would return as would deceased family members. The connection between witchcraft, the evil Great Serpent, and Americans was a central component of Tenskwatawa's preaching, and he helped the Wyandot and Delaware with their witchcraft trials in 1806. Despite his anti-American rhetoric, Tenskwatawa did not advocate ending trade with Anglo-Americans. Instead, he sought to restore order to a system that increasingly resulted in the abuse of Indians. Trade could continue, but only on Native terms.

Tenskwatawa and Tecumseh founded a village for their followers near Greenville, Ohio, but his followers were quickly too numerous for the area. In 1808, they moved to the Tippecanoe River, where they founded Prophetstown. Indiana Governor William Henry Harrison saw the town as a threat and destroyed it. The Indians rebuilt the village and became active participants in the ensuing War of 1812.

when they break the last stick, a great sign would further mark their early morning attack. Early on December 16, 1812, just after the last stick was broken, the New Madrid Earthquake shook the Mississippi Valley. Aftershocks would continue for several months, and many Creeks were literally shaken into action. Creeks felt it in southern Alabama, where the Mississippi River temporarily flowed north, and the rumblings could be felt as far north as Canada. Tecumseh's message rumbled across terrain unfamiliar to earthquakes, and it gained strength in many Indian villages. Almost immediately, his following grew, and many Red Stick Creeks and other Native Americans began to wage war on American settlers.

Tecumseh's message and the New Madrid Earthquake did not convince all Native Americans that violently purging the influence of the United States would restore order to their lives. Many Natives rejected Tecumseh's belief that American culture was corrupting their society, instead pointing to the benefits of trade and alliances with the United States. Some Native Americans tried to maintain their neutrality from the growing war, and still others were declared accommodationists by Tecumseh's followers and therefore enemies of the growing pan-Indian alliance. This was especially the case

In the 1813 Battle of the Thames, Tenskwatawa retreated with his British allies across the Canadian border, while Tecumseh and other Indian warriors tried to keep the Americans at bay. These efforts were short-lived, and Tecumseh and many of the other warriors were killed.

After the war ended, Tenskwatawa remained in Canada until 1824, when he was finally able to get permission to return to the United States. Tenskwatawa would be forced out of Ohio again in 1826, when his Shawnee community was ultimately removed to a reservation in Kansas. He died in 1836.

A Shawnee mystic and the brother of Tecumseh, Tenskwatawa was the first of two influential Indians to be called The Prophet, appointing himself prophet in 1805. Laulewasika was his given name, but he adopted the name Elkswatawa, and later Tenskwatawa, The Prophet. (*McKenney, Thomas L. and James Hall.* The Indian Tribes of North America, *1836–1844*)

among the Creeks, where supporters of Hawkins's civilization plan opposed his detractors. The resulting Creek civil war quickly enveloped the Lower South. When the War of 1812 broke out between the United States and Great Britain, it further inflamed the Indian conflicts and the two conflicts often became indistinguishable. Many of Tecumseh's followers obtained arms and support from British allies, and American soldiers obtained Indian allies of their own.

While Tecumseh and his allies fought the United States, much of the continental violence was among Indians. The Creeks in Georgia fought a civil war among themselves that was resolved only by the intervention of General Andrew Jackson's Army of the Tennessee. The Red Stick War, as it became known, did more than divide Creek society. It also served to demonstrate to Americans that the civilization plan was a failure. Most Americans became first aware of the fighting because of the so-called massacre at Fort Mims. At this August 30, 1813 attack, approximately 500 Americans, black slaves, and Indian allies were killed when their refuge was destroyed by Red Stick warriors. The attack was reported nationwide, and American politicians used it as propaganda to bring war on the Red Sticks.

The participation of Red Stick Creeks like William Weatherford and Josiah Francis, men who otherwise appeared to be civilized children of intermarriages, made many Americans question Hawkins's civilization plan. As the fighting spread, Red Stick Creeks further destroyed many of the physical manifestations of civilization. They burned frame houses, killed cattle, destroyed looms and spinning wheels, and they attacked Creeks who were associated with Hawkins.

While the Creeks fought their civil war, the Cherokees and the Osages also fought an 1813 war that was connected to the civilization plan. The Cherokees, widely considered the most advanced Native American nation, proclaimed that they were forced to fight the Osages because they were "provoked beyond bearing" by people who had murdered a Cherokee citizen through "ferocious and barbarian treachery" (DuVal 2006a, 43). The rhetoric, in large part, worked inasmuch as it helped attract the assistance of the United States in the Cherokee cause. In truth, however, many Cherokee planters used the fighting to get the United States to provide them the title to Osage lands that they had illegally squatted on in recent years.

Forced Removal

Tecumseh's pan-Indian alliance collapsed after he was killed at the Battle of the Thames in 1813. In its aftermath, many Americans concluded that the civilization plans had failed and that Indian removal was inevitable. The Seminole Indians in Florida were among the first to face this new sentiment about removal. The social composition of the Seminoles proved to many Americans that they were not on the path toward civilization. In part, the animosity toward the Seminoles resulted because they took in many Red Stick Creeks who had recently opposed Hawkins' civilization plan and fought the United States. They also forged alliances with maroon communities formed by neighboring runaway slaves, and they had a large contingent of runaway slaves and other African American residents in their villages. In 1818, the Seminoles fought the first of three wars with the United States. They successfully avoided attempts to remove them out of the South by moving into the Florida interior. In the years that followed, though, they remained a thorn in the side of Southern planters. After the First Seminole War, Southern planters renewed their efforts to claim the fertile Seminole lands as well as prevent the Seminoles from offering a safe haven for runaway slaves. The resulting Second Seminole War proved to be a much more costly and drawn-out affair than the first. Once again, the Florida Seminoles were able to resist their complete removal west. Although a third Seminole war would eventually lead to the forced relocation of most members of the Seminole tribe, a few hundred successfully resisted and permanently remained in the wetlands of Florida's southern interior.

As the Seminole resisted their removal west, other Natives were even less fortunate. Demands for their removal, which began decades earlier, grew louder. Some Native Americans voluntarily moved west, hoping to claim the best hunting and farming lands in Indian Territory. Others who moved west usually took over lands already claimed by other Indian nations. The election of Andrew Jackson in 1828 convinced others that moving was a better alternative than resisting. After all, Jackson's rationale for removal was that the civilization plan had failed and that white society would inevitably destroy the Indians if removal did not take place.

> Surrounded by the whites with their arts of civilization, which by destroying the resources of the savage doom him to weakness and decay, the fate of the Mohegan, the Narragansett, and the Delaware is fast overtaking the Choctaw, the Cherokee, and the Creek. That this fate surely awaits them if they remain within the limits of the States does not admit of a doubt. Humanity and national honor demand that every effort should be made to avert so great a calamity. (Richardson 1897, 458)

Jackson clearly misstated his own knowledge of the Creeks and Cherokees. He personally knew several Creeks and Cherokees who could pass for the planter-politicians in the American South. Yet Jackson recognized that the civilization plan had failed.

The Failure of Civilization

The civilization plan failed for many reasons. Inroads were uneven, at best, and largely rejected in many Native American communities. Perhaps most importantly, it failed because most Native Americans had no interest in becoming American citizens, the linchpin to the entire system. They may have wanted to employ certain skills and embrace the customs that suited them, but they had no interest in ceding their sovereignty to the United States. Even the most acculturated Native Americans rarely became American citizens. Instead, many of the most so-called civilized Indians threw their progress in the face of their American enemies. Nu-Tah-E-Tuil, for example, questioned the presumption in Arkansas that the Cherokees were not civilized enough to be trusted neighbors. "What is civilization? Is it a practical knowledge of agriculture," he asked in the *Arkansas Gazette* on April 23, 1828. If so, he explained, "Then I am willing to compare the farms and gardens of this nation with those of the mass of white population in the Territory. The advantage will be on our side." Nu-Tah-E-Tuil continued to pose a series of rhetorical questions. "Does civilization consist in good and comfortable buildings? . . . Does it consist of morality and religion? . . . Does it consist in school and the education of youth?" On all of these the Cherokee leader proclaimed a Cherokee advantage. After all, if removal was to go forward, it required them to leave farms, courts, churches, cotton fields, and schools behind.

Indeed, many of the so-called civilized Cherokees led the fight against forced removal. Rather than acquiesce to demands of the United States, Chief John Ross, a child of a white father and Cherokee mother, led a legal fight against Georgia and the United States. This fight eventually resulted in legal and moral victories in court but could not prevent the eventual removal of the Cherokees. Ross, the elected chief of the nation, epitomized the civilization plan. He was a slaveholder, lived in a plantation-style home, spoke English, practiced Christianity, and had a white father and white grandfathers on both sides of his family. Yet all of these civilized attributes could not alter his allegiance to his Indian nation. When the United States passed the Indian Removal Act in 1830, editor Elias Boudinot and Chief John Ross filled the recently created *Cherokee Phoenix* with antiremoval and anti-American arguments. The Cherokees were "prospering under the exhilarating rewards of agriculture, the rifle is again put into our hands, and the brass kettle swung to our backs, and we are led into the deep forest where game is plenty, by the hands of those who would once have had us abandon the chase" (*Cherokee Phoenix* September 17, 1828). The Cherokees chastised the Americans for demanding that the Cherokees civilize themselves and then forcing them to become savages to make room for the expansion of American settlements.

As the early republic came to a close, many Native Americans continued to resist removal and otherwise maintain that they were sovereign and independent nations. They made treaties, made choices about their cultural and social futures, and otherwise tried to maintain control over their own communities. In some ways they succeeded, but their lives and place on the continent became increasingly redefined by the United States. Their new place was confirmed, if not created, by Supreme Court Chief Justice John Marshall. In *Cherokee Nation v. Georgia* (1831), Marshall determined that the Supreme Court did not have jurisdiction over the matter, but he chose to define the Cherokees as "a domestic, dependent nation." They had some sovereignty over their affairs, but they did not have complete control. Instead, the United States should govern and assist the Cherokees, as a guardian would help a ward. The true meaning of Marshall's term became clear the following year in *Worcester v. Georgia*. In this case, Marshall had to determine whether Georgia had the right to arrest a missionary (Samuel Worcester) for living among the Cherokees without first adhering to a state law that required him to take an oath of allegiance to Georgia. Marshall, whose ruling would be summarily ignored by both Georgia and President Jackson, determined that the Cherokees were a "distinct community, occupying its own territory . . . in which the law of Georgia can have no right to enter but with the assent of the Cherokees." With these rulings, Indian nations became part of the United States and subject to federal law, but they maintained some boundaries that states could not defy. This ambiguous and yet powerful definition continues to define Native American nations today.

References and Further Reading

Calloway, Colin G. *The American Revolution in Indian Country: Crisis and Diversity in Native American Communities*. New York: Cambridge University Press, 1995

Calloway, Colin G. *The World Turned Upside Down: Indian Voices from Early America*. Boston: Bedford/St. Martins, 1994

Carson, James Taylor. *Searching for the Bright Path: The Mississippi Choctaw from Prehistory to Removal*. Lincoln: University of Nebraska Press, 1999

Caughey, John Walton. *McGillivray of the Creeks*. Norman: University of Oklahoma Press, 1938

Cayton, Andrew R. L., and Fredrika J. Teute, eds. *Contact Points: American Frontiers from the Mohawk Valley to the Mississippi, 1750–1830*. Chapel Hill: University of North Carolina Press, 1998

Cherokee Phoenix. 1828.

Dowd, Gregory Evans. *A Spirited Resistance: The North American Indian Struggle for Unity, 1745–1815*. Baltimore, MD: Johns Hopkins University Press, 1992

Drake, Samuel Gardner. *Biography and History of the Indians of North America*. Boston, MA: Antiquarian Institute, 1837

DuVal, Kathleen. "Debating Identity, Sovereignty, and Civilization: The Arkansas Valley after the Louisiana Purchase." *Journal of the Early Republic* 26 (Spring 2006a): 25–58

DuVal, Kathleen. *The Native Ground: Indians and Colonists in the Heart of the Continent*. Philadelphia: University of Pennsylvania Press, 2006b

Ford, Paul Leicester, ed. *The Works of Thomas Jefferson*. New York: G. P. Putnam's Sons, 1892–1899

Frank, Andrew K. *Creeks and Southerners: Biculturalism on the Early American Frontier*. Lincoln: University of Nebraska Press, 2005

Green, Michael D. "The Expansion of European Colonization to the Mississippi Valley, 1780–1880." In Bruce G. Trigger and Wilcomb E. Washburn, eds. *The Cambridge History of the Native Peoples of the Americas: Volume 1: North America: Part 1*, 460–538. New York: Cambridge University Press, 1996

Martin, Joel. *Sacred Revolt: The Muskogees' Struggle for a New World*. Boston: Beacon Press, 1991

McLoughlin, William G. *Cherokee Renascence in the New Republic*. Princeton, NJ: Princeton University Press, 1986

Merrell, James H. *The Indian's New World: Catawbas and Their Neighbors from European Contact Through the Era of Removal*. New York: W. W. Norton, 1989

Moquin, Wayne, ed. *Great Documents in American Indian History*. Westport, CT: Praeger, 1973

Perdue, Theda. *Cherokee Women: Gender and Culture Change, 1700–1835*. Lincoln: University of Nebraska Press, 1988

Perdue, Theda, and Michael Green, *The Cherokee Nation and The Trail of Tears*. New York: Viking, 2007

Richardson, James Daniel. *A Compilation of the Messages and Papers of the Presidents, 1789–1897*, Washington, DC: U.S. Government Printing Office, 1897

Saunt, Claudio. *A New Order of Things: Power, Property, and the Transformation of the Creek Indians, 1733–1816*. New York: Cambridge University Press, 1999

Tanner, Helen Hornbeck. "The Glaize in 1792: A Composite Indian Community." *Ethnohistory* 25 (Winter 1978): 15–39

Usner, Daniel H. Jr. *American Indians in the Lower Mississippi Valley: Social and Economic Histories*. Lincoln: University of Nebraska Press, 1998

Waselkov, Gregory A. *A Conquering Spirit: Fort Mims and the Redstick War of 1813–1814*. Tuscaloosa: University of Alabama Press, 2006

Vanderworth, W. C. *Indian Oratory: Famous Speeches by Noted Indian Chieftains*. Norman: University of Oklahoma Press, 1971

Wallace, Anthony F. C. *The Death and Rebirth of the Seneca*. New York: Alfred A. Knopf, 1969

White, Richard. *The Middle Ground: Indians, Empires, and Republics in the Great Lakes Region, 1650–1815*. New York: Cambridge University Press, 1991

Young, Mary. "The Cherokee Nation: Mirror of the Republic." *American Quarterly* 33 (Winter 1981): 502–524

The Fires of Evangelicalism in the Cauldron of the Early Republic: Race, Class, and Gender in the Second Great Awakening

9

Anna M. Lawrence

Introduction

The era of the Second Great Awakening encompasses a long period of revitalization and growth for Protestant American churches. This growth occurred through a series of small and large evangelical revivals, which took place throughout the country but were particularly focused in the areas of westward expansion. At these revivals, converts committed themselves to God and sometimes experienced a so-called rebirth into new religious lives. This movement reflects the major themes of the early republic: westward expansion, industrialization and market growth, and the country's democratization on a variety of levels. In terms of religious history, this period was instrumental in establishing what would become the modern religious landscape, a competitive and diverse spiritual marketplace. The Second Great Awakening established America's tremendous religious variety, the dominance of evangelical Protestantism, and freedom from state control, all characteristics that have come to define modern American religious life.

This movement occurred over a long span of time, starting in the late 1790s and extending into the 1840s. Revivals occurred in both urban and rural settings, in the North, South, East, and West. Unlike the Great Awakening of the 18th century, a much broader, more diverse group of people were involved in the Second Great Awakening, including a significantly larger proportion of African Americans. In fact, one of the most important outcomes of this movement is the extent to which African Americans formed their own churches and separate leadership structures. In addition, the effect of democratization can be seen in the fact that women were many of the central actors of this awakening. The movement challenged racial hierarchies in some arenas and social hierarchies in others. Particularly when examining the sectarian growth in this movement, one can see a preoccupation with settling the ideal social order. The Shakers envisioned a new society of strict sexual separation and spiritual equality, while the Mormons sought a patriarchal community of true Christians. This period of revivalism fomented such a wide variety of groups, with diverse and often opposing viewpoints on social order, that it is difficult to characterize and generalize the movement as a whole. Yet the attention to social order gave primacy to the private, moral concerns within a public religious sphere. These concerns gave rise to the vast networks of social and moral reform in the antebellum era, a series of reform movements that were built on an evangelical bedrock.

The Rise of Evangelicalism

During the American Revolution, churches were generally weakened due to the fact that the war had curtailed, disrupted, and scattered many religious meetings and congregations. The number of Baptists, who had seen remarkable growth in the colonies during the 1750s and 1760s, started to level off during the Revolution. While many churches saw at least a tapering off of membership and growth, the evangelical Methodists were only beginning their expansion (Isaac 1982, 260–64). However, even previously vibrant evangelical churches noted a sense of religious dissipation, a general spiritual slumbering by the middle of the 1790s (Mathews 1977, 49).

By the 1790s, churches were also facing a new economic reality. Due to the disestablishment of churches on a variety of levels during and after the American Revolution, there was a newly freed religious environment, wherein churches were no longer funded by state, local, or national funds. This release from governmental control was not welcome by many churches, which were forced to seek their daily bread by competing for congregants, rather than drawing on an established tax base. In the face of this lack of economic support from government, standing churches saw the pressing need to find creative ways to attract congregants and their support. However, evangelicals were happier with the disestablishment of churches. They saw the ideal church as based on voluntary membership and on authority constantly reinforced by the democratic principle of individual conversion (Mathews 1977, 57).

The revivals of the day reflected and encouraged the growing diversity and individualistic spirit of the early American republic. Historian Nathan Hatch argues that the revivals democratized religious institutions, following the political expansion of ideas about liberty and freedom of individual choice (Hatch 1989, 5–7, 22–26). Theologically, the movement embraced the idea of salvation as subject to human will, in contrast to the dominant Calvinism of the first Great Awakening. The Methodist idea of salvation provided men and women with numerous opportunities in their lifetime to receive God's grace and to convert (Mathews 1977, 31). Methodist models of salvation also allowed for people to backslide and lose their way, acknowledging that this was a common human occurrence. Conversion narratives, such as Jarena Lee's, include many periods of doubt and questioning their worthiness. Lee even considered suicide because she despaired for the state of her soul following conversion (Lee 1849). Many preachers now underlined the tenets of universal salvation, which opened up the possibility that a broad base of society could be saved, as long as they had the individual will to work toward their conversion and salvation. Converts also focused on individual sin and on elements of their character in an effort to prevent the almost inevitable backsliding. Evangelicalism came to embody the promise of a newly democratic nation in its focus on individualism.

However, historians have differed in assessing the meaning of this individualism and whether it truly translated into a democratic ethos. Individualism does not equate to egalitarianism, politically or socially. Historians have persuasively argued that the early republican period emphasized the political promise of the Revolution by expanding democratic ideals for white men, while reinforcing racial and gender hierarchies in the political and social spheres. As historian Susan Juster states,

> A Southern planter could experience fellowship with his slave during worship without accepting him as an equal, socially or morally. Without overstating the degree of equality implicit in the evangelical notion of fellowship, one can discern a new disjuncture in postrevolutionary evangelical Protestantism between the rhetoric of spiritual equality and the reification of social differences within the community. (Juster 1996, 24)

Camp Meetings and the Attraction of Revivals

In the disorganized and impious landscape of post-Revolutionary America, two major denominations, the Baptists and the Methodists, were the most successful at convincing new converts to commit themselves to God. By 1850, about two-thirds of all churchgoers were either Baptist or Methodist (Hatch 1989, 3). It is not a coincidence that these denominations were also evangelical. Both Baptists and Methodists established itinerant preaching circuits, where single traveling preachers could cover a large network of communities, often visiting places that lacked established churches. In addition, these preachers organized camp meetings and large outdoor meetings that attracted a huge number of new adherents. Camp meetings were creative and popular social events that gathered in rural, wooded areas. As people had become more mobile with the growing transportation networks in this period, religion had become disassociated from the traditional church building. Camp meetings achieved a massive popularity. In 1801, the Cane

Ridge, Kentucky, camp meeting drew an estimated crowd of up to 25,000 people gathered to listen to preaching for a week, and they came from a variety of denominations. This is an extraordinary number of people, considering that Lexington, the largest city in Kentucky, had a population of just 2,000 people (Ahlstrom 1972, 433).

Early 19th-century camp meetings were loud, popular, riotous events. People came in large numbers and shared their religious experiences, alongside the preachers. Because these events lasted at least a few days and up to a week, many people took the stage over the span of the event. The laity participated actively as well, adding their own accounts, shouts, songs and prayers. As Hatch describes the meetings, "Those who led the meeting made overt attempts to have the power of God 'strike fire' over a mass audience; they encouraged the uncensored testimonials by personas without respect to age, gender or race; the public sharing of private ecstasy; overt physical display and emotional release; loud and spontaneous response to preaching; and the use of folk music that would have chilled the marrow of Charles Wesley" (Hatch 1989, 50). Hatch refers to Charles Wesley, the prolific hymn writer, brother to John Wesley, and cofounder of Methodism. Camp meetings were a natural development from the open-air revivals of the first Great Awakening, but, as Hatch argues, their open enthusiasm and extravagant physicality may have been well beyond what the fathers of evangelicalism had envisioned.

Some critics of camp meetings doubted that these events were all about religious awakening. For instance, there are drawings that depict the meetings as unguarded spaces where anything might, and did, happen. In depictions by Alexander Rider, men and women are talking to each other, not listening to the preacher. In the center of one picture, a woman has fainted. She has fallen back into the arms of an older man, who has taken advantage of the moment by cupping the swooning woman's breasts (Hatch 1989, 51). Still, camp meetings persisted in America, despite their occasional bad reputation. They were simply too popular to stop.

Antievangelicals commonly leveled accusations of sexual impropriety toward preachers and their followers. Yet the reality was that the morality of evangelicalism tended to be more conservative than in the standing churches. Preachers often pledged themselves to a period of celibacy while they were engaged in the most arduous years of their circuit riding (Lawrence 2004; Wigger 1998). Historian Donald Mathews writes, "Human sexuality especially became a persistent and terrifying personal problem for Evangelicals, as they lashed themselves in a spiritual masochism of restraint and self-denial" (Mathews 1977, 62). Evangelicals scrutinized their every thought and action to avoid stepping out of the strict moral behavior required by their faith (Lawrence 2004).

Camp meetings represented a revision of religious culture. Camp meetings were held outdoors, where traditional hierarchical structures would be meaningless or at least limited. The lack of structure was in contrast to the

Methodist camp meeting, circa 1829. Camp meetings were a major part of the Second Great Awakening of the early 19th century. Illustration by Alexander Rider. (*Library of Congress*)

strict seating arrangements of Anglican churches in the South, for instance, where the upper classes filled the front pews and the slaves and the poorest were consigned to the galleries or the back of churches (Frey and Wood 1998, 76–77). At camp meetings, the social arrangements were much looser. The upper classes rubbed elbows with the lower classes, women and men commingled, and black and white people also mixed. However, social divisions remained. The black and white campgrounds were explicitly segregated, with blacks confined to the outlying campsites. (Frey and Wood 1998, 140–41; Latrobe 1809).

The Burned-Over District

A newly settled area of upstate New York, the area surrounding the new canals and roads reaching into western New York, became one of the primary areas of evangelical revivalism. Led by one of the most well-known leaders of the Second Great Awakening, Charles Finney, the revivalist movement in this area was especially effective and well organized.

Upstate New York was called the burned-over district because it was supposedly scorched by the fires of evangelicalism. A map of the areas of religious growth traces the areas directly around Erie Canal, where new

Charles Finney (1792–1875)

Finney was born in Warren, Connecticut, on August 29, 1792. His family relocated to upstate New York when he was a toddler, and the area became his lifelong home. At this time, New York was largely backcountry, and formal institutions like schools and churches were sparse. Finney was able to go to high school and became a law student in upstate New York in 1818 (Finney 1977, 7). His life underscores the central tenets of the Second Great Awakening: individualism and the disdain of formal theological education. "I say that God taught me, and I know it must have been so, for surely I never had obtained these ideas from man . . . schools are to a great extent spoiling the ministers" (Finney, 1977, 72).

Finney's spiritual journey takes a common route to faith in this period, an independent course, belonging to no church and shaped by his own reading of the Bible and observation of the world. His description of conversion rang of self-determination and free will: "I made up my mind that I would settle the question of my soul's salvation at once" (Finney 1977, 13). After his conversion in 1821, Finney quit his legal studies and became devoted to preaching in western New York, along the Erie Canal. In the beginning, he was an unaffiliated, itinerant lay preacher in upstate New York, preaching to Congregationalists, Baptists, Deists, and Lutherans, sparking successful revivals in each town he visited. He was indefatigable. He wrote, "I preached outdoors; I preached in barns; I preached in schoolhouses; and a glorious revival spread all over that new region" (Finney 1977, 69). He preached using the common language and experience of the farmers, mechanics, and skilled tradesmen. But he was equally at ease with middle-class professionals and merchants, and he adapted the language of evangelicalism to their experiences when preaching to them.

Charles Grandison Finney was the leading Protestant evangelist of the great religious revival that swept 19th-century America and helped to spark the many social reform movements of the midcentury. (*Library of Congress*)

From 1825 to 1830, he gained national prominence through his phenomenal success in these frontier towns in western New York and toured nationally to great acclaim (Hatch 1989, 196). He capped his success with a revival crusade in Rochester in 1830, where he preached nearly every night and three times on Sundays for six months. He maintained his focus on converting the souls of upstate New York throughout the 1830s and 1840s, while also preaching in Philadelphia, New York City, London, and elsewhere. He married Elizabeth (Lydia) Finney, who also became a religious leader and an advocate of moral reform of women. The couple eventually moved to Oberlin, Ohio, where he died in 1875.

manufacturing towns were springing up. Although revivalism also occurred in New England towns, the Second Great Awakening was largely not urban in focus; the hottest revival areas were in the West and the frontier. Following the land acquisitions after the American Revolution and during Thomas Jefferson's presidency, revivals followed the expansive path of these Western acquisitions, filling the areas that had no institutional religion and thus the greatest potential for growth. The backcountry was also an area where revivalism, traveling preachers, and outdoor meetings were particularly valuable tools.

A debate emerges in the historiography about the function of religion in these new market towns. Did the awakening effectively restore a sense of moral community in the face of the growing sense of individualism and money-oriented economic growth? Or did it, in fact, confirm and encourage the growth of the economy and individualistic pursuits by underscoring the moral basis for a good work ethic among adherents? In the end, these arguments are not necessarily mutually exclusive.

The relationship between the emerging market economy and the Second Great Awakening is complex and disputable. Although the movement reflected the market realities of the period, it was also a release from the real marketplace—from the driven, harsh, economic realities of the market. As a respite, the evangelical congregations and sectarian communities tried to offer communities and connections among individuals. Individuals might compete in the marketplace, but they had reason to find moral and spiritual solace in each other in their religious meetings.

In many ways, the moral emphasis of this religious movement promoted the values of the middle class. Historian Paul Johnson has been the most persuasive voice for explaining this period of revivalism as one driven by the economic forces of industrialization and a growing bourgeois middle class. According to Johnson, religion provided the moral tool for spurring conformity to a dominant middle-class revision of society, with a particular focus on economic goals. "To put it simply, the middle class became resolutely bourgeois between 1825 and 1835. And at every step, that transformation bore the stamp of evangelical Protestantism" (Johnson 1978, 8). Johnson emphasizes the importance of the revivals of 1831 and of the upstate New York arena, particularly Rochester. Johnson contends that this movement's lasting legacy was to make religion an indispensable tool for the bosses of the market economy; by promoting the values of evangelicalism among their workers, bosses would guarantee a clean, sober, upright, hardworking, and punctual workforce. Johnson claims that bosses coerced workers into attending revivals and promoted churchgoing men over their irreligious counterparts (Johnson 1978, 121–23).

Of course, coercing workers undermined the theological emphasis on free will and the democratic element of the revivals. Religion, instead, was everywhere supporting the power structures in society, bolstering the well-connected, stable, and wealthy owners. Yet, although Rochester was extraordinary as a center of evangelical uprising, it was not representative of other cities. Furthermore, even in the same region, by the 1830s one can see other ideas about evangelicalism emerging, such as the millennial and decidedly antibourgeois impulses of Mormonism or the alternative, sexually innovative spirit of the utopian Oneida community. Also, anyone who lived in upstate New York during the early 1800s might have witnessed female preachers touring through the area, such as the visionary spiritualist preacher Jemima Wilkinson or the first African American female preacher, Jarena Lee. These women did not entirely embody the middle-class virtues of femininity.

A Women's Awakening

An important way that the revival movement has been linked to middle class mores is in evangelicalism's confirmation of the ideas about women's nature and their inherent religiosity. Historian Mary Ryan argued that this was a women's awakening, where approximately two-thirds of the converts were women (Ryan 1978, 603). The movement was led, in many important ways, by women. While Charles Finney was the well-known, leading minister of mainstream revivalism, he employed women as the primary organizers. Finneyite evangelical women organized the men; women heard preachers and then went home to convert their husbands and children. Women formed prayer circles and societies to keep the revival going after the preacher left town. In this way, they performed the essential tasks of ensuring the success of the revivals by sustaining their power in areas where there were no standing ministers or churches.

The role of women as so-called domestic clergy (Welter 1966)—converting their families and conducting religious meetings in their homes—gave them a certain amount of authority and made women religious leaders in the domestic realm. This seemed to be a significant shift from the ideal Puritan family, where the father was the religious, domestic, social, and political authority of the family. This shift toward female domestic religious authority was especially disturbing to men in the standing traditional churches. An anonymous writer criticized Finney by writing, "He *stuffed* my wife with tracts, and alarmed her fears, and nothing short of meetings, night and day, could atone for the many fold sins my poor, simple spouse had committed, and at the same time, she made the miraculous discovery, that she had been 'unevenly yoked.' From this unhappy period, peace, quiet, and happiness have fled from my dwelling, never, I fear to return" (Johnson 1978, 108). In this depiction, evangelicalism led to the religious empowerment of women, which produced the nightmare scenario for the secular men so unfortunately yoked to born-again women.

The role of women in 19th-century revivalism went hand in hand with the rise of the "Cult of True Womanhood," a term coined by Historian Barbara Welter to describe a set of ideas about the essential roles and responsibilities of women. In her survey of prescriptive literature in the early 1800s, Welter identifies characteristics that she sees as associated with women—to be nurturing, emotional, pious, and submissive. Early 19th-century society increasingly essentialized men's and women's roles, in part in reaction to the growth of separate spheres of activity during the period of industrialization. As women were more identified with the domestic sphere, what was seen as their natural traits seemed to derive from qualities associated with that sphere. The domestic sphere was an important space for the revivals, as homes became equivalent to the church and women were seen as domestic clergy(Welter 1966).

However, the Cult of True Womanhood concept had its faults. One obvious problem is that it is an ideal, based on a composite picture of prescriptive literature, not on a description of actual behavior. Another issue with the religious ideas of this theory is that it holds the seeds of its own dissolution. While the ideal 19th-century woman was submissive and pious, evangelical religion itself was not passive. Active, noisy, physical, and enthusiastic conversions were anything but passive. In addition, if religiosity and piety were the natural provenance of women, then they could not be contained by the domestic sphere; religion naturally took them out of the home and into churches, revivals, and eventually moral and social reform movements (Braude 1997).

Evangelicalism became the backbone of movements for temperance, the elimination of poverty and slavery, moral reform, and women's rights. The multiple moral reform movements that followed the revivalist period were emblematic of the myriad ways in which a new wave of morality changed 19th-century society. In the 1820s and 1830s, Americans formed a seemingly endless number of moral reform and benevolent associations, all of which extended the role of religious missionaries into the social arena (Evans 1997, 67–68). There was the American Bible Society, the American Tract Society, the American Female Moral Reform Society, the American Temperance Society, the American Peace Society, and the Society for the Prevention of Pauperism, just to name a few of the hundreds of societies that came out of this evangelical movement. The temperance movement grew directly out of the Methodist's and Baptist's strict avoidance of alcoholic beverages and other social diversions.

Emerging from evangelicalism was a new vision of how American society should be ordered, and society was expected to be self-disciplined and moral on all fronts. Charles Finney's wife, Lydia Finney, led the moral reform cause. In 1834, she founded the New York Female Moral Reform Society, a group dedicated to saving prostitutes, ending prostitution, and protecting single women from moral and sexual corruption altogether. In six years, Finney was overseeing a national society with 555 local chapters. Women ran this group on every level, and it typified the centrality of women's involvement in the revivals and their moral reform outgrowth (Evans 1997, 74–75). The public reform that came out of the spirit of evangelicalism had a great influence on the beginnings of the antislavery movement in America, which in turn led to the founding of the early feminist movement. Each of these reform impulses had women at their center. And each pulled women out of the home, where they had enjoyed their particular moral influence, into public realms of influence.

The Birth of the Black Church

One of the most important and long lasting outcomes of the awakening was the formation of African American churches. A phenomenal growth of conversions and religious societies took place among slave and free black populations, in the North and the South, in rural and urban groups. This movement sparked mass conversions among slaves, marking the beginning of organized African American religious groups in the plantation South. Significant numbers of black preachers were now ministering to other African Americans, both free and slave. Although the first Great Awakening had converted many African Americans, they remained an inconsequential proportion of the larger societies. Following the American Revolution, however, African Americans converted in much larger numbers and began to form their own societies. The increased attraction of African Americans to evangelicalism had many causes; the methods and spirit of evangelicalism, its increased attention to spirituality, and congregational participation were all appealing characteristics to African Americans. Traditional African spirituality was more participatory than traditional Christian churches, and so many blacks picked up on the newfound evangelical attention to lay participation. In addition, evangelical leaders were more likely than traditional churches to regard African American communities as a previously untapped arena for new souls in the new competitive marketplace for religiosity (Frey and Wood 1998, 119).

African Americans had begun to join evangelicals in some numbers during the latter part of the Great Awakening, when the South saw its greatest revivals in the 1760s with Separate Baptist groups springing up in Virginia. Methodist revivals, which began sweeping the South in the 1770s and found new urgency toward the turn of the 19th century, found an interested African American population. Religious historians Sylvia Frey and Betty Wood see this relationship between African Americans and the growth of evangelical expression as a collaborative one. The swapping of religious practices and influences between African Americans and European Americans was an ongoing process. Baptists and Methodists had been embracing a physical form of worship, one that included tears, shouts, and extravagant displays of religious enthusiasm, from the 1760s and 1770s. In early 19th-century revivals, blacks started to innovate with this open, lay-oriented revival mode. They also emphasized lay participation and the importance of visions, music, and other aspects that are characteristic of African spirituality (Frey and Wood 1998).

Early Methodist preachers noted, sometimes with ambivalence, that they were particularly popular among African Americans (Lawrence 2004). Methodists were especially ardent in their pursuit of African American converts, who, Mathews argues, "were often more responsive to the evocative Methodist preaching than were whites" (Mathews 1977, 66). Still, while the initial forays by white Methodist leaders led to many conversions of slaves, the result was not an egalitarian religious community. However, as Mathews contends, African American conversion "did offer blacks a means of establishing their claim upon the Christian care, respect, and love of their newfound comrades [white evangelicals]" (Mathews 1977, 67). To be sure, these claims were somewhat limited. Mathews points out that evangelical culture privileged individual experience; it relied on conversion narratives and on the links they drew among members of the evangelical community, black and white. This sort of religious community had revolutionary possibilities.

To what extent did evangelicalism's spiritual equality translate into social equality for African Americans in the early republic? In England, a coalition of evangelicals and Quakers successfully challenged and overturned the British slave trade in 1807. Methodists, maintaining their ties to church leaders in England and their early antislavery arguments, were among the early antislavery activists in America as well. In 1780, Methodist leaders argued that slavery was "contrary to the laws of God, man, and nature, and hurtful to society, contrary to the dictates of conscience and pure religion" (Methodist Conference 1780). Circuit preachers agreed to not hold slaves themselves. In 1784, the leadership vowed to expel any Methodist members who did not free their slaves within two years. Other evangelical Presbyterians and Baptists followed suit by issuing antislavery stances in the late 1780s (Mathews 1977, 69).

Methodists also encouraged black preaching and, to some extent, black leadership. Francis Asbury, a leading preacher and Bishop of American Methodists, toured in Virginia with Harry Hosier, who was an inspired black preacher. He regularly appeared alongside white Methodist preachers, drawing throngs of white and black converts on their circuits and occasionally outraging white audiences. Leading Methodists realized that they had talented black speakers in their midst and that these speakers would be helpful aides in converting more African Americans. However, black male and female preachers did not commonly become official preachers with their own Methodist circuits; rather, like white female preachers, they were more commonly given the roles of exhorters or lay speakers. Occasionally, these black male exhorters, who were more compelling to black audiences, threatened to upstage their white counterparts (Frey and Wood 1998, 124–25).

By the 1790s, Baptists had biracial churches and black preachers who lobbied for more official power within their churches. There were various responses to this push for power, because Baptist congregations were largely autonomous. Many churches tried to limit the positions of black preachers by giving them a separate function from the white preachers, who retained the ministerial powers of the sacraments (Frey and Wood 1998, 126).

Although the evangelical push to recognize black preachers and to repudiate slaveholding members held a strong potential, the Methodists dropped these radical ideas within a relatively short period, caving in to vociferous objections by the slaveholding membership. The Methodist leadership had to step down from their previously promised excommunication, replacing their prior radicalism with a program of "education and moral suasion" (Mathews 1977, 69). In the end, the Second Great Awakening proved to conform to some of the more conservative elements of Southern society by confirming the existing hierarchies. As Frey and Wood argue, this revivalist period confirmed certain power structures:

> namely the accommodation reached by evangelical leadership and slavehold-
> ing society on the question of slavery; the formation of a proslavery version of
> Christianity and the acceleration of the movement toward evangelical Protes-
> tantism by the upper ranks of Southern society that accompanied it; and the
> emergence of a coherent patriarchal ideology based on the subordination of
> women and the enslavement of Africans. (Frey and Wood 1998, 140)

The potential for radicalism was realized by the African American converts themselves. Instead of waiting quietly by for the white leadership to recognize them, many formed their own congregations. Perhaps the most powerful of Black preachers was Reverend Richard Allen, who rose up through the ranks of the Methodist church. Allen was increasingly frustrated with the acceptance of slaveholding Methodists, and he decided to separate and form the African Methodist Episcopal (AME) Church in 1816. His church was centered in Philadelphia, and there were AME congregations in New York, Long Island, and Baltimore as well. Though black Methodists were once the majority of members in the Methodist churches in Baltimore, they became a minority in the white-led Methodist churches as African Americans joined Allen's church. Similarly, Virginia had high numbers of all-black Baptist churches. These churches were highly oriented to the community of believers and tended to be less hierarchical than their white counterparts, according to Frey and Wood. Still, as the case of Jarena Lee points out, there were significant limits to women's leadership within these churches. Lee sought to be confirmed as a female preacher in the AME Church, but she faced stiff opposition from Reverend Allen and the AME church as a whole.

Yet, as Frey and Wood argue, even though black women were not given leadership roles, they had more meaningful, active lay roles in church business and lay leadership than their white counterparts (Frey and Wood 1998, 181).

The Proliferation of Religious Choice

One of the most enduring outcomes of this movement was how it transformed the American religious landscape into one of great variety. An overwhelming number of new churches were established in mainstream Protestant denominations. Alongside the mainstream growth of the Second Great Awakening was a dramatic increase in new sect formation, some of

Jarena Lee (1783–d.?)

Jarena Lee's autobiography acts as a useful lens for seeing the typical effects of the Second Great Awakening, even as she gives us an extraordinary, unusual life story. She published her own autobiography at the age of 53, after struggling to be recognized as a female preacher in the African Methodist Episcopal Church. She was born in 1783 in Cape May, New Jersey. At the age of 21, she converted while listening to a Methodist preacher (Lee 1849, 5). In 1811, she married Joseph Lee, the pastor of a Black Methodist church in Snow Hill, Pennsylvania, near Philadelphia. The same year she was married, she felt her first call to preach, but she was initially rebuffed by the leader of the African Methodist Episcopal Church, Reverend Bishop Richard Allen. Jarena Lee partially fulfilled her calling by "exhorting," a sort of preaching that involved leading prayer or explicating biblical passages, an approved role for women in Methodist churches.

After six years of marriage, she had given birth to six children, only to see four of them die alongside her husband in 1817. Now a widow with two young children, she went back to Bishop Allen and asked whether she could take on more responsibility in the church, specifically if she could lead prayer meetings in her home. He granted her permission, and she began to hold regular meetings, but she still felt she should be a preacher. In 1819, she dramatically interrupted a minister who was preaching to give her own interpretation of God's word. After this bold move, Bishop Allen surprisingly relented to Lee's demands, and she became an itinerant preacher, touring through New Jersey, New York, New England, and Ohio. In a typical year, she traveled about 2,500 miles and gave almost 200 sermons (Lee 1849, 51). After several years of traveling, she wrote her own conversion narrative and autobiography,

Jarena Lee, frontispiece from her autobiography, *Religious Experience and Journal of Mrs. Jarena Lee,* 1849. (*Library of Congress*)

detailing especially how she felt that her preaching was ordained by God. She had an uneasy relationship with the official African Methodist Episcopal Church. Although she was an effective preacher, the official church position was that women were lay leaders only, not fit for occupying the pulpit, even though they were the vast majority of converts during the Second Great Awakening. The historical record of the end of her life is disappointingly vague. We know very little about her life following the publication of an expanded version of her autobiography in 1849. We do not even know how long she lived or where she died.

which differed greatly from the mainstream revivals in their methods, message, and impact.

The Church of Latter Day Saints has to be the most important group to emerge from this sectarian growth. Like the Finneyites, Mormons sprang forth from the burned-over district of New York. In 1827, Joseph Smith, a farmer and treasure hunter, had a vision that there was a treasure for him to find, a cache of golden plates. He claimed to have found a new scripture on these golden tablets buried in the ground near his home in Palmyra, New York (Ahlstrom 1972, 502). In writing the new bible, the Book of Mormon, he also formed the most significant, thriving, modern American religion. Smith protested against the market forces of the early American republic by explicitly championing the poor over the rich, proud, and educated. In the end of the Book of Mormon, rich folks get their comeuppance and die a fiery death. In other ways too, Mormonism was a countercultural religion. In 1843, Smith announced that he had a private revelation from God that Mormons should be polygamous. In 1844, Smith was jailed for polygamy and murdered in jail. After his death, Brigham Young took over leadership, and persecution drove the Mormons westward until they found some peace in Salt Lake City. Overall, the movement was very patriarchal, under the leadership of one man who was the father over all. The polygamous arrangement echoed early biblical narratives that holy men had a number of wives. The religious group was structured as a strict, male-dominated hierarchical society, one that was oriented toward the family (Foster 1991; Kern 1981).

As an almost diametrically opposed example, the Shakers also came out of the early republican period, but they proposed a very different gender organization. They were led by Mother Ann Lee, who had emigrated from England in 1774. Early Shakers shaped exciting religious practices, by which they sang, danced, shook themselves, and shouted in religious exultation. The Shakers sought to establish gender equality in religious leadership. Men and women were also expected to remain celibate and to live in monastic, industrious, tightly-regulated communities. Celibacy had come out of Ann Lee's desire for women to avoid the suffering of childbearing (she had lost several children of her own before founding the group). By the 1830s, Shakers were at the height of their popularity, having garnered about 4,000 members who lived in approximately 60 communities scattered throughout the United States. Although they practiced religious equality between the sexes, this did not, as Lawrence Foster argues, translate to an egalitarian community; this group was very hierarchical and strict in its organization and regulations (Foster 1991).

Conclusion

The Shakers and the Mormons represent two very different examples of sectarian growth in the early 1800s, but they also demonstrate some of the central themes of this period. One can see how open the questions of gender organization were during this early republican era. In many ways, the sec-

An emotional meeting of the United Society of Believers in Christ's Second Coming, a utopian community in New York state founded by Anne Lee in 1774. Known as the Shakers for their vigorous dancing, the group favored communal work over specialized duties of men and women. Both sexes participated in domestic labor, and profits from sales of canned goods and furniture were shared by all. Because of the requirement for absolute chastity, the group's numbers declined from a high of over 5,000 to virtual extinction by 1988. (*Library of Congress*)

tarian movements, including some of the utopian experiments like the Oneida Community, demonstrate the heterodoxy of dissenting groups in early America. They also throw into sharp relief the ways in which the Second Great Awakening, while providing a platform for the early women's movement, did little to change women's roles. A more radical challenge was offered by the Methodists and Baptists when they tested the normative social order, specifically racial hierarchy. Even in this arena, however, the accommodation of slavery over time created a split between the black and white churches, a racial divide that largely still exists today. While the Second Great Awakening provided innumerable choices for religious individuals, it also came to segment society.

References and Further Reading

Ahlstrom, Sydney E. *A Religious History of the American People.* New Haven, CT: Yale University Press, 1972

Andrews, William L., ed. *Sisters of the Spirit: Three Black Women's Autobiographies of the Nineteenth Century.* Bloomington: Indiana University Press, 1986

Baker, Gordon Pratt. *Those Incredible Methodists: A History of the Baltimore Conference of the United Methodist Church*. Baltimore, MD: Commission on Archives and History, Baltimore Conference, 1972

Braude, Ann. "Women's History *Is* Religious History." In Thomas A. Tweed, ed. *Retelling U. S. Religious History*, 7–107. Berkeley: University of California Press, 1997

Carwardine, Richard. "The Second Great Awakening in Urban Centers: An Examination of Methodism and the 'New Measures.'" *Journal of American History* 59 (September 1972): 327–40

Evans, Sara M. *Born for Liberty: A History of Women in America*, 2nd ed. New York: Simon & Schuster, 1997

Finney, Charles G. *The Autobiography of Charles G. Finney*. Edited by Helen Wessel. Minneapolis, MN: Bethany House Publishers, 1977

Foster, Lawrence. *Women, Family and Utopia: Communal Experiments of the Shakers, the Oneida Community, and the Mormons*. Syracuse, NY: Syracuse University Press, 1991

Frey, Sylvia, and Betty Wood. *Come Shouting to Zion: African American Protestantism in the American South and British Caribbean to 1830*. Chapel Hill: University of North Carolina Press, 1998

Hatch, Nathan O. *The Democratization of American Christianity*. New Haven, CT: Yale University Press, 1989

Hempton, David. *Methodism: Empire of the Spirit*. New Haven, CT: Yale University Press, 2005

Isaac, Rhys. *The Transformation of Virginia, 1740–1790*. Chapel Hill: University of North Carolina Press, 1982

Johnson, Paul E. *A Shopkeepers Millennium: Society and Revivals in Rochester, New York, 1815–1837*. New York: Hill and Wang, 1978

Johnson, Paul E., and Sean Wilentz. *The Kingdom of Matthias: A Story of Sex and Salvation in Nineteenth-Century America*. New York: Oxford University Press, 1994

Juster, Susan. *Disorderly Women: Sexual Politics and Evangelicalism in Revolutionary New England*. Ithaca, NY: Cornell University Press, 1994

Juster, Susan. "To Slay the Beast: Visionary Women in the Early Republic." In Susan Juster and Lisa MacFarlane, eds. *A Mighty Baptism: Race, Gender and the Creation of American Protestantism*, 19–37. Ithaca, NY: Cornell University Press, 1996

Kern, Louis J. *An Ordered Love: Sex Roles and Sexuality in Victorian Utopias—the Shakers, the Mormons and the Oneida Community*. Chapel Hill: University of North Carolina Press, 1981

Latrobe, Benjamin. Journal. August 23, 1806–August 8, 1809, "Plan of the Camp, August 8, 1809," Latrobe Papers, Maryland Historical Society, Baltimore.

Lawrence, Anna M. "The Transatlantic Methodist Family: Gender, Revolution and Evangelicalism in America and England, c. 1730–1815." PhD thesis. University of Michigan, 2004

Lee, Jarena. *Religious Experience and Journal of Mrs. Jarena Lee, Giving an Account of Her Call to Preach the Gospel, Revised and Corrected from the Original Manuscript, Written by Herself.* Philadelphia: Author, 1849 (Digital Schomburg Collection, New York Public Library)

Mathews, Donald G. *Religion in the Old South.* Chicago: University of Chicago Press, 1977

Methodist Conference. *American Discipline.* 1780

Raboteau, Albert J. *Slave Religion: The "Invisible Institution" in the Antebellum South.* New York: Oxford University Press, 1978

Ryan, Mary P. "A Women's Awakening: Evangelical Religion and the Families of Utica, New York, 1800–1840." *American Quarterly* 30 (Winter 1978): 602–23

Taves, Ann. *Fits, Trances, and Visions: Experiencing Religion and Explaining Experience from Wesley to James.* Princeton, NJ: Princeton University Press, 1999

Welter, Barbara. "The Cult of True Womanhood: 1820–1860." *American Quarterly* 18 (Summer 1966): 151–74

Wigger, John H. *Taking Heaven by Storm: Methodism and the Rise of Popular Christianity in America.* New York: Oxford University Press, 1998

Primary Documents

Rules and Maxims for Promoting Matrimonial Happiness (1784)

In this article, which was "Addressed to the Ladies," an anonymous author delineates the proper place for women and wives in society. Subservience to one's husband is advocated as the only means to assuring a successful marriage and personal happiness. This advice correlates with the rise of the cult of true domesticity and the separation of the home from the workplace.

The likeliest way, either to obtain a good husband, or keep one, so, is to be good yourself.

Never use a lover ill whom you design to make your husband, lest he should either upbraid you with it, or return it, afterwards; and, if you find at any time an inclination to play the tyrant, remember these two lines of truth and justice:

Gently shall those be rul'd who gently sway'd
Abject shall those obey who baughty were obey'd

Battle of the Sexes
Avoid, both before and after marriage, all thoughts of managing your husband. Never endeavour to deceive or impose on his understanding; nor give him uneasiness, (as some do very foolishly) to try his temper; but treat him always, beforehand, with sincerity, and afterwards, with affection and respect.

Be not over sanguine before marriage, nor promise yourself felicity without alloy; for that's impossible to be attainted in this present state of things. Consider, beforehand, that the person you are going to spend your days with is a man, and not an angel; and if, when you come together, you discover any thing in his humour or behaviour, that is not . . . so agreeable as you expect, pass it over as a human frailty; smooth your brow; compose your temper; and try to amend it by cheeriness and good nature.

Remember always, that, whatever misfortunes may happen to either, they are not to be changed to the account of matrimony, but to the accounts and indemnities of human life. . . . Therefore, instead of murmurs, reflections, and disagreement, whereby the weight is rendered abundantly more grievous, readily put your shoulder to the yoke, and make it easier to both.

Resolve, every morning, to be good natured and cheerful that day; and, if any accident should happen to break that resolution, suffer it not to put you out of temper with every thing besides;—and especially with your husband.

Dispute not with him, be the occasion what it will; but much rather deny yourself the trivial satisfaction of having your own will, or gaining the better of an argument, than to risqué a quarrel, or create a heart burning, which it is impossible to know the end of.

Be assured, a woman's power, as well as happiness, has no other foundation but her husband's esteem and love, which, consequently, it is her undoubted interest, but all means possible, to preserve and increase.—Do you therefore study his temper, and command your own; enjoy his satisfaction with him, share and soothe his cares, and with the utmost diligence conceal his infirmities.

Read frequently with due attention, the Matrimonial services; and take care, in doing so, not to overlook the word Obey.

Always wear your wedding ring, for therein lies more virtue than is usually imagined. If you are ruffled unawares, assaulted with improper thoughts, or tempted in any kind against your duty, cast your eyes upon it, and call to mind who gave it you, where it was received, and what passed at that solemn time.

Source: The Gentleman and Lady's Town and Country Magazine *(May 1784): 28*

Alexander Falconbridge Describes the African Slave Trade (1788)

The African slave trade was the most condemned aspect of slavery in the early republic. The middle passage—the journey between West Africa and the Americas—was criticized even as the institution of slavery was defended. In the following excerpt, Alexander Falconbridge describes many of the horrors that he witnessed aboard a slave ship. Falconbridge, who was employed as a surgeon aboard the ship, later served as the governor of a British colony for freed slaves in Sierra Leone. The conditions on board the ships convinced enough Americans, even slave owners, to prohibit future slave imports. As a result, the United States ended its participation in the transatlantic slave trade in 1808. This predated the abolition of slavery by five and a half decades.

. . . The men Negroes, on being brought aboard the ship, are immediately fastened together, two and two, by handcuffs on their wrists and by irons rivetted on their legs. They are then sent down between the decks and placed in an apartment partitioned off for that purpose. The women also are placed in a separate apartment between decks, but without being ironed. An adjoining room on the same deck is appointed for the boys. Thus they are all placed in different apartments.

But at the same time, however, they are frequently stowed so close, as to admit of no other position than lying on their sides. Nor will the height between decks, unless directly under the grating, permit the indulgence of an erect posture; especially where there are platforms, which is generally the case. These platforms are a kind of shelf, about eight or nine feet in breadth, extending from the side of the ship toward the centre. They are placed nearly midway between the decks, at the distance of two or three feet from each deck, Upon these the Negroes are stowed in the same manner as they are on the deck underneath.

In each of the apartments are placed three or four large buckets, of a conical form, nearly two feet in diameter at the bottom and only one foot at the top and in depth of about twenty-eight inches, to which, when necessary, the Negroes have recourse. It often happens that those who are placed at a distance from the buckets, in endeavoring to get to them, rumble over their companions, in consequence of their being shackled. These accidents, although unavoidable, are productive of continual quarrels in which some of them are always bruised. In this distressed situation, unable to proceed and prevented from getting to the tubs, they desist from the attempt; and as the necessities of nature are not to be resisted, ease themselves as they lie. This becomes a fresh source of boils and disturbances and tends to render the condition of the poor captive wretches still more uncomfortable. The nuisance arising from these circumstances is not infrequently increased by the tubs being much too small for the purpose intended and their being usually emptied but once every day. The rule for doing so, however, varies in different ships according to the attention paid to the health and convenience of the slaves by the captain. . . .

Upon the Negroes refusing to take sustenance, I have seen coals of fire, glowing hot, put on a shovel and placed so near their lips as to scorch and burn them. And this has been accompanied with threats of forcing them to swallow the coals if they any longer persisted in refusing to eat. These means have generally had the desired effect. I have also been credibly informed that a certain captain in the slave-trade, poured melted lead on such of his Negroes as obstinately refused their food. . . .

The hardships and inconveniences suffered by the Negroes during the passage are scarcely to be enumerated or conceived. They are far more violently affected by seasickness than Europeans. It frequently terminates in death, especially among the women. But the exclusion of fresh air is among the most intolerable. For the purpose of admitting this needful refreshment, most of the ships in the slave trade are provided, between the decks, with five or six air-ports on each side of the ship, of about five inches in length and four in breadth. In addition, some ships, but not one in twenty, have what they denominate wind-sails. But whenever the sea is rough, and the rain heavy it becomes necessary to shut these and every other conveyance by which the air is admitted. The fresh air being thus excluded, the Negroes' rooms soon grow intolerable hot. The confined air, rendered noxious by the effluvia exhaled from their bodies and being repeatedly breathed, soon produces fevers and fluxes which generally carries off great numbers of them.

During the voyages I made, I was frequently witness to the fatal effects of this exclusion of fresh air. I will give one instance, as it serves to convey some idea, though a very faint one, of their terrible sufferings. . . . Some wet and blowing weather having occasioned the port-holes to be shut and the grating to be covered, fluxes and fevers among the Negroes ensued. While they were in this situation, I frequently went down among them till at length their room became so extremely hot as to be only bearable for a very short time. But the excessive heat was not the only thing that rendered their situation intolerable. The deck, that is the floor of their rooms, was so covered with the blood and mucus which had proceeded from them in consequence of the flux, that it resembled a slaughter-house. It is not in the power of the human imagination to picture a situation more dreadful or disgusting. Numbers of the slaves having fainted, they were carried upon deck where several of them died and the rest with great difficulty were restored. It had nearly proved fatal to me also. The climate was too warm to admit the wearing of any clothing but a shirt and that I had pulled off before I went down. . . . In a quarter of an hour I was so overcome with the heat, stench and foul air that I nearly fainted, and it was only with assistance I could get back on deck. The consequence was that I soon after fell sick of the same disorder from which I did not recover for several months. . . .

Source: Alexander Falconbridge, An Account of the Slave Trade on the Coast of Africa *(London: J. Phillips, 1788), 19–25*

Hints for Young Married Women (1789)

In the early republic, many women publicly recognized the importance and vagaries of finding a husband. They also questioned the perceived salvation that women felt upon attaining married status. In the following essay, an unknown author explores many of the experiences that women faced when they married, all but dismissing the idea that marriage was the solution to all of women's problems. At the same time, this essay also reveals the inequity that shaped marriage and offers advice on how to deal with it.

It has often been thought, that the first year after marriage is the happiest of a woman's life. We must first suppose that she marries from motives of affection, or, what the world calls love; and, even in this case, the rule admits of many exceptions, and she encounters many difficulties. She has her husband's temper to study, his family to please, household cares to attend, and, what is worse than all, she must cease to command, and learn to obey. She must learn to submit, without repining, where she has been used to have even her looks studied.

Would the tender lover treat his adored mistress like a rational being, rather than a goddess, a woman's task would be rendered much easier, and her life much happier. Would the flatterer pay his devoirs to her understanding, rather than her person, he would soon find his account in it. Would he consult her on his affairs, converse with her freely upon all subjects, and make her his companion and friend, instead of flattering her beauty, admiring her dress, and exalting her beyond what human nature merits, for what can at best be only called fashionable accomplishments, he would find himself less disappointed, and she would rattle the marriage chains with less impatience and difficulty. Now, can a sensible man expect that the poor vain trifler, to whom he pays so much court, should make an intelligent, agreeable companion, and assiduous and careful wife, a fond and anxious mother?

When a man pays court only to a woman's vanity, he can expect nothing but a fashionable wife, who may shine as a fine lady, but never in the softer intercourse of domestic endearments. How often is it owing to these lords of the creation, that the poor women become, in reality, what their ridiculous partiality made them suppose themselves? A pretty method this is of improving the temper, informing the mind, engaging the affections, and exciting our esteem, for those objects that we entrust with our future happiness.

I will not give my fair friends a few hits with regard to their conduct in the most respectable of all characters, a wife, a mother, and a friend. But first let me assert, and I do it with confidence, that nothing can be more false, than the idea that "a reformed rake makes the best husband!" this is a common opinion, but it is not mine: at least, there are too many chances against it.

A libertine, by the time he can bear to think of matrimony, has little left to boast, but a shattered constitution, empty pocket, trademen's bills, bad habits, and a taste for dress, and vices of every denomination. The poor wife's fortune will supply the rake with these fashionable follies a little longer. When money, the last resource, fails, he becomes peevish, sour, and discontented; angry that she can indulge him no longer, and ungrateful and regardless of her past favours. Disease, with all her miserable attendants, next steps in! ill is he prepared, either in body or mind, to cope with pain, sickness, poverty, and wretchedness. The poor wife has spent her all in supporting his extravagancies. She may now pine for want, with a helpless infant crying for bread; shunned and despised by her friends, and neglected by her acquaintance.

This, my beloved fair, is too often the case with many of our sex. The task of reforming a rake, is much above our capacity. I wish our inclinations, in this instance, were as limited as our abilities; but, alas! we vainly imagine we shall be rewarded for our resolution, in making such trial, by the success that will attend our undertaking.

If a young woman marries an amiable and virtuous young man, she has nothing to fear; she may even glory in giving up her own wishes to his! Never marry a man whose understanding will not excite your esteem, and whose virtues will not engage your affections. If a woman once thinks herself superior to her husband, all authority ceases, and she cannot be brought to obey, where she thinks she is so well entitled to command.

Sweetness and gentleness are all a woman's eloquence; and sometimes they are too powerful to be resisted especially when accompanied with youth and beauty. They are then enticements to virtue, preventatives from vice, and affection's security.

Never let your brow be clouded with resentment! never triumph in revenge! Who is it that you afflict? The man upon earth that should be dearest to you! Upon whom all your future hopes of happiness must depend. Poor the conquest, when our dearest friend must suffer; and ungenerous must be the heart, that can rejoice in such a victory.

Let your tears persuade: these speak with most irresistible language, with which you can assail the heart of a man. But even these sweet fountains of sensibility must not flow too often, lest they degenerate into weakness, and we lose our husband's esteem and affection, by the very methods which were given us to ensure them.

Study every little attention in your person, manner, and dress, that you find please. Never be negligent in your appearance, because you expect no body but your husband. He is the person whom you should chiefly endeavour to oblige. Always make home agreeable to him: receive him with ease, good humour, and cheerfulness; but be cautious how you enquire too minutely into his engagements abroad. Betray neither suspicion nor jealousy. Appear always gay and happy in his presence. Be particularly attentive to his favourite friends, even if they intrude upon you. A welcome reception will, at all times, counterbalance indifferent fare. Treat his relations with respect and affection: ask their advice in your household affairs, and always follow it, when you can confidently with propriety.

Treat your husband with the most unreserved confidence, in everything that regards yourself; but never betray your friend's letters or secrets to him. This, he cannot, and indeed, ought not to expect. If you do not use him to it, he will never desire it. Be careful never to intrude upon his studies or his pleasures: be always glad to see him, but do not be laughed at, as a fond, foolish wife. Confine your endearments to your own fireside. Do not let the young envy you, not the old abuse you, for a weakness, which, upon reflexion, you must condemn.

These hints will, I hope, be of some service to my fair country-women. They will, perhaps, have more weight. When they are known that the author of them has been married about a year, and has often, with success, practiced those rules herself, which she now recommends to others.

Source: The American Museum, or, Universal Magazine *(September 1789): 198*

Judith Sargent Murray Writes of the Equality of the Sexes (1790)

Writing under the pseudonym Constantia, Judith Sargent Murray rejects the assumption that women are the weaker sex or satisfied by their domestic chores. This rejection of the separate sphere declares that nurture rather than nature creates most of the distinctions between the sexes. Murray's statement is made at a time when the ideals of republican motherhood physically and morally separate men and women into separate spheres. This essay was originally published in the *Massachusetts Magazine* and almost immediately reprinted elsewhere in the United States and England.

Is it upon mature consideration we adopt the idea, that nature is thus partial in her distributions? Is it indeed a fact, that she hath yielded to one half of the human species so unquestionable a mental superiority? I know that to both sexes elevated understandings, and the reverse, are common. But, suffer me to ask, in what the minds of females are so notoriously deficient, or unequal. May not the intellectual powers be ranged under these four heads—imagination, reason, memory and judgment. The province of imagination hath long since been surrendered to us, and we have been crowned and undoubted sovereigns of the regions of fancy. Invention is perhaps the most arduous effort of the mind; this branch of imagination hath been particularly ceded to us, and we have been time out of mind invested with that creative faculty. Observe the variety of fashions (here I bar the contemptuous smile) which distinguish and adorn the female world: how continually are they changing, insomuch that they almost render the wise man's assertion problematical, and we are ready to say, *there is something new under the sun.* Now what a playfulness, what an exuberance of fancy, what strength of inventine imagination, doth this continual variation discover? Again, it hath been observed, that if the turpitude of the conduct of our sex, hath been ever so enormous, so extremely ready are we, that the very first thought presents us with an apology, so plausible, as to produce our actions even in an amiable light. Another instance of our creative powers, is our talent for slander; how ingenious are we at inventive scandal? what a formidable story can we in a moment fabricate merely from the force of a prolifick imagination? how many reputations, in the fertile brain of a female, have been utterly despoiled? how industrious are we at improving a hint? suspicion how easily do we convert into conviction, and conviction, embellished by the power of eloquence, stalks abroad to the surprise and confusion of unsuspecting innocence. Perhaps it will be asked if I furnish these facts as instances of excellency in our sex. Certainly not; but as proofs of a creative faculty, of a lively imagination. Assuredly great activity of mind is thereby discovered, and was this activity properly directed, what beneficial effects would follow. Is the needle and kitchen sufficient to employ the operations of a soul thus organized? I should conceive not, Nay, it is a truth that those very departments leave the intelligent principle vacant, and at liberty for speculation. Are we deficient in reason? we can only reason from what we know, and if an opportunity of acquiring knowledge hath been denied us, the inferiority of our sex cannot fairly be deduced from thence. Memory, I believe, will be allowed us in common, since everyone's experience must testify, that a loquacious old woman is as frequently met with, as a communicative man; their subjects are alike drawn from the fund of other times, and the transactions of their youth, or of maturer life, entertain, or perhaps fatigue you, in the evening of their lives.

"But our judgment is not so strong—we do not distinguish so well."—Yet it may be questioned, from what doth this superiority, in this determining faculty of the soul, proceed. May we not trace its source in the difference of education, and continued advantages? Will it be said that the judgment of a male of two years old, is more sage than that of a female's of the same age? I believe the reverse is generally observed to be true. But from that period what partiality! how is the one exalted, and the other depressed, by the contrary modes of education which are adopted! the one is taught to aspire, and the other is early confined and limitted. As their years increase, the sister must be wholly domesticated, while the brother is led by the hand through all the flowery paths of science. Grant that their minds are by nature equal, yet who shall wonder at the *apparent* superiority, if indeed custom becomes *second nature*; nay if it taketh place of nature, and that it doth the experience of each day will evince. At length arrived at womanhood, the uncultivated fair one feels a void, which the employments allotted her are by no means capable of filling. What can she do? to books she may not apply; or if she doth, *to those only of the novel kind,* lest she merit the appellation of a *learned lady;* and what ideas have been affixed to this term, the observation of many can testify. Fashion, scandal, and sometimes what is still more reprehensible, are then called in to her relief; and who can say to what lengths the liberties she takes may proceed. Meantimes she herself is most unhappy; she feels the want of a cultivated mind. Is she single, she in vain seeks to fill up time from sexual employments or amusements. Is she united to a person whose soul nature made equal to her own, education hath set him so far above her, that in those entertainments which are productive of such rational felicity, she is not qualified to accompany him. She experiences a mortifying consciousness of inferiority, which embitters every enjoyment. Doth the person to whom her adverse fate hath consigned her, possess a mind incapable of improvement, she is equally wretched, in being so closely connected with an individual whom she cannot but despise. Now, was she permitted the same instructors as her brother, (with an eye however to their particular departments) for the employment of a rational mind an ample field would be opened. In astronomy she might catch a glimpse of the immensity of the Deity, and thence she would form amazing conceptions of the august and supreme Intelligence. In geography she would admire Jehovah in the midst of his benevolence; thus adapting this globe to the various wants and amusements of its inhabitants. In natural philosophy she would adore the infinite majesty of heaven, clothed in condescension; and as she traversed the reptile world, she would hail the goodness of a creating God. A mind, thus filled, would have little room for the trifles with which our sex are, with too much justice, accused of amusing themselves, and they would thus be rendered fit companions for those, who should one day wear them as their crown. Fashions, in their variety, would then give place to conjectures, which might perhaps conduce to the improvements of the literary world; and there would be no leisure for slander or detraction. Reputation would not then be blasted, but serious speculations would occupy the lively imaginations of the sex. Unnecessary visits would only be indulged by way of relaxation, or to answer the demands of consanguinity and friendship. Females would become discreet, their judgments would be invigorated, and their partners for life being circumspectly chosen, an unhappy Hymen would then be as rare, as is now the reverse.

Will it be urged that those acquirements would supersede our domestick duties. I answer that every requisite in female economy is easily attained; and, with truth I can add, that when once attained, they require no further *mental attention*. Nay, while we are pursuing the needle, or the superintendency of the family, I repeat, that our minds are at full liberty for reflection; that imagination may exert itself in full vigor; and that if a just foundation is early laid, our ideas will then be worthy of rational beings. If we were industrious we might easily find time to arrange them upon paper, or should avocations press too hard for such an indulgence, the hours allotted for conversation would at least become more refined and rational. Should it still be vociferated, "Your domestick employments are sufficient"—I would calmly ask, is it reasonable, that a candidate for immortality, for the joys of heaven, an intelligent being, who is to spend an eternity in contemplating the works of the Deity, should at present be so degraded, as to be allowed no other ideas, than those which are suggested by the mechanism of a pudding, or the sewing the seams of a garment? Pity that all such censurers of female improvement do not go one step further, and deny their future existence; to be consistent they surely ought.

Yes, ye lordly, ye haughty sex, our souls are by nature *equal* to yours; the same breath of God animates, enlivens, and invigorates us; and that we are not fallen lower than yourselves, let those witness who have greatly towered above the various discouragements by which they have been so heavily oppressed; and though I am unacquainted with the list of celebrated characters on either side, yet from the observations I have made in the contracted circle in which I have moved, I dare confidently believe, that from the commencement of time to the present day, there hath been as many females, as males, who, by the *mere force of natural powers,* have merited the crown of applause; who, *thus unassisted*, have seized the wreath of fame. I know there are who assert, that as the animal power of the one sex are superiour, of course their mental faculties also must be stronger; thus attributing strength of mind to the transient organization of this earth born tenement.

But if this reasoning is just, man must be content to yield the palm to many of the brute creation, since by not a few of his brethren of the field, he is far surpassed in bodily strength. Moreover, was this argument admitted, it would prove too much, for occular demonstration evinceth, that there are many robust masculine ladies, and effeminate gentlemen. Yet I fancy that Mr. Pope, though clogged with an enervated body, and distinguished by a diminutive stature, could nevertheless lay claim to greatness of soul; and perhaps there are many other instances which might be adduced to combat so unphilosophical an opinion. Do we not often see, that when the clay built tabernacle is well nigh dissolved, when it is just ready to mingle with the parent soil, the immortal inhabitant aspires to, and even attaineth heights the most sublime, and which were before wholly unexplored. Besides, were we to grant that animal strength proved any thing, taking into consideration the accustomed impartiality of nature, we should be induced to imagine, that she had invested the female mind with superiour strength as an equivalent for the bodily powers of man. But waving this however palpable advantage, for *equality only,* we wish to contend.

Source: Judith Sargent Murray, "On the Equality of the Sexes," Massachusetts Magazine 2 *(March 1790): 132–135*

The Postwar Migration to America (1792)

During the American Revolution, immigration slowed to a trickle. Then a postwar peace, available Western lands, and an economic boom encouraged a new wave of European immigration. The following article enthusiastically describes a perceived change in the nature of immigration to the United States after independence was secured. These new immigrants contrasted sharply with their colonial counterparts—most of whom were poor, landless, and unskilled. These new immigrants came to America because of its stability and its industrial potential. They brought financial resources and skills, and they hoped to escape the political turmoil that characterized their European homes.

At no period since the discovery of America has the spirit of emigration been so general as it is at present. Instead of servants by indentures, sent out from Great Britain, Ireland, and Germany, we find several respectable families come from these countries with an intention of establishing factories and little colonies, in various parts of our frontier towns, and back settlements.

A vessel, arrived at one of our ports, a few days ago, brought near 500, and another 750 passengers, many of whom were of the class above mentioned. These people have given it as their opinion, that no less than ten thousand would emigrate this fall from one port in Ireland, if an opportunity offered on board American vessels, which in general are preferred to those of their own country. It is ever confidently asserted from late information, received in different parts of the continent, that upwards of four thousand mechanics, merchants, gentlemen, and nobles, from the Netherlands, and who, with respect to the present contests there, meant to be altogether neuter, and wishing on that account, though in vain, to steer clear of the storms, which they, for some time past, saw gathering in their political horizon, came to a resolution of quitting their native country forever—and to seek that peace and happiness in a foreign clime, which hath been denied both to them, and to their ancestors, for above 300 years; the low countries, as they are called, having been always made the theatre of war upon the continent of Europe.

Some time ago, 200 of these people, who had invested part of their money in the Dutch funds, met with considerable opposition from different parties, who suspected their intention; and, under pretence of their being factious persons, who wished to join some of the belligerent powers, inimical to their interest, prevailed on the directors of the bank to impede their design as much as possible. Those who had money in the English funds, were more successful; for although it was well known that they proposed coming to America, and settling here, no stumbling block was thrown in their way—and they are all now ready to embark by the first vessels that sail either from Holland or England, to the number of 4,000 upon a moderate calculation—with cash and other valuable effects. . . .

Source: "Migration to America" in The American Museum, or, Universal Magazine, Containing, Essays on Agriculture—Commerce—Manufacturers—Politics—Morals—and Manners. Sketches of National Characters—Natural and Civil History—and Biography *(August 1792): 112–113*

A Toast on the Fourth of July (1798)

In the years following the Revolution, Americans fought over its meaning, as well as the meaning of liberty and equality. Americans routinely used toasts to publicly declare their patriotism while defining their particular vision of the American dream. The following toast was originally given at a July Fourth celebration at Patterson, New Jersey. In it, the deliverer appeals to the individualism of citizens and a workingman's definition of liberty.

The Continuation of this country—May the Citizens thereof be ever ready to protect and defend it, to its primary purity.

The RIGHTS of MAN—May they be rightly understood, and firmly established, throughout the world on the ruins of tyranny.

The *youthful* Fair of Columbia—May they detest as the world of evils, the very idea of despotism, and prefer a union with a *Republican cobbler*, to an *Aristocratic Nobleman*.

May the God of Empires speedily dispel the gloomy cloud that overshadows our political hemisphere; and in purest light demonstrate to the citizens of this seemingly devoted country, who those are, that are justly entitled to be branded with the epithets of *deluded* and *degraded*.

May every American have liberty imprinted in his mind, his tongue free to express it, and strength in his arm to support it.

May all engines of despotism be annihilated, and the State prisons lately erected in this country, for the mitigation of punishments, never be converted into political Bastiles.

Source: The Time Piece; and Literary Companion *(July 16, 1798), 2*

John James Audubon Describes the Squatters of the Mississippi (1831)

While much of the United States underwent dramatic economic transformations during the early 19th century, many settlers on the backcountry remained largely unconnected with the industrial world and mired in poverty. In the following excerpt famed naturalist John James Audubon describes their livelihood and speculates how their community formed. In the process Audubon declares that even the most impoverished American should be able to rise out of squalor and obtain economic stability.

Although every European traveller who has glided down the Mississippi, at the rate of ten miles an hour, has told his tale of the Squatters, yet none has given any other account of them than that they are "a sallow, sickly-looking sort of miserable beings," living in swamps, and subsisting on pig-nuts, Indian corn and bear's flesh. It is obvious, however, that none but a person acquainted with their history, manners, and condition, can give any real information respecting them.

The individuals who become squatters choose that sort of life of their own free will. They mostly remove from other parts of the United States, after finding that land has become too high in price; and they are persons who, having a family of strong and hardy children, are anxious to enable them to provide for themselves. They have heard from good authorities, that the country extending along the great streams of the West, is of all parts of the Union the richest in its soil, the growth of its timber, and the abundance of its game; that, besides, the Mississippi is the great road to and from all the markets in the world; and that every vessel borne by its waters, affords to settlers some chance of selling their commodities, or of exchanging them for others. To these recommendations is added another, of ever greater weight with persons of the above denomination, namely, the prospect of being able to settle on land, and perhaps to hold it for a number of years, without purchase, rent or tax of any kind. How many thousands of individuals in all parts of the globe would gladly try their fortune with such prospects, I leave to you, reader, to determine.

. . . The land which they and their ancestors have possessed for a hundred years, having been constantly forced to produce crops of one kind or other, is now completely worn out. It exhibits only a superficial layer of red clay, cut up by deep ravines, through which much of the soil has been conveyed to some more fortunate neighbour, residing in a yet rich and beautiful valley. Their strenuous efforts to render it productive have failed. They dispose of every thing too cumbrous or expensive for them to remove, retaining only a few horses, a servant or two, and such implements of husbandry and other articles as may be necessary on their journey, or useful when they arrive at the spot of their choice.

I think I see them at this moment harnessing their horses, and attaching them to their wagons, which are already filled with bedding, provisions, and the younger children; while on their outside are fastened spinning-wheels and looms; and a bucket, filled with tar and tallow, swings between the hind wheels. Several axes are secured to the bolster, and the feeding trough of the horses contains pots, kettles, and pans. The servant, now become a driver, rides the near saddled horse, the wife is mounted on another, the worthy husband shoulders his gun, and his sons, clad in plain substantial homespun, drive the cattle ahead, and lead the procession, followed by the hounds and other dogs. Their day's journey is short and not agreeable: — the cattle, stubborn or wild, frequently leave the road for the woods, giving the travellers much trouble; the harness of the horses here and there gives away, and needs immediate repair; a basket, which has accidentally dropped, must be gone after, for nothing that they have can be spared; the roads are bad, and now and then all hands are called to push on the wagon, or prevent it from upsetting. Yet by sunset they have proceeded perhaps twenty miles. Rather fatigued, all assemble round the fire, which has been lighted, supper is prepared, and a camp being erected, there they pass the night.

. . . October tinges the leaves of the forest, the morning dews are heavy, the days hot, the nights chill, and the unacclimated family in a few days are attacked with ague. The lingering disease almost prostrates their whole faculties, and one seeing them at such a period might well call them sallow and sickly. Fortunately the unhealthy season soon passes over, and hoar-frosts make their appearance. Gradually each individual recovers strength. The largest ash trees are felled; their trunks are cut, split, and corded in front of the building; a large fire is lighted under night on the edge of the water, and soon a steamer calls to purchase the wood, and thus add to their comforts during the winter.

This first fruit of their industry imparts new courage to them; their exertions multiply, and when spring returns, the place has a cheerful look. Venison, bear's flesh, wild turkeys, ducks, and geese, with now and then some fish, have served to keep up their strength, and now their enlarged field is planted with corn, potatoes, and pumpkins. Their stock of cattle, too, has augmented; the steamer, which now stops there as if by preference, buys a calf or a pig, together with the whole of their wood. Their store of provisions is renewed, and brighter rays of hope enliven their spirits.

Who is he of the settlers on the Mississippi that cannot realize some profit? Truly none who is industrious. When the autumnal months return, all are better prepared to encounter that ague, which then prevails. Substantial food, suitable clothing, and abundant firing, repel its attacks; and before another twelvemonth has elapsed, the family is naturalized.

Every successive year has increased their savings. They now possess a large stock of horses, cows, and hogs, with abundance of provisions, and domestic comfort of every kind. The daughters have been married to the sons of neighbouring Squatters, and have gained sisters to themselves by the marriage of their brothers. The government secures to the family the lands, on which twenty years before, they settled in poverty and sickness. Larger buildings are erected on piles, secure from the inundations; where a single cabin once stood, a neat village is now to be seen; warehouses, stores, and work-shops, increase the importance of the place. The squatters live respected and in due time die regretted, by all who knew them.

Thus are the vast frontiers of our country peopled, and thus does cultivation, year after year, extend over the western wilds. Time will no doubt be, when the great valley of the Mississippi, still covered with primeval forests, interspersed with swamps, will smile with corn-fields and orchards, while crowded cities will rise at intervals along its banks, and enlightened nations will rejoice in the bounties of Providence.

Source: John James Audubon, Delineations of American Scenery and Character *(New York: G. A. Baker & Co., 1926)*

Speech of Tecumseh to Indiana Governor William Harrison (1810)

In this fiery speech, the Shawnee warrior and leader Tecumseh rejects calls to leave Indiana. Instead, he explains why neither he nor any Shawnee chief has the ability to make such an agreement as the so-called whisky treaty that cedes land without the consent of the entire tribe. In the following years, Tecumseh and his brother Tenskwatawa (The Prophet) led a pan-Indian alliance against the United States that corresponded with the War of 1812.

It is true I am a Shawnee. My forefathers were warriors. Their son is a warrior. From them I take only my existence; from my tribe I take nothing. I am the maker of my own fortune; and oh! that I could make that of my red people, and of my country, as great as the conceptions of my mind, when I think of the Spirit that rules the universe. I would not then come to Governor Harrison to ask him to tear the treaty and to obliterate the landmark; but I would say to him: "Sir, you have liberty to return to your own country."

The being within, communing with past ages, tells me that once, nor until lately, there was no white man on this continent; that it then all belonged to red men, children of the same parents, placed on it by the Great Spirit that made them, to keep it, to traverse it, to enjoy its productions, and to fill it with the same race, once a happy race, since made miserable by the white people, who are never contented but always encroaching. The way, and the only way, to check and to stop this evil, is for all the red men to unite in claiming a common and equal right in the land, as it was at first, and should be yet; for it never was divided, but belongs to all for the use of each. For no part has a right to sell, even to each other, much less to strangers—those who want all, and will not do with less.

The white people have no right to take the land from the Indiana, because they had it first; it is theirs. They may sell, but all must join. Any sale not made by all is not valid. The late sale is bad. It was made by a part only. Part do not know how to sell. It requires all to make a bargain for all. All red men have equal rights to the unoccupied land. The right of occupancy is as good in one place as in another. There can not be two occupations in the same place. The first excludes all others. It is not so in hunting or traveling; for there the same ground will serve many, as they may follow each other all day; but the camp is stationary, and that is occupancy. It belongs to the first who sits down on his blanket or skins which he has thrown upon the ground; and till he leaves it no other has a right.

Source: William Jennings Bryan, ed., World's Greatest Orations, *10 vols. (New York: Funk & Wagnalls, 1906), 4:14–15.*

John Doyle Describes His Arrival at Philadelphia (1818)

John Doyle was one of many Irish immigrants who came to the United States in the early 19th century. Doyle came to Philadelphia in 1818. In the following letter, Doyle describes his journey and new home to his wife, whom he left behind. Doyle hoped that he could quickly use his skills as a printer to save enough money for his wife and childrens' passage. A changing economy and an influx of similarly skilled immigrants convinced Doyle that his ambition would have to be achieved through other means. Doyle would eventually save enough money to pay his family's passage to Pennsylvania.

We were safely landed in Philadelphia on the 7th of October and I had not so much as would pay my passage in a boat to take me ashore. My distress and confusion for the want of three or four pence was very great, and such was the jealousy and miserableness of the passengers that there was not one who would lend another even that sum. I, however, contrived to get over, and God is my witness that at that moment, I would as soon the ground would open and swallow me up. It was not long till I made out my father, whom I instantly knew, and no one could describe our feelings when I made myself known to him, and received his embraces, after an absence of seventeen years. The old man was quite distracted about me. He done nothing that entire day but bringing me about to his friends. Their manner of receiving me was quite amusing; one would say you are welcome, sir, from the old country; another, you are welcome to this free country; you are welcome to this wooden country; you are welcome to this free country—you are welcome to this land of liberty. Pray sir, are you not happy to have escaped from the tyranny of the old country? When you would deny the tyranny and give the preference to home, they would look amazed and say, "What sir, would you not rather live in a free country than in slavery?" In short they imagine here that we can not act or speak in Ireland but as the authorities please. Their ignorance and presumption are disgusting, their manners worse. As to politeness and good nature, they are totally unknown and though they all pretend to be well acquainted with the affairs of Europe they are utterly ignorant of all transactions there, or at the best know them imperfectly. If my father's love could do me any good I did not want it, for it amounted to jealousy.

The morning after landing I went to work to the printing and to my great surprise I found that my hand was very little out. There is an immensity of printing done in America, still it is not as good as other businesses, and I think a journeyman printer's wages might be averaged at 7½ dollars a week all the year round. In New York it may not be so much as they are often out of work. The bookbinding may be put upon a footing with the printing; they execute their work here remarkably well.

I worked in Philadelphia for five and one-half weeks and saved 6 [pounds], that is counting four dollars to the pound (in the currency) of the United States the dollar is worth five shillings Irish at all times. They give the name of shillings to one-eighth of a dollar which are common here . . . This name is what blinds many immigrants to the value of their money here and about the price of dollars and flatters them with the idea of such enormous wages. . . .

I found the printing and bookbinding overpowered with hands in New York. I remained idle for twelve days in consequence; when finding there was many out of employment like myself I determined to turn myself to something else, seeing that there was nothing to be got by idleness. The trifle which I had saved was going from me fast. I drove about accordingly and was engaged by a bookseller to hawk maps for him at 7 dollars a week. This I done much to his satisfaction but when the town was well supplied he discharged me and instead of paying me my entire bill he stopped 9 dollars for maps which he said I made him no return for. I had to look for justice but was defeated for want of a person to prove my account. I lost the 9 dollars which I reckon to be 45 shillings. However I got such an insight into the manners and customs of the natives whilst going among them with the maps as served me extremely. I now had about 60 dollars of my own saved, above every expense. These I laid out in the purchase of pictures on New Year's Day, which I sell ever since. I am doing astonishingly well, thanks be to God and was able on the 16th of this month to make a deposit of 100 dollars in the bank of the United States.

Thus you see, my dearest Fanny, God has at length done something for us; every penny of it is my own hard earnings and I am now convinced that it is only by deserving His blessing that we can hope or expect to merit His favors; apropos, I must inform you that I made a solemn promise to God while at sea that if it was His goodness to spare my life till I get ashore I would make a hearty confession of my sins, which I thank Him for having granted me time and grace to perform, and this I mention, my love, because I know that it will be a source of pleasure to you; though living happy in the midst of my brother's family whom you know that I always loved and being as yet very successful in dealing in the pictures and indeed I may say in everything I have taken in hand since I came to America, I feel, particularly in the evenings, when I return home, a lonesomeness and lowness of spirits which oppress me almost to fainting. . . .

There are poor houses charity schools and even soup houses here which shows that there are a number of destitute poor; of course there is misery in every part of the world, but none of the real actual poverty and distress which is in all parts of Ireland. . . .

One thing I think is certain that if the emigrants knew before hand what they have to suffer for about the first six months after leaving home in every respect they would never come here. However, an enterprising man, desirous of advancing himself in the world will despise everything for coming to this free country, where a man is allowed to thrive and flourish, without having a penny taken out by government; no visits from tax gatherers, constables or soldiers, every one at liberty to act and speak as he likes, provided it does not hurt another, to slander and damn government, abuse public men in their office to their faces, wear your hat in court and smoke a cigar while speaking to the judge as familiarly as if he was a common mechanic, hundreds go unpunished for crimes for which they would be surely hung in Ireland; in fact, they are so tender of life in this country that a person should have a very great interest to get himself hanged for anything! . . .

I can not say any more but for ever and ever your loving husband. John.

Source: Journal of the American Irish Historical Society *12 (1913): 201–204*

The First Discipline of the African Methodist Episcopal Church (1817)

In this public statement of the beliefs and practices of the African Methodist Episcopal (AME) Church, the authors describe the origins of the church. An outgrowth of the Second Great Awakening, the AME Church explains its history of separation from the Methodist Church in Philadelphia in both spiritual as well as racial terms. In this passage, the founders of the church explain how the AME Church emerged out of the general mistreatment of African Americans in the country as well as in the church itself.

We deem it necessary to annex to our book of discipline, a brief statement of our rise and progress, which we hope will be satisfactory, and conducive to your edification and growth in the knowledge of our Lord Jesus Christ. In

November, 1787, the coloured people belonging to the Methodist Society in Philadelphia, convened together, in order to take into consideration the evils under which they laboured, arising from the unkind treatment of their white brethren, who considered them a nuisance in the house of worship, and even pulled them off their knees while in the act of prayer, and ordered them to the back seats. From these, and various other acts of unchristian conduct, we considered it our duty to devise a plan in order to build a house of our own, to worship God under our own vine and fig tree: in this undertaking, we met with great opposition from an elder of the Methodist church (J. McC.) who threatened, that if we did not give up the building, erase our names from the subscription paper, and make acknowledgments for having attempted such a thing, that in three months we should all be publicly expelled from the Methodist society. Not considering ourselves bound to obey this injunction, and being fully satisfied we should be treated without mercy, we sent in our resignations. . . .

In 1793, the number of serious people of colour, being greatly increased, they were of different opinions respecting the mode of religious worship; and, as many felt a strong partiality for that adopted by the Methodists, Richard Allen, with the advice of some of his brethren, proposed erecting a place of worship on his own ground, and at his own expense, as an African Methodist Meetinghouse. As soon as the preachers of the white Methodist church, in Philadelphia, came to the knowledge of this, they opposed it with all their might, insisting that the house should be made over to the conference, or they would publish us in the newspapers as imposing on the public, as we were not Methodists. However, the building went on, and when finished, we invited Francis Asbury, then bishop of the Methodist Episcopal Church, to open the house for Divine service; which invitation he accepted, and the house was named BETHEL . . . .

In this situation, we experienced grievances too numerous to mention: at one time, the elder (J. S.) demanded the keys of the house, with the books and papers belonging to the church; telling us at other times, we should have no more meetings without his leave—and, that the house was not ours, but belonged to the Methodist conference. Finding ourselves thus embarrassed, we consulted a lawyer, who informed us that by means of a supplement, we could be delivered from the grievances we laboured under. The congregation were unanimous, in signing the petition for a supplement, which the legislature of Pennsylvania readily granted; and we were liberated from the difficulties which, for ten years, we experienced. We now hoped to be free from any further perplexity; but we soon found, that our proceedings respecting the supplement, exasperated our opponents. In order to accommodate matters, they proposed supplying us with preaching, if we would give them $600 per year. The congregation not consenting to this sum, they fell to $400; but the people were not willing to give more than $200 per year. For which sum, they were to preach for us twice a week, during the

year. But it proved to be only six or seven times; and sometimes by such
preachers as were not acceptable to the Bethel people, and not in much
esteem among the white Methodists, as preachers. The Bethel people being
dissatisfied with such conduct, induced the trustees to pass a resolution to
give but $100 per year, to the white ministers. When a quarterly payment of
the $100 was tendered, it was refused, and sent back, insisting on the $200,
or we should have no more preaching from them. At this time they strongly
pressed us to repeal the supplement; this we could not comply with.

We waited on bishop Asbury, and proposed taking a preacher to ourselves, and supporting him in boarding and salary, provided he would attend
to the duties of the church; such as, visiting the sick, burying the dead, bap-
tising, and administering the sacrament. The bishop observed, "He did not
think there was more than one preacher belonging to the conference who
would attend to those duties." It was then asked, "Who was to do the
duties?" the bishop answered, "You," referring to Richard Allen. The bishop
being informed that if we paid a preacher four or five hundred dollars per
year, we should expect that preacher to do his duty, replied, that "We would
not be served on them terms."

Shortly after this, an elder (S. R.) then in Philadelphia, declared that
unless we would repeal the supplement, neither he nor any white preacher,
travelling or local, should preach any more for us: so we were left to ourselves. At length, the preachers and stewards belonging to the Academy,
proposed serving us on the same terms that we had offered to the St.
George's preachers: and they preached for us better than twelve months,
and then demanded $150 per year; this not being complied with, they
declined preaching for us, and we were once more left to ourselves, as an
edict was passed by the elder, that if any local preacher should serve us, he
should be expelled. . . .

. . . Our coloured friends at Baltimore, were treated in a similar manner,
by the white preachers and trustees, and many of them drove away; who were
disposed to seek a place of worship for themselves, rather than go to law.

Many of the coloured people, in other places, were in a situation nearly
like those of Philadelphia and Baltimore, which induced us, last April, to call
a general meeting, by way of conference. Delegates from Baltimore, and
other places, met those of Philadelphia, and taking into consideration their
grievances, and in order to secure their privileges, promote union and harmony among themselves, it was resolved, "That the people of Philadelphia,
Baltimore, &c. &c. should become one body, under the name of the African
Methodist Episcopal Church." We have deemed it expedient to have a form
of Discipline, whereby we may guide our people in the fear of God, in the
unity of the Spirit, and in the bonds of peace, and preserve us from that spiritual despotism which we have so recently experienced—remembering, that
we are not to Lord it over God's heritage, as greedy dogs, that can never have
enough; but with long suffering, and bowels of compassion, to bear each

other's burthens, and so fulfil the law of Christ; praying that our mutual striving together, for the promulgation of the gospel, may be crowned with abundant success, we remain your affectionate servants in the kingdom and patience of the Prince of Peace.

RICHARD ALLEN,
DANIEL COKER,
JAMES CHAMPION.

Source: The Doctrines and Discipline of the African Methodist Episcopal Church *(Philadelphia, PA: J. H. Cunningham, 1817): 1–8*

A Cherokee Memorial (1830)

In the early 19th century, white Americans increasingly pressured Native Americans to move west of the Mississippi River. The United States used treaties to claim some Indian lands, but this did not satisfy many Americans who coveted arable Indian hunting grounds and corn fields. As squatters increasingly settled on Indian lands and tensions mounted on the frontier, many Americans declared that removal was in the best interest of everyone involved. Removal would provide white society with additional lands for slavery and cotton, and it was the only means to protect Native Americans from hostile Western settlers and intrusive American culture. In the following memorial, the Cherokees reject this logic for removal.

We are aware that some persons suppose it will be for our advantage to remove beyond the Mississippi. We think otherwise. Our people universally think otherwise. Thinking that it would be fatal to their interests, they have almost to a man sent their memorial to Congress, deprecating the necessity of a removal. This question was distinctly before their minds when they signed their memorial. Not an adult person can be found, who has not an opinion on the subject; and if the people were to understand distinctly, that they could be protected against the laws of the neighboring States, there is probably not an adult person in the nation, who would think it best to remove; though possibly a few might emigrate individually. There are doubtless many who would, flee to an unknown country, however beset with dangers, privations and sufferings, rather than be sentenced to spend six years in a Georgia prison for advising one of their neighbors not to betray his country. And there are others who could not think of living as outlaws in their native land, exposed to numberless vexations, and excluded from being parties or witnesses in a court of justice. It is incredible that Georgia should ever have enacted the oppressive laws to which reference is here made, unless she had supposed that something extremely terrific in its character was necessary, in order to make the Cherokees willing to remove. We are not willing to remove; and if we could be brought to this extremity, it would be, not by argument; not because our judgment was satisfied; not because our condition will be improved—but only because we cannot endure to be deprived of our national and individual rights, and subjected to a process of intolerable oppression.

We wish to remain on the land of our fathers. We have a perfect and original right to claim this, without interruption or molestation. The treaties with us, and laws of the United States made in pursuance of treaties, guaranty our residence, and our privileges, and secure us against intruders. Our only request is, that these treaties may be fulfilled, and these laws executed. But if we are compelled to leave our country, we see nothing but ruin before us. The country west of the Arkansas territory is unknown to us. From what we can learn of it, we have no prepossessions in its favor. All the inviting parts of it, as we believe, are pre-occupied by various Indian nations, to which it has been assigned. They would regard us as intruders, and look upon us with an evil eye. The far greater part of that region is, beyond all controversy, badly supplied with wood and water; and no Indian tribe can live as agriculturists without these articles. All our neighbors, in case of our removal, though crowded into our near vicinity, would speak a language totally different from ours, and practice different customs. The original possessors of that region are now wandering savages, lurking for prey in the neighborhood. They have always been at war, and would be easily tempted to turn their arms against peaceful emigrants. Were the country to which we are urged much better than it is represented to be, and were it free from the objections which we have made to it, still it is not the land of our birth, nor of our affections. It contains neither the scenes of our childhood, nor the graves of our fathers.

The removal of families to a new country, even under the most favorable auspices, and when the spirits are sustained by pleasing visions of the future, is attended with much depression of mind and sinking of heart. This is the case, when the removal is a matter of decided preference, and when the persons concerned are in early youth or vigorous manhood, Judge, then, what must be the circumstances of a removal, when a whole community, embracing persons of all classes and every description, from the infant to the man of extreme old age, the sick, the blind, the lame, the improvident, the reckless, the desperate, as well as the prudent, the considerate, the industrious, are compelled to remove by odious and intolerable vexations and persecutions, brought upon them in the forms of law, when all will agree only in this, that they have been cruelly robbed of their country, in violation of the most solemn compacts which it is possible for communities to form with each other; and that, if they should make themselves comfortable in their residence, they have nothing to expect hereafter but to be the victims of a future legalized robbery!

Source: E. C. Tracy, Memoir of the Life of Jeremiah Evarts *(Boston, MA: Crocker and Brewster, 1845), 446–447.*

Reference

Adams, John (1735–1826) Second president of the United States. He served at the first Continental Congress, suggested Washington as the leader of the army, aided in the drafting and signed the Declaration of Independence, and served as the first vice president of the United States (1788, 1792) and as president of the United States (1796).

Adams, John Quincy (1767–1848) Sixth president of the United States. He served as minister to Russia (1809) during Napoleon's invasion, as head of the United States delegation for the Treaty of Ghent (1814), and as minister to Great Britain; worked out the principles of the Monroe Doctrine; was president of the United States (1825–1829); and was defeated by Andrew Jackson for reelection.

Alien and Sedition Acts The collective name applied to a series of four acts passed by Congress in 1798. Curtailed freedom of speech and the freedom of foreigners residing in the United States.

American Colonization Society (1817–1912) Purchased the freedom of slaves and colonized them in Liberia. After the abolition of slavery, provided aid for freed slaves in Liberia.

American System A program of government subsidies favored by Henry Clay to promote American economic growth and to protect domestic manufacturers from foreign competition. Clay chose this name in support of the Tariff of 1824.

Anglo-American Accords Series of agreements, reached during the British-American Conventions of 1818, that fixed the western boundary between the United States and Canada. Also restored American fishing rights.

Annapolis Convention (September 1786) Met at Annapolis, Maryland and consisted of 12 delegates from five states (New Jersey, New York, Pennsylvania, Delaware, and Virginia). Called for the establishing of a Continental Congress.

Anti-Federalists Opponents of the Constitution in the debate over its ratification.

Asbury, Francis (1745–1816) In 1784, John Wesley named Asbury the superintendent of the Methodist Church in America. Under his leadership, the Methodist Church grew from five thousand members in 1776 to 214,000 at the time of his death.

Audubon, John James (1785–1851) An ornithologist and artist, one of America's foremost naturalists. His most famous work is *The Birds of America* (4 vols., 1827–1838).

Bartram, William (1739–1823) Native-born traveler and naturalist. Documented 18th-century life in the Southeastern United States. In 1791, published his work, *Travels through North and South Carolina, Georgia, East and West Florida, the Cherokee Country, etc.* (1791).

Becknell, William (ca.1787–1856) Missouri trader, followed the route that later became known as the Santa Fe Trail (1821).

Blount, William (1749–1800) Served with North Carolina troops in the Revolution; member of the Continental Congress; state senator; governor of the territory south of the Ohio River; president of the Tennessee constitutional convention; elected as one of Tennessee's first senators; expelled from the Senate for inciting Creek and Cherokee Indians to cooperate with the British fleet in an attack on Spanish Florida and Louisiana.

Brown, Charles Brockden (1771–1810) Novelist and editor. Considered to be the first professional American novelist.

Burr, Aaron (1756–1836) Revolutionary officer and political leader most famous for his rivalry and duel with Hamilton at Weehawken, New Jersey. Mortally wounded his opponent, bringing about the end of his political career.

Carroll, John (1735–1815) First Roman Catholic bishop, first archbishop of Baltimore, and founder of the Roman Catholic hierarchy in the United States. In 1791, founded Georgetown University.

Census Act (March 1, 1790) Provided for the collection of census information. The first census, in August of 1790, indicated over four million residents in the United States.

Chesapeake Incident Attack in 1807 by the British ship *Leopard* on the American ship *Chesapeake* in American waters, nearly triggering war, as a result of public outcry. Jefferson responded with the passage of the Embargo Act of 1807.

Clark, William (1770–1838) Appointed by Thomas Jefferson as leader of the expedition to explore the Louisiana Purchase territories. Along with Captain Meriwether Lewis, he made his way to the Pacific Ocean and back to St. Louis.

Clinton, George (1739–1812) American soldier and pioneer. Served as the governor of New York and as the vice president of the United States under both Thomas Jefferson and James Madison.

Coke, Thomas (1747–1814) Father of Methodist Missions. Mostly remembered as the first bishop of the Methodist Episcopal Church in America.

Crockett, Davy (1786–1836) Frontiersman. Served under Jackson during the Creek Wars (1813–1814) and as a member of the Tennessee state legislature and the U.S. House of Representatives. Joined with the Texas forces in their fight for independence in the battle of the Alamo in 1836. Died at the Alamo on March 6, 1836.

Dartmouth College v. Woodward (1819) Supreme Court decision that prohibited states from interfering with the privileges granted to private corporations.

Davis, Captain John In February of 1821, Davis arguably became the first man to set foot on the continent of Antarctica.

Deism Enlightenment religious philosophy that had become popular with the leaders of the Revolutionary era, now being seen among ordinary citizens. Rejects divine revelation and holds that the workings of nature alone reveal God's design for the universe.

Democratic Party Political party formed in the 1820s under the direction of Andrew Jackson. Favored states' rights and a limited role for the federal government.

Denmark Vesey Conspiracy The most carefully devised slave revolt in which rebels planned to seize control of Charleston in 1822 and escape to freedom in Haiti, a free black republic. Other slaves betrayed them, leading to the execution of 35 slaves. Historians are now in debate over the accuracy of the actual conspiracy.

Dwight, Timothy (1752–1817) President of Yale University and famous author and educator.

Ellicott, General Andrew (1754–1820) A United States surveyor who helped map territories west of the Appalachians.

Embargo Act of 1807 Act passed by Congress prohibiting American ships from leaving port for any nation until Britain and France resumed trade with neutral shippers.

Equiano, Olaudah (1745–1797) An 18th-century African writer. Published books that furthered the abolitionist cause.

Era of Good Feelings (1817–1823) Ushered in the era of Republican rule.

Fanning, Edmund (1769–1841) Trader and explorer responsible for discovering Fanning Island in the South Pacific, which led to greater explorations of the region.

Federalists Supporters of Hamilton's program. The most fully integrated into the market economy and in control of it.

Federal Judiciary Act (September 22, 1789) Established a six-member Supreme Court, attorney general, 13 federal district courts, and three circuit courts.

Fletcher v. Peck Supreme Court decision of 1810 that overturned a state law by ruling that it violated a legal contract.

Fourier, Francois Marie Charles (1772–1837) A social scientist, reformer, and Utopian. Greatly influenced ideas of the day.

Franco-American Accord of 1800 Brought about an end to the Quasi-War and released the United States from its 1778 alliance with France.

Franklin, Benjamin (1706–1790) From electricity to politics, Franklin made his mark on America. Born January 17, 1706, eventually left his hometown and settled in Philadelphia, where he worked as an apprentice printer. Later bought the *Philadelphia Gazette*, lobbied for better living conditions, joined the Masons, helped stem fire outbreaks, published *Poor Richard's Almanac*, proved the existence of electricity, and then finally entered into politics. Became the ambassador to France and contributed greatly to the writing and ideas of the Declaration of Independence.

Fries, John (1750?–1818) Leader of the Fries' Rebellion in Pennsylvania. Opposed the federal property tax and gathered Pennsylvania Germans to fight the tax assessors. Authorities arrested and sentenced Fries to death, but the president later pardoned him in 1800.

Fulton, Robert (1765–1815) Engineer, inventor, and artist. Patented a machine for sawing marble and a machine for twisting hemp into rope, invented the submarine (1797–1806), and commissioned the first successful steamboat. Also designed other steamboats, a torpedo boat, a ferry, and built a steam frigate at the request of the government. Author of *A Treatise on the Improvement of Canal Navigation* (1796).

Gabriel's Rebellion Ultimately unsuccessful rebellion of a thousand slaves for an attack on Richmond in 1800, organized by Gabriel Prosser, a slave preacher and blacksmith.

Gaillard, Peter (1783–1843) Patented the first horse-drawn mower in 1812.

Gallaudet, Thomas Hopkins (1787–1851) An educator. Studied at Trinity College and served as the Head of the Columbia Institution for the Deaf and Dumb in Washington, D.C. Made important progress in the education of the handicapped. Gallaudet's father, Thomas, first taught the deaf in America.

Graham, Charles In 1822, patented false teeth.

Hamilton, Alexander (1755 or 1757–1804) Served as a secretary to Washington during the Revolution. Worked out the problems in the Articles of Confederation and suggested a plan for a stronger central government. Later contributed to the Federalist Papers and assisted during the ratification of the Constitution. Washington appointed Hamilton as the first U.S. secretary of the Treasury.

Handsome Lake (1735–1815) A Seneca religious leader of the Iroquois people. Encouraged the adoption of some European-style customs, yet preached the preservation of Native American heritage.

Hicks, Elias (1748–1830) A Quaker preacher. Worked as a farmer and carpenter in New York. Became well-known among Quakers nationwide; instituted a liberal element within the Society of Friends, with followers named Hicksites.

Hopkins, Samuel (1721–1803) A Congregational theologian. Authored the *System of Doctrines Contained in Divine Revelation, Explained and Defended* (2 vols., 1793).

Hopper, Isaac Tatem (1771–1852) Abolitionist and member of the Society of Friends. Played a key role in the Underground Railroad.

Horseshoe Bend, Battle of (March 29, 1814) Battle on the Tallapoosa River in Alabama, in which Andrew Jackson defeated the Creek Indians.

Humphreys, David (1752–1818) Revolutionary officer and diplomat. Imported first Merino sheep to the United States (1801). Author of *A Poem on the Happiness of America* (1786).

Humphreys, Joshua (1751–1838) Ship designer. Appointed as the first United States naval constructor. Designs included the *President, United States, Chesapeake, Constitution,* ships that were instrumental during the War of 1812.

Indian Removal Act (1830) President Andrew Jackson's Congressional measure that authorized to reinstate land cessions directly with eastern tribes. Allowed for the removal of Southeastern Indians to territory west of the Mississippi.

Jackson, Andrew (1767–1845) Seventh president of the United States (1828 and 1832). Served during the American Revolution, served as a United States senator and judge, served as the governor of Florida, became major general of the Tennessee militia (1820), and became the major general in the regular army after defeating the Creek Indians at Horseshoe Bend in 1814. His defense of New Orleans against the British made him a hero in the War of 1812. Waged campaigns against the Seminole Indians. His Indian removal Act forced thousands of Native Americans to lands in Oklahoma.

Jay, John (1745–1829) Jurist and statesman. Served as a member of the Continental Congress, as minister to Spain, and as one of the commissioners to negotiate peace in Paris. He wrote the *Federalist* with Hamilton and Madison, served as the first chief justice of the Supreme Court, negotiated the Jay Treaty with Great Britain, and served as governor of New York from 1795 to 1801.

Jay's Treaty Treaty with Britain negotiated in 1794, in which the United States made major concessions to avert a war over the British seizure of American ships.

Johnson, Reverend Thomas With his wife, founded the Shawnee Methodist Mission, the largest and historically most important of all the Kansas missions, on the site of present-day Turner (part of Greater Kansas City).

Judiciary Act of 1789 Act of Congress that implemented the judiciary clause of the Constitution. Established the Supreme Court and a system of lower federal courts.

Judiciary Act of 1801 Enlarged the judiciary and filled it with Adams's appointees. The Republican Congress appealed it. A conflict ensued, which resulted in *Marbury v. Madison* in 1803.

Key, Francis Scott (1779–1843) A lawyer. While watching the bombardment of Fort McHenry by the British, sighted the American flag still flying over the fort. Then penned *The Star Spangled Banner* on the back of an envelope. Went back to his law practice and wrote no other poetry of note.

Land Ordinance of 1785 Act passed by Congress under the Articles of Confederation that created the grid system of surveys by which all subsequent public land became available for sale.

Leavenworth, Colonel Henry (1783–1834) Established Fort Leavenworth, first known as Cantonment Leavenworth, on the Missouri River's right bank of Salt Creek. The cantonment served as an army post to protect the Western frontier and travelers on the Santa Fe Trail.

Lewis, Meriwether (1774–1809) Served as a captain in the Whiskey Rebellion and Northwest campaigns, and as private secretary to President Thomas Jefferson, who appointed him to explore lands gained by the Louisiana Purchase.

Long, Stephen H. (1784–1864) In 1819, Long's party explored portions of Kansas.

Louisiana Purchase (1803) purchase of territory from the French that doubled the size of the United States. President Thomas Jefferson purchased the land from Napoleon for $15 million.

Macdonough, Commodore Thomas (1783–1825) Naval officer. Served with Decatur during the War with Tripoli and later commanded an American fleet on Lake Champlain (1812–1814), in which he defeated a superior British squadron at Plattsburg.

Macon, Nathaniel (1758–1837) A strong supporter of states' rights, a speaker of the House, and a United States senator. Strongly opposed the Alien and Sedition Acts and the Bank of the United States.

Madison, James (1751–1836) Fourth president of the United States. Played the leading role of the drafting of the Constitution and probably most deserves the title "father of the Constitution."

Major Ridge (1771–1839) A Cherokee leader. Led a wayward party in the signing of the Treaty of New Echota, effectively removing the Cherokees from their homelands. Fellow Cherokees assassinated him after arriving in Oklahoma.

Marbury v. Madison Supreme Court decision of 1803 that created the precedent of judicial review by ruling as unconstitutional part of the Judiciary Act of 1789.

Marshall, John (1755–1835) Served in the Continental Army through the Revolution. John Adams later appointed him as the United States secretary of State (1800–1801) and chief justice of the United States Supreme Court (1801–1835). His decisions established the fundamental doctrines of American constitutional laws. Generally considered to be the greatest chief justice in the history of the Supreme Court.

McClary, John United States Army Lieutenant. Took possession of Fort St. Stephens from the Spanish, and the United States flag is raised for the first time on soil that would eventually belong to Alabama.

McCulloch v. Maryland (1819) Unanimous court decision in which the Congress was authorized to charter a national bank and thereby regulate the nation's finances and currency.

McGillivray, Alexander (1759–1793) Creek Indian chief educated in Charleston and Savannah. Played the Spanish against the Americans in hope of obtaining the best deal for his people. Worked to establish a Creek national identity and centralized leadership as a means for resisting American encroachments on Creek territory.

Missouri Compromise Sectional compromise in Congress in 1820 that admitted Missouri to the Union as a slave state and Maine as a free state. Also prohibited slavery in the northern Louisiana Purchase territory.

Monroe Doctrine (December 1823) Doctrine declared by President James Monroe to Congress that America is not to be considered for future colonization by any European power and that the United States would not interfere in the internal affairs of European nations.

Morse, Samuel F. B. (1791–1872) Inventor and artist. Most famous for his invention of the telegraph and Morse code. Also introduced the daguerreo-type to the United States.

Murray, Judith Sargent (1751–1820) Author of feminist work, *On the Equality of the Sexes,* which strongly advocated equal educational opportuni-ties for women. Regularly contributed to the *Massachusetts Magazine.*

Newbold, Charles (1764–1835) Patented the first cast-iron plow in 1797.

New Orleans, Battle of (January of 1815) Decisive American battle of the War of 1812 and a victory over British troops. Troops fought the battle two weeks after the war's end.

Niles, Hezekiah (1777–1839) Journalist and editor for the Baltimore *Evening Post.* Founded *Niles' Weekly Register* in 1811. Greatly influenced peo-ple during his time, opposed Jackson, and advocated a protective tariff.

Northwest Ordinance of 1787 Legislation that prohibited slavery in the Northwest Territories and that provided the model of the incorporation of future territories into the Union.

Osceola (1803–1838) Predominant Seminole leader opposed to Indian removal. Led in the Second Seminole War. His name derives from Asiyahola, the cry made during the ceremonial black drink rituals.

Palmer, Captain Nathaniel In 1820, discovered the continent of Antarctica.

Pan-Indian military resistance movement Movement calling for the political and cultural unification of Indian tribes during the late 18th and early 19th centuries.

Pike, Lieutenant Zebulon (1779–1813) Army officer and explorer. Dis-covered a peak in Colorado, now named Pike's Peak. Also pioneered the Santa Fe Trail.

Pinckney, Charles (1757–1824) Represented South Carolina at the Consti-tutional Convention. Later served as the South Carolina governor for four terms, as well as in many other governmental positions.

Poe, Edgar Allen (1809–1849) Poet and author. Published many well-known stories. Lived in poverty and despondency for most of his life. Some of his most famous stories are included in his *Tales of the Grotesque and Arabesque* (1839).

Put-in-Bay, Battle of American naval victory over Britain during the War of 1812. Denied the British the control over the Great Lakes Region.

Quasi-War (1797–1800) Undeclared naval war in the Caribbean between the United States and France.

Quock Walker decision (April 1783) Decision resulting in the abolishing of slavery in Massachusetts.

Republican Jeffersonian Party Political party headed by Thomas Jefferson that formed in opposition to the financial and diplomatic policies of the Federalist Party. Republicans favored limiting the national government and placing the interests of farmers over commercial and financial groups.

Residency Act (July 10, 1790) Act passed by the House of Representatives that locates the national capital on a 10-square-mile site along the Potomac River, with President George Washington choosing the exact location.

Ross, Betsy (Elizabeth Griscom Ross) (1752–1836) Believed to have been commissioned by George Washington, Robert Morris, and George Ross to create the new stars and stripes flag.

Ross, John (Indian name, Coowescoowee) (1790–1866) Democratically elected Cherokee Indian chief, who resisted the policy of moving the Cherokee nation into Indian Territory but eventually led them west.

Roulstone, George (1767–1804) Editor of the first newspaper in Tennessee, the *Knoxville Gazette.*

Rowson, Susannah (1762–1824) Wrote *Charlotte, A Tale of Truth.*

Rush, Benjamin (1746–1813) Physician and political leader. Belonged to the Pennsylvania convention to ratify the Constitution, established the first dispensary in the United States (1786), served as treasurer of the United States Mint, and founded the first American Antislavery Society.

Rush-Bagot Agreement (1817) Treaty between the United States and Britain that effectively demilitarized the Great Lakes. The treaty limited the number of ships each country could station on them.

Sacagawea (ca. 1787–ca. 1812) Shoshone Indian. Became the interpreter for the Lewis and Clark Expedition.

Second Bank of the United States National bank chartered by Congress in 1816 with extensive regulatory powers over currency and credit.

Second Great Awakening Series of religious revivals during the early 19th century characterized by great emotionalism in large public meetings.

Sequoyah (ca. 1767–1843) Cherokee blacksmith who developed the Cherokee syllabary.

Sevier, John (1745–1815) One of Tennessee's most illustrious citizens. Served as the first and only governor of the aborted state of Franklin and served as the governor of Tennessee for six terms. Also rose to the rank of general in the North Carolina militia. Died in 1815 while trying to ascertain the accurate Creek boundary in Alabama.

Shay's Rebellion (Shay's Uprising) (1786–1787) Rebellion in western Massachusetts. Daniel Shay led fellow farmers in an uprising to protest high taxes and debtor's prisons. Eventually squelched, the rebellion played a pivotal role in the beginnings of the Constitutional Convention in 1787.

Sibley, George C. Completed an official survey of the Appalachian Trail in 1825.

Slater, Samuel (1768–1835) Contributed to the building of the first successful water-powered textile mill in America.

Spencer, Peter (1782–1843) Born a slave, founder of the first independent black Christian denomination in the United States in 1812, the African Union Methodist Protestant Church (AUMPC).

Stevens, John (1749–1838) Inventor and shipbuilder. Greatly influenced the inception of the U.S. system of patent laws in 1790. He built the *Phoenix* and sent it from New York to Philadelphia, the first successful steamboat trip on the ocean.

Sublette, William L. (1779–1845) Took the first wagons along a route (Oregon Trail) to the Rocky Mountains.

Tariff Act of 1789 First tariff passed by Congress, intended to raise revenue and not to protect American manufacturers from foreign competition.

Tecumseh (1768–1813) Shawnee Indian and one of their most famous chiefs. Tecumseh's younger brother, Tenskwatawa, helped him unite Indians to stave off white customs and products. His defeat at the Battle of Tippecanoe tremendously weakened Tecumseh's Confederation, and in 1813 Tecumseh died in battle. His death signified the end of the unified resistance.

Temperance Reform movement originating in the 1820s that sought to curtail the consumption of alcohol.

Tenskwatawa (1775–1836) A brother to Tecumseh, who led a religious movement in the Ohio Valley during the early 1800s. Taught that white Americans initiated all evil in the world and forbade his people to use European goods.

Thomson, Charles (1729–1824) Revolutionary patriot. Became the first secretary of the Continental Congress from 1774 to 1789.

Tonnage Act of 1789 Duty levied on the tonnage of incoming ships to U.S. ports. Favored American ships due to higher taxes on foreign-owned ships.

Trans-Continental Treaty of 1819 Treaty between the United States and Spain in which Spain ceded Florida to the United States, agreed to a boundary between the Louisiana Purchase territory and the Spanish Southwest, and surrendered all claims to the Pacific Northwest.

Treaty of Ghent Signed on Christmas Eve, 1814, treaty that officially ended the War of 1812.

Treaty of Greenville (1795) Treaty in which the United States government forced Native Americans in the Old Northwest to cede most of the present state of Ohio.

Treaty of Paris (September 3, 1783) Treaty between the United States and Britain that ended the Revolutionary War.

Treaty of San Lorenzo (Pickney's Treaty) (1795) Treaty between the United States and Spain, in which Spain recognized the 31st parallel as being the boundary between the United States and Spanish Florida.

United States Army The first army established by Congress on September 29, 1789. Consisted of a total of one thousand men.

Walker, David (1785–1830) Free African American. Published *Appeal to the Coloured Citizens of the World.*

War Hawks Members of Congress who adamantly pushed for a war against Britain. Led by Henry Clay of Kentucky and John C. Calhoun of South Carolina, they contributed to Madison's growing aggression toward Britain.

War of 1812 (June 1812–January 1815) A war fought between the United States and Britain mainly over British restrictions on American shipping. The war included three failed U.S. offensives against Canada.

Warren, John (1753–1815) Revolutionary surgeon. Founded Harvard Medical School.

Warren, John Collins (1778–1856) Surgeon and professor at Harvard Medical School and Massachusetts General Hospital, Boston. Well-known for being the first physician to use ether as anesthesia.

Washington, George (1732–1799) First president of the newly formed United States. Privately educated, initially worked as a surveyor in Virginia. Later commanded the Virginia troops, became a member of the Virginia House of Burgesses, led opposition to the British in his colony, member of the First and Second Continental Congresses, assumed command of all Continental armies in 1775, presided at the convention in Philadelphia (1787), and became unanimously elected as the first president of the United States under the new Constitution (1789) and reelected in 1793. Declined the offer of a third term and made his famous Farewell Speech in 1796.

Wayne, General Anthony (1745–1796) Revolutionary general, colonel in the Pennsylvania regiment in the Continental Army, placed in command at Ticonderoga, member from Georgia of the United States House of Representatives, major general in command of American troops at the Battle of Fallen Timbers, successfully negotiated the Treaty of Greenville in 1795.

Webster, Noah (1758–1843) Father of American Scholarship and Education. His spellers and dictionaries have made his name synonymous with "dictionary."

Whiskey Rebellion (1794) Armed uprising by farmers in Pennsylvania who attempted to prevent the collection of the excise tax on whiskey. Showed that the United States government would not hesitate to utilize military force to compel obedience.

Whitney, Eli (1765–1825) Inventor of the cotton gin (March 1794).

Wood, Jethro Patented the iron plow with interchangeable parts in 1819.

Wright, Frances "Fanny" (1795–1852) First American woman to speak publicly against slavery and for the equality of women. Later established Nashoba, a colony for free blacks near Memphis.

XYZ Affair Diplomatic incident in 1798 in which Americans were outraged by the demand of the French for a bribe as a condition for negotiating with American diplomats.

Bibliography

Abernethy, T. Perkins. *From Frontier to Plantation in Tennessee.* Chapel Hill: University of North Carolina Press, 1932

Abernethy, T. Perkins. *The South in the New Nation, 1789–1819.* Baton Rouge: Louisiana State University Press, 1961

Adams, John. *Rules and Regulations Respecting the Recruiting Service.* United States War Department, 1798. George Washington Papers, 1741–1799: Series 6. Military Papers. 1755–1798. Washington, DC: Library of Congress

Additional Rules and Regulations for Recruiting the Army. Broadside, Army Papers, Missouri Historical Society, St. Louis, 1814

Ahlstrom, Sydney E. *A Religious History of the American People.* New Haven, CT: Yale University Press, 1972

Alexander, John K. *Render Them Submissive: Responses to Poverty in Philadelphia, 1760–1800.* Amherst: University of Massachusetts Press, 1980

American State Papers, Miscellaneous. 2 vols. Washington, DC: Gales and Seaton, 1834

Andrews, William L., ed. *Sisters of the Spirit: Three Black Women's Autobiographies of the Nineteenth Century.* Bloomington: Indiana University Press, 1986

Appleby, Joyce. *Capitalism and a New Social Order: The Republican Vision of the 1790s.* New York: New York University Press, 1984

Appleby, Joyce. "Commercial Farming and the 'Agrarian Myth' in the Early Republic." *Journal of American History* 68 (March 1982): 833–849

Aron, Stephen. *How the West Was Lost: The Transformation of Kentucky from Daniel Boone to Henry Clay.* Baltimore, MD: Johns Hopkins University Press, 1996

Aron, Stephen. "Pioneers and Profiteers: Land Speculation and the Homestead Ethic in Frontier Kentucky." *Western Historical Quarterly* 23 (May 1992): 179–198

Ashworth, John. *Slavery, Capitalism, and Politics in the Antebellum Republic. Vol. 1: Commerce and Compromise, 1820–1850.* New York: Cambridge University Press, 1995

Bailyn, Bernard. *The Ideological Origins of the American Revolution.* Cambridge, MA: Belknap Press, 1992

Baker, Gordon Pratt. *Those Incredible Methodists: A History of the Baltimore Conference of the United Methodist Church.* Baltimore, MD: Commission on Archives and History, Baltimore Conference, 1972

Ball, Charles. *Slavery in the United States: A Narrative of the Life and Adventures of Charles Ball, a Black Man, Who Lived Forty Years in Maryland, South Carolina and Georgia, as a Slave under Various Masters, and was One Year in the Navy with Commodore Barney, During the Late War.* Lewistown, PA: J. W. Shugert, 1837

Barney, William L. *The Passage of the Republic: An Interdisciplinary History of Nineteenth-Century America.* Lexington, MA: D. C. Heath and Company, 1987

Barnhart, John D. *Valley of Democracy: The Frontier Versus the Plantation in the Ohio Valley, 1775–1818.* Bloomington: Indiana University Press, 1953

Baptist, Edward E. *Creating an Old South: Middle Florida's Plantation Frontier before the Civil War.* Chapel Hill: University of North Carolina Press, 2002

Basch, Norma. *Framing American Divorce: From the Revolutionary Generation to the Victorians.* Berkeley: University of California Press, 1999

Baseler, Marilyn C. *"Asylum for Mankind": America, 1607–1800.* Ithaca, NY: Cornell University Press, 1998

Bates, Frederick. *The Life and Papers of Frederick Bates.* Edited by Thomas Marshall. 2 vols. St. Louis: Missouri Historical Society, 1926

Baylor, Ronald H. *Race and Ethnicity in America: A Concise History.* New York: Columbia University Press, 2003

Beeman, Richard R. *The Evolution of the Southern Backcountry: A Case Study of Lunenburg County, Virginia, 1746–1832.* Philadelphia: University of Pennsylvania Press, 1984

Belue, Ted Franklin. *The Long Hunt: Death of the Buffalo East of the Mississippi.* Mechanicsburg, PA: Stackpole Books, 1996

Berkus, Catherine A. *Strangers and Pilgrims: Female Preaching in America, 1740–1845.* Chapel Hill: University of North Carolina Press, 2001

Berlin, Ira. *Generations of Captivity: A History of African-American Slaves.* Cambridge, MA: Harvard University Press, 2003

Berlin, Ira. *Many Thousands Gone: The First Two Centuries of Slavery in North America.* Cambridge, MA: Harvard University Press, 1998

Berthoff, Rowland. "Celtic Mist over the South." *Journal of Southern History* 52 (November 1986): 523–546

Bilhartz, Terry D. *Urban Religion and the Second Great Awakening: Church and Society in Early National Baltimore.* Rutherford, NJ: Fairleigh Dickinson University Press, 1986

Billington, Ray Allen. *America's Frontier Heritage.* New York: Holt, Rinehart, and Winston, 1966

Birkbeck, Morris. *Letters from Illinois.* London: Taylor and Hessey, 1818

Birkbeck, Morris. *Notes on a Journey in America.* London: Severn and Co., 1818

Birtle, Andrew J. "The Origins of the Legion of the United States." *Journal of Military History* 67 (October 2003): 1249–1262

Blane, William. *An Excursion Through the United States and Canada in the Years 1822 and 1823.* London: Baldwin, Craddock, and Joy, 1824

Blassingame, John W. *The Slave Community: Plantation Life in the Antebellum South,* rev. ed. New York: Oxford University Press, 1979

Blewett, Mary H. "Work, Gender and the Artisan Tradition in New England Shoemaking, 1780–1860." In Peter N. Stearns, ed. *Expanding the Past: A Reader in Social History,* 119–146. New York: New York University Press, 1988

Blumin, Stuart M. *The Emergence of the Middle Class: Social Experience in the American City, 1760–1900.* New York: Cambridge University Press, 1989

Bolster, W. Jeffrey. *Black Jacks: African American Seamen in the Age of Sail.* Cambridge, MA: Harvard University Press, 1997

Bolster, W. Jeffrey. "'To Feel Like a Man': Black Seamen in the Northern States, 1800–1860." *Journal of American History* 76 (March 1990): 1173–1199

Bolton, S. Charles. *Territorial Ambition: Land and Society in Arkansas, 1800–1840.* Fayetteville: University of Arkansas Press, 1993

Bordley, John B. *Essays and Notes on Husbandry and Rural Affairs,* 2nd ed. Philadelphia: Thomas Dobson, 1801

Bowling, Kenneth R., and Donald R. Kennon, eds. *Neither Separate nor Equal: Congress in the 1790s.* Athens: Ohio University Press, 2000

Boydston, Jeanne. *Home and Work: Housework, Wages, and the Ideology of Labor in the Early Republic.* New York: Oxford University Press, 1990

Boylan, Anne M. *The Origins of Women's Activism New York and Boston, 1797–1840.* Chapel Hill: University of North Carolina Press, 2002

Bradbury, John. "Travels in the Interior of America, 1809–1811." In *Early Western Travels, 1748–1846*, Volume 5. Edited by Reuben Gold Thwaites. 31 vols. Cleveland, OH: A. H. Clark, 1904

Branson, Susan. "Women and the Family Economy in the Early Republic: The Case of Elizabeth Meredith." *Journal of the Early Republic* 16 (Spring 1996): 47–71

Brasseaux, Carl A. *The Founding of New Acadia: The Beginnings of Acadian Life in Louisiana, 1765–1803*. Baton Rouge: Louisiana University Press, 1996

Braude, Ann. "Women's History *Is* Religious History." In Thomas A. Tweed, ed. *Retelling U. S. Religious History*, 7–107. Berkeley: University of California Press, 1997

Braund, Kathryn E. Holland. *Deerskins and Duffels: The Creek Indian Trade with Anglo-America, 1685–1815*. Lincoln: University of Nebraska Press, 1993

Breen, T. H. "'Baubles of Britain': The American and Consumer Revolutions of the Eighteenth Century." *Past and Present* 119 (May 1988): 73–104

Breen, T. H. *The Marketplace of Revolution: How Consumer Politics Shaped American Independence*. New York: Oxford University Press, 2004

Breen, T. H. "Narrative of Commercial Life: Consumption, Ideology, and Community on the Eve of the American Revolution." *William and Mary Quarterly*, 3rd ser. 50 (July 1993): 471–501

Brekus, Catherine A. *Strangers and Pilgrims: Female Preaching in America, 1740–1845*. Chapel Hill: University of North Carolina Press, 1998

Brewer, John, and Roy Porter, eds. *Consumption and the World of Goods*. New York: Routledge, 1993

Bridenbaugh, Carl. *The Colonial Craftsman*. New York: Oxford University Press, 1950

Brown, John. *Slave Life in Georgia: A Narrative of the Life, Sufferings, and Escape of John Brown, a Fugitive Slave, Now in England*. London: M. W. Watts, 1855

Bruchey, Stuart. *The Roots of American Economic Growth, 1607–1801: An Essay in Social Causation*. New York: Harper and Row, 1968

Bruegel, Martin. *Farm, Shop, Landing: The Rise of a Market Society in the Hudson Valley, 1780–1860*. Durham, NC: Duke University Press, 2002

Bullock, Steven C. *Revolutionary Brotherhood: Freemasonry and the Transformation of the American Social Order, 1730–1840*. Chapel Hill: University of North Carolina Press, 1996

Burgett, Bruce. *Sentimental Bodies: Sex, Gender, and Citizenship in the Early Republic*. Princeton, NJ: Princeton University Press, 1998

Burke, Martin J. *The Conundrum of Class: Public Discourse on the Social Order in America*. Chicago, IL: University of Chicago Press, 1995

Bushman, Richard L. "Markets and Composite Farms in Early America." *William and Mary Quarterly* 3rd ser. 55 (July 1998): 351–374

Bushman, Richard L. *The Refinement of America: People, Cities, Houses*. New York: Vintage, 1993

Butler, Jon. *Becoming America: The Revolution Before 1776*. Cambridge, MA: Harvard University Press, 2000

Calloway, Colin G. *The American Revolution in Indian Country: Crisis and Diversity in Native American Communities*. New York: Cambridge University Press, 1995

Calloway, Colin G. "Neither White nor Red: White Renegades on the American Indian Frontier." *Western Historical Quarterly* 17 (January 1986): 43–66

Calloway, Colin G. *New Worlds for All: Indians, Europeans, and the Remaking of Early America*. Baltimore, MD: Johns Hopkins University Press, 1997

Calloway, Colin G. *The World Turned Upside Down: Indian Voices from Early America*. Boston: Bedford/St. Martins, 1994

Carey, Henry Charles. *The Credit System in France, Great Britain, and the United States*. Philadelphia, PA: Carey, Lea, & Blanchard, 1838

Carr, Jacqueline Barbara. *After the Siege: A Social History of Boston, 1775–1800*. Boston, MA: Northeastern University Press, 2004

Carson, James Taylor. *Searching for the Bright Path: The Mississippi Choctaw from Prehistory to Removal*. Lincoln: University of Nebraska Press, 1999

Carson, W. Wallace. "Transportation and Traffic on the Ohio and Mississippi Before the Steamboat." *Mississippi Valley Historical Review* 7 (June 1920): 26–38

Carwardine, Richard. "The Second Great Awakening in Urban Centers: An Examination of Methodism and the 'New Measures.'" *Journal of American History* 59 (September 1972): 327–340

Cashin, Joan. *A Family Venture: Men and Women on the Southern Frontier*. New York: Oxford University Press, 1991

Caughey, John Walton. *McGillivray of the Creeks*. Norman: University of Oklahoma Press, 1938

Cayton, Andrew R. L. *Frontier Indiana*. Bloomington: Indiana University Press, 1996

Cayton, Andrew R. L. *Frontier Republic: Ideology and Politics in the Ohio Country, 1780–1825*. Kent, OH: Kent State University Press, 1986

Cayton, Andrew R. L., and Fredrika J. Teute, eds. *Contact Points: American Frontiers from the Mohawk Valley to the Mississippi, 1750–1830.* Chapel Hill: University of North Carolina Press, 1998

Cayton, Andrew R. L. and Stuart D. Hobbs, eds. *The Center of a Great Empire: The Ohio Country in the Early American Republic.* Athens: Ohio University Press, 2005

Cecil-Fronsman, Bill. *Common Whites: Class and Culture in Antebellum North Carolina.* Lexington: University Press of Kentucky, 1992

Chambers-Scheller, Virgina Lee. *Liberty a Better Husband: Single Women in America: The Generations of 1780–1840.* New Haven, CT: Yale University Press, 1984

Chaplin, Joyce E. *An Anxious Pursuit: Agricultural Innovation and Modernity in the Lower South, 1730–1815.* Chapel Hill: University of North Carolina Press, 1993

Cherokee Phoenix. 1828.

Chused, Richard H. *Private Acts in Public Places: A Social History of Divorce in the Formative Era of American Family Law.* Philadelphia: University of Pennsylvania Press, 1994

Clark, Christopher. *The Roots of Rural Capitalism: Western Massachusetts, 1780–1860.* Ithaca, NY: Cornell University Press, 1990

Clark, Christopher. "The View from the Farmhouse: Rural Lives in the Early Republic." *Journal of the Early Republic* 24 (Summer 2004): 198–207

Clark, Thomas D., and John D. W. Guice. *Frontiers in Conflict: The Old Southwest, 1795–1830.* Albuquerque: University of New Mexico Press, 1989

Cleaves, Freeman. *Old Tippecanoe: William Henry Harrison and His Time.* New York: Charles Scribner's Sons, 1939

Clemens, Paul G. E., and Lucy Simler, "Rural Labor and the Farm Household in Chester County, Pennsylvania, 1650–1820." In Stephen Innes, ed. *Work and Labor in Early America.* Chapel Hill: University of North Carolina Press, 1988

Cochran, Thomas G. *Frontiers of Change: Early Industrialism in America.* New York: Oxford University Press, 1981

Coffman, Edward M. *The Old Army: A Portrait of the American Army in Peacetime, 1784–1898.* New York: Oxford University Press, 1986

Cohen, Patricia Cline. *The Murder of Helen Jewett: The Life and Death of a Prostitute in Nineteenth-Century.* New York: Alfred A. Knopf, 1998

Columbian Centinel, July 13, 1803

Corbin, Henry, and Raphael P. Thian, eds. *Legislative History of the General Staff of the Army of the United States (Its Organizations, Duties, Pay, and Allowances), 1775–1901.* Washington, DC: Government Printing Office, 1901

Corfield, Penelope J., ed. *Language, History and Class.* Cambridge, MA: Basil Blackwell, 1991

Cott, Nancy. *The Bonds of Womanhood: "Woman's Sphere" in New England, 1780–1835,* 2nd ed. New Haven, CT: Yale University Press, 1997

Cott, Nancy. "Passionlessness: An Interpretation of Victorian Sexual Ideology, 1790–1850." *Signs: Journal of Women in Culture and Society* 4, no. 2 (1978): 219–236

Cott, Nancy. "Young Women in the Second Great Awakening in New England." *Feminist Studies* 3 (Fall 1975): 15–29

Crass, David Colin, Steven D. Smith, Martha A. Zierden, and Richard D. Brooks, eds. *The Southern Colonial Backcountry: Interdisciplinary Perspectives on Frontier Communities.* Knoxville: University of Tennessee Press, 1998

Cray, Robert E. Jr. *Paupers and Poor Relief in New York and its Rural Environs, 1700–1830.* Philadelphia, PA: Temple University Press, 1988

Cress, Lawrence Delbert. *Citizens in Arms: The Army and the Militia in American Society to the War of 1812.* Chapel Hill: University of North Carolina Press, 1982

Crozier, Alan. "The Scotch-Irish Influence on American English." *American Speech* 59 (Winter 1984): 310–331

Cusick, James G. *The Other War of 1812: The Patriot War and the American Invasion of Spanish East Florida.* Gainesville: University Press of Florida, 2003

Daniels, Roger. *Coming to America: A History of Immigration and Ethnicity in American Life.* New York: HarperCollins, 1990

Davidson, Victor. *History of Wilkinson County, Georgia.* Macon, GA: J. W. Burke, 1930

Davis, James. *Frontier Illinois.* Bloomington: Indiana University Press, 1998

Davis, Janet M. *The Circus Age: Culture and Society Under the American Big Top.* Chapel Hill: University of North Carolina Press, 2002

Davis, Lance E., Jonathan R. T. Hughes, and Duncan M. McDougall. *American Economic History: The Development of a National Economy.* Homewood, IL: R. D. Irwin, 1965

Davis, Susan G. *Parades and Power: Street Theater in Nineteenth-Century Philadelphia.* Philadelphia, PA: Temple University Press, 1986

Dawley, Alan. *Class and Community: The Industrial Revolution in Lynn.* Cambridge, MA: Harvard University Press, 1976

Dawson, John Charles. "The French in Alabama: The Vine and Olive Colony." *French Review* 18 (December 1944): 92–95

De Tocqueville, Alexis. *Democracy in America*. New York: Knopf, 1945 (Originally printed in 1835)

Demos, John. *Circles and Lines: The Shape of Early America*. Cambridge, MA: Harvard University Press, 2004

Dinnerstein, Leonard, and David M. Reimers. *Ethnic Americans: A History of Immigration and Assimilation*. New York: Dodd, Mead and Company, 1975

Donaldson, Gary A. *The History of African-Americans in the Military*. Malabar, FL: Krieger, 1991

Dooley, Patricia L. *The Early Republic: Primary Documents on Events from 1799 to 1820*. Westport, CT: Greenwood Press, 2004

Douglass, Frederick. *My Bondage and My Freedom*. New York: Miller, Orton & Mulligan, 1855

Douglass, Frederick. "To Our Oppressed Countrymen." January 2, 1848. Typescript. The Frederick Douglass Papers. Washington, DC: Library of Congress

Dowd, Gregory Evans. *A Spirited Resistance: The North American Indian Struggle for Unity, 1745–1815*. Baltimore, MD: Johns Hopkins University Press, 1992

Drake, Samuel Gardner. *Biography and History of the Indians of North America*. Boston, MA: Antiquarian Institute, 1837

Drew, Benjamin. *A North-Side View of Slavery. The Refugee: or the Narratives of Fugitive Slaves in Canada. Related by Themselves, with an Account of the History and Condition of the Colored Population of Upper Canada*. Boston: J. P. Jewett and Co., 1856

Duane, William, ed. *Extracts from the Diary of Christopher Marshall 1774–1781*. Albany: *New York Times*, 1877

Duane, William. *A Handbook for Infantry: Containing the First Principles of Military Discipline*. Philadelphia, PA: Author, 1813

Dublin, Thomas, ed. *Farm to Factory: Women's Letters, 1830–1860*, 2nd ed. New York: Columbia University Press, 1993

Dublin, Thomas. *Immigrant Voices: New Lives in America, 1773–1986*. Urbana: University of Illinois Press, 1993

Dublin, Thomas. *Women at Work: The Transformation of Work and Community in Lowell, Massachusetts, 1826–1860*. New York: Columbia University Press, 1979

Dunaway, Wilma. "Rethinking Cherokee Acculturation: Women's Resistance to Agrarian Capitalism and Cultural Change, 1800–1838." *American Indian Culture and Research Journal* 21 (1997): 155–192

Dunaway, Wilma A. *The First American Frontier: Transition to Capitalism in Southern Appalachia, 1700–1860*. Chapel Hill: University of North Carolina Press, 1996

Dunn, Richard S. "After Tobacco: The Slave Labour Pattern on a Large Chesapeake Grain-and-Livestock Plantation in the Early Nineteenth Century." In *The Early Modern Atlantic Economy*, eds. John J. McCusker and Kenneth Morgan, 344–363. Cambridge: Cambridge University Press, 2000

Dupree, Daniel S. *Transforming the Cotton Frontier: Madison County, Alabama, 1800–1840*. Baton Rouge: Louisiana State University Press, 1997

DuVal, Kathleen. "Debating Identity, Sovereignty, and Civilization: The Arkansas Valley After the Louisiana Purchase." *Journal of the Early Republic* 26 (Spring 2006): 25–58

DuVal, Kathleen. *The Native Ground: Indians and Colonists in the Heart of the Continent*. Philadelphia: University of Pennsylvania Press, 2006

Edmunds, R. David. *The Shawnee Prophet*. Lincoln: University of Nebraska Press, 1983

Edmunds, R. David. *Tecumseh and the Quest for Indian Leadership*. Boston, MA: Little, Brown and Company, 1984

Egerton, Douglass. *Gabriel's Rebellion: The Virginia Slave Conspiracies of 1800 and 1802*. Chapel Hill: University of North Carolina Press, 1993

Elaw, Zilpha. *Memoirs of the Life, Religious experience, Ministerial Travels and Labors of Mrs. Zilpha Elaw. Sisters of the Spirit*. Edited by William L. Andrews. Bloomington: Indiana University Press, 1986 (Orig. pub. 1846)

Elkins, Stanley, and Erik McKitrick. *The Age of Federalism: The Early American Republic, 1788–1800*. New York: Oxford University Press, 1993

Erickson, Charlotte. *Invisible Immigrants: The Adaptation of English and Scottish Immigrants in Nineteenth-Century America*. Coral Gables, FL: University of Miami Press, 1972

Eslinger, Ellen, ed. *Running Mad for Kentucky: Frontier Travel Accounts*. Lexington: University Press of Kentucky, 2004

Essah, Patience. *A House Divided: Slavery and Emancipation in Delaware, 1638–1865*. Charlottesville: University of Virginia Press, 1996

Estes, J. Worth. *Naval Surgeon: Life and Death at Sea in the Age of Sail*. Canton, MA: Science History Publications, 1998

Etchison, Nicole. *The Emerging Midwest: Upland Southerners and the Political Culture of the Old Northwest, 1787–1861*. Bloomington: Indiana University Press, 1996

Ethridge, Robbie. *Creek Country: The Creek Indians and their World*. Chapel Hill: University of North Carolina Press, 2003

Evans, Sara M. *Born for Liberty: A History of Women in America*, 2nd ed. New York: Simon & Schuster, 1997

Faler, Paul G. *Mechanics and Manufacturers in the Early Industrial Revolution*. Albany: State University of New York Press, 1981

Faragher, John Mack. *Daniel Boone: The Life and Legend of an American Pioneer*. New York: Henry Holt and Company, 1992

Faragher, John Mack. *Sugar Creek: Life on the Illinois Prairie*. New Haven, CT: Yale University Press, 1986

Finney, Charles G. *The Autobiography of Charles G. Finney*. Edited by Helen Wessel. Minneapolis, MN: Bethany House Publishers, 1977

Fiske, John. *The Critical Period of American History, 1783–1789*. Boston, MA: Houghton Mifflin, 1888

Fogleman, Aaron S. "From Slaves, Convicts, and Servants to Free Passengers: The Transformation of Immigration in the Era of the American Revolution." *Journal of American History* 85 (June 1998): 43–76

Foner, Eric. *Free Soil, Free Labor, Free Men: The Ideology of the Republican Party Before the Civil War*. New York: Oxford University Press, 1970

Foner, Eric. *Story of American Freedom*. New York: W. W. Norton, 1998

Foner, Philip S. *William Heighton: Pioneer Labor Leader of Jacksonian Philadelphia. With Selections from Heighton's Writings and Speeches*. New York: International Publishers, 1991

Ford, Paul Leicester, ed. *The Works of Thomas Jefferson*. New York: G. P. Putnam's Sons, 1892–1899

Formisano, Ronald P. *The Transformation of Political Culture: Massachusetts Parties, 1790s–1840s*. New York: Oxford University Press, 1984

Foster, A. Kristen. *Moral Visions and Material Ambitions: Philadelphia Struggles to Define the Republic, 1776–1836*. Lanham, MD: Lexington Books, 2004

Foster, Lawrence. *Women, Family and Utopia: Communal Experiments of the Shakers, the Oneida Community, and the Mormons*. Syracuse, NY: Syracuse University Press, 1991

Frank, Andrew K. *Creeks and Southerners: Biculturalism on the Early American Frontier*. Lincoln: University of Nebraska Press, 2005

Frank, Andrew K. "Taking the State Out: Seminoles and Creeks at a Transnational Moment." *Florida Historical Quarterly* 84 (Summer 2005): 10–27

Franklin, Benjamin. *Writings*. Edited by J. A. Leo Lemay. New York: Library of America, 1987

Freeman, Joanne B. *Affairs of Honor: National Politics in the New Republic*. New Haven, CT: Yale University Press, 2001

Frey, Sylvia, and Betty Wood. *Come Shouting to Zion: African American Protestantism in the American South and British Caribbean to 1830*. Chapel Hill: University of North Carolina Press, 1998

Fried, Marc. *The World of the Urban Working Class*. Cambridge, MA: Harvard University Press, 1973

Friend, Craig T. *Along the Maysville Road: The Early American Republic in the Trans-Appalachian West*. Knoxville: University of Tennessee Press, 2005

Friend, Craig T., ed. *The Buzzel About Kentuck: Settling the Promised Land*. Lexington: University Press of Kentucky, 1999

Friend, Craig T. "Merchants and Markethouses: Reflections on Moral Economy in Early Kentucky." *Journal of the Early Republic* 17 (Winter 1997): 553–574

Fruchtman, Jack Jr. *Atlantic Cousins: Benjamin Franklin and His Visionary Friends*. New York: Thunder's Mouth Press, 2005

Gemery, Henry A. "Disarray in the Historical Record: Estimates of Immigration to the United States, 1700–1860." Symposium on the Demographic History of the Philadelphia Region, 1600–1860. *Proceedings of the American Philosophical Society* 133, no. 2 (June 1989): 123–127

Gilbert, Bil. *God Gave Us This Country: Tekamthi and the First American Civil War*. New York: Atheneum, 1989

Gilje, Paul A. *Liberty on the Waterfront: American Maritime Culture in the Age of Revolution*. Philadelphia: University of Pennsylvania Press, 2004

Gilje, Paul, ed. *Wages of Independence: Capitalism in the Early American Republic*. Madison, WI: Madison House, 1997

Gilje, Paul A. *The Road to Mobocracy: Popular Disorder in New York City, 1763–1834*. Chapel Hill: University of North Carolina Press, 1987

Gilje, Paul A., and Howard B. Rock, eds. *Keepers of the Revolution: New Yorkers at Work in the Early Republic*. Ithaca, NY: Cornell University Press, 1992

Gillespie, Joanna Bowen. *The Life and Times of Martha Laurens Ramsay, 1759–1811*. Columbia: University of South Carolina Press, 2001

Gilmore, William J. *Reading Becomes a Necessity of Life: Material and Cultural Life in Rural New England, 1780–1835*. Knoxville: University of Tennessee Press, 1989

Goodfriend, Joyce D., and Claudia M. Christie, eds. *Lives of American Women: A History with Documents*. Boston: Little, Brown and Company, 1981

Grabbe, Hans-Jurgen. "European Immigration to the United States in the Early National Period, 1783–1820." Symposium on the Demographic History of the Philadelphia Region, 1600–1860. *Proceedings of the American Philosophical Society* 133, no. 2 (June 1989): 190–214

Green, James R., and Hugh Carter Donahue. *Boston's Workers: a Labor History*. Boston, MA: Trustees of the Public Library of the City of Boston, 1979

Green, Michael D. "The Expansion of European Colonization to the Mississippi Valley, 1780–1880." In Bruce G. Trigger and Wilcomb E. Washburn, eds. *The Cambridge History of the Native Peoples of the Americas: Volume 1: North America: Part 1*, 460–538. New York: Cambridge University Press, 1996

Green, Michael D. *The Politics of Indian Removal: Creek Government and Society in Crisis*. Lincoln: University of Nebraska Press, 1982

Griswold, Bert J., ed. *Fort Wayne, Gateway of the West, 1802–1813: Garrison Orderly Books; Indian Agency Account Book*. Indianapolis: Historical Bureau of the Indiana Library and Historical Department, 1927

Groneman, Carol, and Mary Beth Norton, eds. *"To Toil the Livelong Day": America's Women at Work, 1780–1980*. Ithaca, NY: Cornell University Press, 1987

Grubb, Farley. "The End of European Immigrant Servitude in the United States: An Economic Analysis of Market Collapse, 1772–1835." *Journal of Economic History* 54 (December 1994): 794–824

Gruenwald, Kim. *River of Enterprise: The Commercial Origins of Regional Identity in the Ohio Valley, 1790–1850*. Bloomington: Indiana University Press, 2002

Gudmestad, Robert H. *A Troublesome Commerce: The Transformation of the Interstate Slave Trade*. Baton Rouge: Louisiana State University Press, 2003

Guthman, William H. *March to Massacre, a History of the First Seven Years of the United States Army*. New York: McGraw Hill, 1975

Gutman, Herbert. *The Black Family in Slavery and Freedom, 1750–1925*. New York: Pantheon, 1976

Hackett, David G. *The Rude Hand of Innovation: Religion and Social Order in Albany, New York, 1652–1836*. New York: Oxford University Press, 1991

Hahn, Steven, and Jonathan Prude, eds. *The Countryside in the Age of Capitalist Transformation*. Chapel Hill: University of North Carolina Press, 1985

Hale, Sarah J. "Education." *Ladies Magazine* 1 (September 1828): 422–423

Hale, Sarah J. "Introduction." *Ladies Magazine* 1 (January 1828): 1–4

Hammon, Neal O., ed. *My Father Daniel Boone: The Draper Interviews with Nathan Boone*. Lexington: University Press of Kentucky, 1999

Hanger, Kimberly S. *Bounded Lives, Bounded Places: Free Black Society in Colonial New Orleans, 1769–1803*. Durham, NC: Duke University Press, 1997

Harper, R. Eugene. *The Transformation of Western Pennsylvania, 1770–1800*. Pittsburgh, PA: University of Pittsburgh Press, 1991

Harper, Robert Goodloe. *Observations on the North American Land Company*. London: H. L. Gallabin, 1796

Harris, Thaddeus. *Journal of a Tour into the Territory Northwest of the Allegheny Mountains*. Boston: Manning and Loring, 1805

Hassler, Warren W. Jr. *With Shield and Sword: American Military Affairs, Colonial Times to the Present*. Ames: Iowa State University Press, 1982

Hatch, Nathan O. *The Democratization of American Christianity*. New Haven, CT: Yale University Press, 1989

Hauptman, Laurence M., and L. Gordon McLester. *Oneida Indian Journal: From New York to Wisconsin, 1784–1860*. Madison: University of Wisconsin Press, 1999

Heidler, David S., and Jeanne T. Heidler. *Daily Life in the Early American Republic, 1790–1820: Creating a New Nation*. Westport, CT: Greenwood Press, 2004

Hempton, David. *Methodism: Empire of the Spirit*. New Haven, CT: Yale University Press, 2005

Henderson, Archibald. "The Creative Forces in Westward Expansion: Henderson and Boone." *American Historical Review* 20 (October 1914): 86–107

Henretta, James A. *The Evolution of American Society, 1700–1815. An Interdisciplinary Analysis*. Lexington, MA: Heath, 1973

Henretta, James A. "Families and Farms: Mentalité in Pre-Industrial America." *William and Mary Quarterly* 3rd ser. 35 (January 1978): 3–32

Herman, Daniel J. "The Other Daniel Boone: The Nascence of a Middle-Class Hunter Hero, 1784–1860." *Journal of the Early Republic* 18 (Autumn 1998): 429–457

Herndon, Ruth Wallis. *Unwelcome Americans: Living on the Margin in Early New England*. Philadelphia: University of Pennsylvania Press, 2001

Herring, Joseph B. *Kenekuck, the Kickapoo Prophet*. Lawrence: University Press of Kansas, 1988

Hessinger, Rodney. *Seduced, Abandoned, and Reborn: Visions of Youth in Middle-Class America, 1780–1850*. Philadelphia: University of Pennsylvania Press, 2005

Hill, Sarah H. *Weaving New Worlds: Southeastern Cherokee Women and Their Basketry.* Chapel Hill: University of North Carolina Press, 1997

Hinderaker, Eric, and Peter C. Mancall. *At the Edge of Empire: The Backcountry in British North America.* Baltimore, MD: Johns Hopkins University Press, 2003

Hinderaker, Eric. *Elusive Empires: Constructing Colonialism in the Ohio Valley, 1673–1800.* New York: Cambridge University Press, 1997

Hodges, Graham Russell. *Roots and Branch: African Americans in New York and East New Jersey, 1613–1863.* Chapel Hill: University of North Carolina Press, 1999

Hopper, Isaac T. *Narrative of the Life of Thomas Cooper.* New York: I. T. Hopper, 1832

Horsman, Reginald. *Expansion and American Indian Policy, 1783–1812.* Norman: University of Oklahoma Press, 1992

Horton, James Oliver, and Lois E. Horton. *In Hope of Liberty: Culture, Community, and Protest Among Northern Blacks, 1700–1860.* New York: Oxford University Press, 1997

Hurt, R. Douglas. *The Ohio Frontier: Crucible of the Old Northwest, 1720–1830.* Bloomington: Indiana University Press, 1996

Ignatiev, Noel. *How the Irish Became White.* New York: Routledge, 1995

Innes, Stephen, ed. *Work and Labor in Early America.* Chapel Hill: University of North Carolina Press, 1988

Isaac, Rhys. *The Transformation of Virginia, 1740–1790.* Chapel Hill: University of North Carolina Press, 1982

Isaac, Rhys, and Sean Wilentz. *The Kingdom of Matthias: A Story of Sex and Salvation in 19th-Century America.* New York: Oxford University Press, 1994

Isenberg, Andrew. "The Market Revolution in the Borderlands: George Champlin Sibley in Missouri and New Mexico, 1808–1826." *Journal of the Early Republic* 21 (Fall 2001): 445–465

Isenberg, Nancy, and Andrew Burstein, eds. *Moral Remains: Death in Early America.* Philadelphia: University of Pennsylvania Press, 2003

Jabour, Anya. *Marriage in the Early Republic: Elizabeth and William Wirt and the Companionate Ideal.* Baltimore, MD: Johns Hopkins University Press, 1998

Jackson, Andrew. *Correspondence of Andrew Jackson.* Edited by John Spencer Bassett. 7 vols. Washington, DC: Carnegie Institution of Washington, 1926–1935

Jacobson, Matthew Frye. *Whiteness of a Different Color: European Immigrants and the Alchemy of Race.* Cambridge, MA: Harvard University Press, 1998

Jefferson, Thomas. *Notes on the State of Virginia*. Richmond, VA: J. W. Randolph, 1853

Jensen, Laura. *Patriots, Settlers, and the Origins of American Social Policy*. New York: Cambridge University Press, 2003

Johnson, Paul E. *The Early American Republic, 1789–1829*. New York: Oxford University Press, 2006

Johnson, Paul E. *A Shopkeepers Millennium: Society and Revivals in Rochester, New York, 1815–1837*. New York: Hill and Wang, 1978

Johnson, Paul, and Sean Wilentz. *The Kingdom of Matthias: A Story of Sex and Salvation in Nineteenth-Century America*. New York: Oxford University Press, 1994

Johnson, Walter. *Soul by Soul: Life Inside the Antebellum Slave Market*. Cambridge, MA: Harvard University Press, 1999

Jones, Daniel P. *The Economic and Social Transformation of Rural Rhode Island, 1780–1850*. Boston, MA: Northeastern University Press, 1992

Jones, Jacqueline. *A Social History of the Laboring Classes: From Colonial Times to the Present*. Malden, MA: Blackwell Publishing, 1999

Jones, Jacqueline. *Labor of Love, Labor of Sorrow: Black Women, Work, and the Family, from Slavery to the Present*. New York: Basic Books, 1985

Juravich, Tom, William F. Hartford, and James R. Green. *Commonwealth of Toil: Chapters in the History of Massachusetts Workers and Their Unions*. Amherst: University of Massachusetts Press, 1996

Juster, Susan. *Disorderly Women: Sexual Politics and Evangelicalism in Revolutionary New England*. Ithaca, NY: Cornell University Press, 1994

Juster, Susan. "To Slay the Beast: Visionary Women in the Early Republic." In Susan Juster and Lisa MacFarlane, eds. *A Mighty Baptism: Race, Gender and the Creation of American Protestantism*, 19–37. Ithaca, NY: Cornell University Press, 1996

Kann, Mark E. *Punishment, Prisons, and Patriarchy: Liberty and Power in the Early American Republic*. New York: New York University Press, 2005

Kasserman, David Richard. *Fall River Outrage: Life, Murder, and Justice in Early Industrial New England*. Philadelphia: University of Pennsylvania Press, 1986

Kaster, Peter J. *The Nation's Crucible: The Louisiana Purchase and the Making of America*. New Haven, CT: Yale University Press, 2004

Kaufmann, Eric P. *The Rise and Fall of Anglo-America*. Cambridge, MA: Harvard University Press, 2004

Kazin, Michael. *The Populist Persuasion: An American History*. New York: Basic Books, 1995

Kelley, Mary. *Learning to Stand and Speak: Women, Education, and Public Life in America's Republic*. Chapel Hill: University of North Carolina Press, 2006

Kenny, Kevin. *The American Irish: A History*. New York: Longmans, 2000

Kerber, Linda K. *No Constitutional Right to Be Ladies: Women and the Obligations of Citizenship*. New York: Hill and Wang, 1998

Kerber, Linda K. "The Republican Mother: Women and the Enlightenment—An American Perspective." *American Quarterly* 28 (Summer 1976): 187–205

Kerber, Linda K. *Toward an Intellectual History of Women: Essays*. Chapel Hill: University of North Carolina Press, 1997

Kerber, Linda K. *Women of the Republic: Intellect and Ideology in Revolutionary America*. Chapel Hill: University of North Carolina Press, 1980

Kern, Louis J. *An Ordered Love: Sex Roles and Sexuality in Victorian Utopias—the Shakers, the Mormons and the Oneida Community*. Chapel Hill: University of North Carolina Press, 1981

Kidwell, Clara Sue. *Choctaws and Missionaries in Mississippi, 1818–1918*. Norman: University of Oklahoma Press, 1995

Kidwell, Clara Sue. "Choctaw Women and Cultural Persistence in Mississippi." In Nancy Shoemaker, ed. *Negotiators of Change: Historical Perspectives on Native American Women*, 115–134. New York: Routledge, 1995

Kierner, Cynthia A. *Beyond the Household: Women's Place in the Early South 1700–1835*. Ithaca, NY: Cornell University Press, 1998

Klein, Rachel N. *Unification of a Slave State: The Rise of the Planter Class in the South Carolina Backcountry, 1760–1808*. Chapel Hill: University of North Carolina Press, 1990

Klepp, Susan E. *Philadelphia in Transition: A Demographic History of the City and Its Occupational Groups, 1720–1830*. New York: Garland Publishing, 1989

Klinghoffer, Judith Apter, and Lois Elkis. "'The Petticoat Electors': Women's Suffrage in New Jersey, 1776–1807." *Journal of the Early Republic* 12 (Summer 1992): 159–193

Knouff, Gregory. "Soldiers and Violence on the Pennsylvania Frontier." In John Frantz and William Pencak, eds. *Beyond Philadelphia: The American Revolution in the Pennsylvania Hinterland*, 171–193, 243–251. University Park: Pennsylvania State University Press, 1998

Kohn, Richard H. *Eagle and Sword: The Federalists and the Creation of the Military Establishment in America, 1783–1802*. New York: Free Press, 1975

Kolchin, Peter. *American Slavery 1619–1877*. New York: Hill and Wang, 1993

Kornblith, Gary. "Becoming Joseph T. Buckingham: The Artisanal Struggle for Independence in Early-Nineteenth Century Boston." In Howard B. Rock, Paul A. Gilje, and Robert Asher. *American Artisans: Crafting Social Identity, 1750–1850*, 123–134. Baltimore, MD: Johns Hopkins University Press, 1995

Kukla, Jon. *A Wilderness So Immense: The Louisiana Purchase and the Destiny of America*. New York: Alfred A. Knopf, 2003

Kulikoff, Allan. *The Agrarian Origins of American Capitalism*. Charlottesville: University of Virginia Press, 1992

Kulikoff, Allan. *Tobacco and Slaves: The Development of Southern Cultures in the Chesapeake, 1680–1800*. Chapel Hill: University of North Carolina Press, 1986

Kulikoff, Allan. "Uprooted Peoples: Black Migrants in the Age of the American Revolution, 1790–1820." In Ira Berlin and Ronald Hoffman, eds. *Slavery and Freedom in the Age of the American Revolution*, 143–171. Charlottesville: University Press of Virginia, 1983

Lamoreaux, Naomi R. "Rethinking the Transition to Capitalism in the Early American Northeast." *Journal of American History* 90 (September 2003): 437–462

Larcom, Lucy. *A New England Girlhood*. Gloucester, MA: Peter Smith, 1973

Larkin, Jack. *The Reshaping of Everyday Life, 1790–1840*. New York: Harper & Row, 1988

Lasser, Carol. "Gender, Ideology, and Class in the Early Republic." *Journal of the Early Republic* 10 (Autumn 1990): 331–337

Latrobe, Benjamin. "Plan of the Camp, August 8, 1809." Journal. Latrobe Papers. Baltimore: Maryland Historical Society, August 23, 1806–August 8, 1809

Laurie, Bruce. *Artisans into Workers: Labor in Nineteenth-Century America*. Chicago: University of Illinois Press, 1997

Laurie, Bruce. *Working People of Philadelphia, 1800–1850*. Philadelphia, PA: Temple University Press, 1980

Lawrence, Anna M. "The Transatlantic Methodist Family: Gender, Revolution and Evangelicalism in America and England, ca. 1730–1815." PhD thesis. University of Michigan, 2004

Layer, Robert G. *Earnings of Cotton Mill Operatives, 1825–1914*. Cambridge, MA: Harvard University Press, 1955

Lee, Jarena. *Religious Experience and Journal of Mrs. Jarena Lee, Giving an Account of Her Call to Preach the Gospel, Revised and Corrected from the Original Manuscript, Written by Herself*. Philadelphia, PA: Author, 1849 (Digital Schomburg Collection, New York Public Library)

Letters Received by the Office of the Adjutant General, 1805–1821. Microcopy 566, Roll 27. National Archives, Washington, DC

Letters to the Secretary of War. Microcopy 370, Roll 1. National Archives, Washington, DC

Levesque, George A. *Black Boston: African American Life and Culture in Urban America, 1750–1860.* New York: Garland Publishing, 1994

Lewis, Jan. "The Republican Wife: Virtue and Seduction in the Early Republic." *William and Mary Quarterly* 3rd ser. 44 (October 1987): 689–710

Littlefield, Daniel C. *Rice and Slaves: Ethnicity and the Slave Trade in Colonial South Carolina.* Baton Rouge: Louisiana State University Press, 1981

Litwack, Leon F. *North of Slavery: The Negro in the Free States, 1790–1860.* Chicago: University of Chicago Press, 1961

Lockridge, Kenneth. "Land, Population, and the Evolution of New England Society, 1630–1790." *Past and Present* 39 (April 1968): 62–80

Louis-Philippe. *Diary of My Travels in America.* Translation by Stephen Becker. New York: Delacorte Press, 1977

Lubow, Lisa Beth. "From Carpenter to Capitalist: The Business of Building in Post-Revolutionary Boston." In Conrad Edick Wright and Kathryn P. Viens, eds. *Entrepreneurs: The Boston Business Community, 1700–1800*, 181–209. Boston: Massachusetts Historical Society and Northeastern University Press, 1997

Marchalonis, Shirley. *The Worlds of Lucy Larcom, 1824–1893.* Athens: University of Georgia Press, 1989

Martin, Joel. *Sacred Revolt: The Muskogees' Struggle for a New World.* Boston: Beacon Press, 1991

Martin, Scott C., ed. *Cultural Change and the Market Revolution in America, 1789–1860.* Lanham, MD: Rowman & Littlefield, 2005

Mason, Kathryn Harrod. *James Harrod of Kentucky.* Baton Rouge: Louisiana State University Press, 1951.

Mason, Mary. *The Young Housewife's Counsellor and Friend: Containing Directions in Every Department of Housekeeping, Including the Duties of Wife and Mother.* New York: E. J. Hale & Son, 1875

Mason, Matthew. *Slavery and Politics in the Early American Republic.* Chapel Hill: University of North Carolina Press, 2006

Mathews, Donald G. *Religion in the Old South.* Chicago: University of Chicago Press, 1977

McClure, David. *Diary of David McClure, Doctor of Divinity 1748–1820.* New York: Knickerbocker Press, 1899

McCoy, Drew. *The Elusive Republic: Political Economy in Jeffersonian America.* Chapel Hill: University of North Carolina Press, 1980

McCurry, Stephanie. *Masters of Small Worlds: Yeoman Households, Gender Relations, and the Political Culture of the Antebellum South Carolina Low Country.* New York: Oxford University Press, 1995

McGaw, Judith A. *Early American Technology: Making and Doing Things from the Colonial Era to 1850.* Chapel Hill: University of North Carolina Press, 1994

McLoughlin, William G. *Cherokee Renascence in the New Republic.* Princeton, NJ: Princeton University Press, 1986

McLoughlin, William G. *Cherokees and Missionaries, 1789–1838.* New Haven, CT: Yale University Press, 1984

McMichael, Andrew. *Atlantic Loyalties: Americans in Spanish West Florida, 1785–1810.* Athens: University of Georgia Press, 2008

McMillen, Sally G. *Southern Women: Black and White in the Old South,* 2nd ed. Wheeling, IL: Harlan Davidson, 2002

Memoire of Old Elizabeth, a Coloured Woman. Philadelphia, PA: Collins Printer, 1863

Merrell, James H. *The Indian's New World: Catawbas and Their Neighbors from European Contact Through the Era of Removal.* New York: W. W. Norton, 1989

Merrill, Michael, and Sean Wilentz, eds. *The Key of Liberty: The Life and Democratic Writings of William Manning, "A Laborer," 1747–1814.* Cambridge, MA: Harvard University Press, 1993

Mesick, Jane Louise. *The English Traveller in America, 1785–1835.* New York: Columbia University Press, 1922

Methodist Conference. *American Discipline.* 1780

Miller, Marion Mills, ed. *Great Debates in American History.* 14 vols. New York: Current Literature Publishing Company, 1913

Millett, Allen R. *Semper Fidelis, the History of the United States Marine Corps.* New York: Free Press, 1991

Millett, Allan R., and Peter Maslowski. *For the Common Defense: A Military History of the United States of America.* New York: Free Press, 1984

Mitchell, Robert D., ed. *Appalachian Frontiers: Settlement, Society, & Development in the Preindustrial Era.* Lexington: University Press of Kentucky, 1991

Mitchell, Robert D. *Commercialism and Frontier: Perspectives on the Early Shenandoah Valley.* Charlottesville: University Press of Virginia, 1977

Mohl, Raymond A. "Humanitarianism in the Preindustrial City: The New York Society for the Prevention of Pauperism, 1817–1823." *Journal of American History* 57 (December 1970): 576–599

Montgomery, David. "The Working Classes of the Pre-Industrial American City, 1780–1830." *Labor History* 9 (Winter 1968): 3–22

"Monthly Register." *The New York Magazine, or Literary Repository* 4 (September 1793): 574

Moore, John Hebron. *The Emergence of the Cotton Kingdom in the Old Southwest: Mississippi, 1770–1860.* Baton Rouge: Louisiana State University Press, 1988

Moquin, Wayne, ed. *Great Documents in American Indian History.* Westport, CT: Praeger, 1973

Morris, Christopher. *Becoming Southern: The Evolution of a Way of Life. Warren County and Vicksburg, Mississippi, 1760–1860.* New York: Oxford University Press, 1995

Murphy, Teresa Anne. *Ten Hours' Labor: Religion, Reform, and Gender in Early New England.* Ithaca, NY: Cornell University Press, 1992

Mustafa, Sam A. *Merchants and Migration: Germans and Americans in Connection, 1776–1835.* Burlington, VT: Ashgate, 2001

Nash, Gary B. *Forging Freedom: The Formation of Philadelphia's Black Community, 1720–1840.* Cambridge, MA: Harvard University Press, 1988

Nash, Gary B. *The Urban Crucible: The Northern Seaports and the Origins of the American Revolution.* Cambridge, MA: Harvard University Press, 1986

Nettels, Curtis P. *The Emergence of a National Economy, 1775–1815.* Armonk, NY: M. E. Sharpe, 1989, 1962

Newman, Simon P. *Embodied History: The Lives of the Poor in Early Philadelphia.* Philadelphia: University of Pennsylvania Press, 2003

Newman, Simon P. *Parades and the Politics of the Street: Festive Culture in the Early American Republic.* Philadelphia: University of Pennsylvania Press, 1997

Nichols, David. *Red Gentlemen and White Savages: Indians, Federalists, and the Search for Order on the American Frontier.* Charlottesville: University of Virginia Press, 2008

Nichols, Roger L. *General Henry Atkinson: A Western Military Career.* Norman: University of Oklahoma Press, 1965

Nobles, Gregory. *American Frontiers: Cultural Encounters and Continental Conquest.* New York: Hill and Wang, 1997

Nolt, Steven M. *Foreigners in Their Own Land: Pennsylvania Germans in the Early Republic.* University Park: Pennsylvania State University Press, 2002

North, Douglass C. *The Economic Growth of the United States, 1790–1860*. Upper Saddle River, NJ: Prentice-Hall, 1961

Northup, Solomon. *Twelve Years a Slave: Narrative of Solomon Northup, a Citizen of New York, Kidnapped in Washington City in 1841, and Rescued in 1853*. Cincinnati, OH: Henry W. Derby, 1853

Norton, Mary Beth. *Liberty's Daughters: The Revolutionary Experience of American Women, 1750–1800*. Boston, MA: Little, Brown, 1980

O'Brien, Michael Joseph, ed. *The Irish in America: Immigration, Land, Probate, Administrations, Birth, Marriage and Burial Records of the Irish in America in and about the Eighteenth Century*. Baltimore, MD: Genealogical Publishing Company, 1965

Offley, G. W. *A Narrative of the Life and Labors of the Rev. G.W. Offley, a Colored Man, Local Preacher and Missionary; Who Lived Twenty-Seven Years at the South and Twenty-Three at the North; Who Never Went to School a Day in His Life, and Only Commenced to Learn His Letters When Nineteen Years and Eight Months Old; The Emancipation of His Mother and Her Three Children; How He Learned to Read While Living in a Slave State, and Supported Himself from the Time He Was Nine Years Old Until He Was Twenty-One*. Hartfot, CT: [s.n.], 1859

Osterud, Nancy Grey. *Bonds of Community: The Lives of Farm Women in Nineteenth-Century New York*. Ithaca, NY: Cornell University Press, 1991

Owsley, Frank. *Plain Folk of the Old South*. New York: Quadrangle Books, 1965. (Originally published 1949)

Pasley, Jeffrey L., Andrew W. Robertson, and David Waldstreicher. *Beyond the Founders: New Approaches to the Political History of the Early Republic*. Chapel Hill: University of North Carolina Press, 2004

Pennsylvania Gazette. 1791–1799

Perdue, Theda. *"Mixed Blood" Indians: Racial Construction in the Early South*. Athens: University of Georgia Press, 2003

Perdue, Theda. *Cherokee Women: Gender and Culture Change, 1700–1835*. Lincoln: University of Nebraska Press, 1998

Perdue, Theda. *Slavery and the Evolution of Cherokee Society, 1540–1866*. Knoxville: University of Tennessee Press, 1979

Perkins, Elizabeth. *Border Life: Experience and Memory in the Revolutionary Ohio Valley*. Chapel Hill: University of North Carolina Press, 1998

Peskin, Lawrence A. *Manufacturing Revolution: The Intellectual Origins of Early American Industry*. Baltimore, MD: Johns Hopkins University Press, 2003

Pessen, Edward. *Jacksonian America: Society, Personality, and Politics*, rev. ed. Homewood, IL: Dorsey Press, 1978

Phillips, Christopher. *Freedom's Port: The African American Community of Baltimore, 1790–1860*. Urbana: University of Illinois Press, 1997

Pickard, Kate E. R. *The Kidnapped and the Ransomed. Being the Personal Recollections of Peter Still and his Wife "Vina," after Forty Years of Slavery*. Syracuse, NY: W. T. Hamilton, 1856

Prucha, Francis Paul, ed. *Cherokee Removal: The William Penn Essays and Other Writing*. Knoxville: University of Tennessee Press, 1981

Prucha, Francis Paul. *The Sword of the Republic: The United States Army on the Frontier, 1783–1834*. New York: Macmillan, 1969

"Queries Respecting the Slavery and Emancipation of Negroes in Massachusetts, Proposed by the Hon. Judge Tucker of Virginia, and Answered by the Rev. Dr. Belknap. Williamsburg, Virginia, January 24, 1795." In *Collections of the Massachusetts Historical Society, for the year M, DCC, XCV*, 4: 191–211. Boston, MA: Samuel Hall, 1795

Raboteau, Albert J. *Slave Religion: The "Invisible Institution" in the Antebellum South*. New York: Oxford University Press, 1978

Rahe, Paul. *Republics Ancient and Modern: Classical Republicanism and the American Revolution*. 2 vols. Chapel Hill: University of North Carolina Press, 1994

Reese, William S. *The First Hundred Years of Printing in British North America: Printers and Collectors: From the Proceedings of the American Antiquarian Society*, Volume 99, Part 2. Worcester, MA: American Antiquarian Society, 1989

Register of Enlistments, 1798–1815. Microcopy 233. Washington, DC: National Archives,

Resch, John. *Suffering Soldiers: Revolutionary War Veterans, Moral Sentiment, and Political Culture in the Early Republic*. Amherst: University of Massachusetts Press, 2000

Richardson, Harry V. *Dark Salvation: The Story of Methodism as It Developed Among Blacks in America*. New York: Anchor Books/Doubleday, 1976

Richardson, James Daniel. *A Compilation of the Messages and Papers of the Presidents, 1789–1897*, Washington, DC: U.S. Government Printing Office, 1897

Richter, Daniel K. *Facing East from Indian Country: A Native History of Early America*. Cambridge, MA: Harvard University Press, 2001

Rigsby, Allen. Thomas Adams Smith Papers, 1809. Western Historical Manuscript Collection. Kansas City: University of Missouri Archives

Rischin, Moses, ed. *Immigration and the American Tradition*. Indianapolis, IN: Bobbs-Merrill Company, 1976

Rider, Alexander. "Camp Meeting" and "Camp-Meeting," Harry T. Peters Collection. Smithsonian Institution, Washington, DC

Roberts, Mary Louise. "*True Womanhood* Revisited." *Journal of Women's History* 14, 1 (2002): 150–155

Rock, Howard B. *Artisans of the New Republic: The Tradesmen of New York City in the Age of Jefferson*. New York: New York University Press, 1979

Rock, Howard B., ed. *New York City Artisan, 1789–1825: A Documentary History*. Albany: State University of New York, 1989

Rock, Howard B., Paul A. Gilje, and Robert Asher, eds. *American Artisans: Crafting Social Identity, 1750–1850*. Baltimore, MD: Johns Hopkins University Press, 1995

Rogers, Daniel. "Republicanism: The Career of a Concept." *Journal of American History* 79 (June 192): 11–38

Rohrbough, Malcolm. *The Land Office Business: The Settlement and Administration of American Public Lands, 1789–1837*. Belmont, CA: Wadsworth, 1990a

Rohrbough, Malcolm. *The Trans-Appalachian Frontier: People, Societies, and Institutions, 1775–1850*. Belmont, CA: Wadsworth, 1990b

Rollings, Williard H. *The Osage: An Ethnohistorical Study of Hegemony on the Prairie-Plains*. Columbia: University of Missouri Press, 1992

Romans, Bernard. *A Concise Natural History of East and West Florida*. Gainesville: University of Florida Press, 1962 (Reprint of 1775 edition)

Rorabaugh, W. J. *The Alcoholic Republic: An American Tradition*. New York: Oxford University Press, 1979

Rorabaugh, W. J. *The Craft Apprentice: From Franklin to the Machine Age in America*. New York: Oxford University Press, 1986

Roth, Randolph A. *The Democratic Dilemma: Religion, Reform, and the Social Order in the Connecticut River Valley of Vermont, 1791–1850*. New York: Cambridge University Press, 1987

Rothman, Adam. *Slave Country: American Expansion and the Origins of the Deep South*. Cambridge, MA: Harvard University Press, 2005

Rothman, David J. *The Discovery of the Asylum: Social Order and Disorder in the New Republic*. Boston, MA: Little, Brown and Company, 1971

Rothman, Joshua D. *Notorious in the Neighborhood: Sex and Families Across the Color Line in Virginia, 1787–1861*. Chapel Hill: University of North Carolina Press, 2003

Rowe, Mary Ellen. *Bulwark of the Republic: The American Militia in Antebellum West*. Westport, CT: Praeger, 2003

Ruether, Rosemary Radford, and Rosemary Skinner Keller, eds. *Women and Religion in America, Volume 1: The Nineteenth Century: A Documentary History.* Cambridge, MA: Harper & Row, 1981

Ryan, Mary P. *Cradle of the Middle Class: The Family in Oneida County, New York, 1790–1865.* New York: Cambridge University Press, 1981

Ryan, Mary P. "A Women's Awakening: Evangelical Religion and the Families of Utica, New York, 1800–1840." *American Quarterly* 30 (Winter 1978): 602–623

Saunt, Claudio. *A New Order of Things: Property, Power, and the Transformation of the Creek Indians, 1733–1816.* New York: Cambridge University Press, 1999

Schechter, Stephen L., and Wendell Tripp, eds. *The World of the Founders: New York Communities in the Federal Period.* Albany: New York Commission on the Bicentennial of the U.S. Constitution, 1990

Schloesser, Pauline E. *The Fair Sex: White Women and Racial Patriarchy in the Early American Republic.* New York: New York University Press, 2002

Schultz, Ronald. *The Republic of Labor: Philadelphia Artisans and the Politics of Class, 1720–1830.* New York: Oxford University Press, 1993

Scott, Paula A. *Growing Old in the Early Republic: Spiritual, Social, and Economic Issues, 1790–1830.* New York: Garland Publishing, 1997

Sedgwick, Catharine M. "Diary Entry May, 18, 1828." In Nancy Woloch, ed. *Early American Women: A Documentary History 1600–1900*, 2nd ed. 163–165. Belmont, CA: Wadsworth, 1997

Sellers, Charles. *The Market Revolution.* New York: Oxford University Press, 1991

Shackel, Paul A. *Culture Change and the New Technology: An Archaeology of the Early American Industrial Era.* New York: Plenum, 1996

Sheehan, Bernard W. *Seeds of Extinction: Jeffersonian Philanthropy and the American Indian.* Chapel Hill: University of North Carolina Press, 1973

Shelton, Cynthia J. *The Mills of Manayunk: Industrialization and Social Conflict in the Philadelphia Region, 1787–1837.* Baltimore, MD: Johns Hopkins University Press, 1986

Sheppard, George. *Plunder, Profit, and Paroles: A Social History of the War of 1812 in Upper Canada.* Montreal, Can: McGill-Queen's University Press, 1994

Shirley, Michael. *From Congregation Town to Industrial City: Culture and Social Change in a Southern Community.* New York: New York University Press, 1994

Sibley, George Champlin. *The Road to Santa Fe: The Journal and Diaries of George Champlin Sibley.* Edited by Kate L. Gregg. Albuquerque: University of New Mexico Press, 1995

Sidbury, James. *Ploughshares into Swords: Race, Rebellion, and Identity in Gabriel's Virginia, 1730–1810.* Boston, MA: Cambridge University Press, 1997

Siegel, Frederick F. *The Roots of Southern Distinctiveness: Tobacco and Society in Danville, Virginia, 1780–1865.* Chapel Hill: University of North Carolina Press, 1987

Silver, Timothy. *A New Face on the Countryside: Indians, Colonists, and Slaves in the South Atlantic Forests, 1500–1800.* Cambridge: Cambridge University Press, 1990

Siracusa, Carl. *A Mechanical People: Perceptions of the Industrial Order in Massachusetts, 1815–1880.* Middletown, CT: Wesleyan University Press, 1979

Skeen, C. Edward. *Citizen Soldiers in the War of 1812.* Lexington: University Press of Kentucky, 1999

Skelton, William B. "The Confederation's Regulars: A Social Profile of Enlisted Service in America's First Standing Army." *William and Mary Quarterly* 3rd ser. 46 (October 1989): 770–785

Slaughter, Thomas G. *The Whiskey Rebellion: Frontier Epilogue to the American Revolution.* New York: Oxford University Press, 1986

Smith, Billy G., ed. *Life in Early Philadelphia: Documents from the Revolutionary and Early National Periods.* University Park: Pennsylvania State University Press, 1995

Smith, Billy G. *The "Lower Sort": Philadelphia's Laboring People, 1750–1800.* Ithaca, NY: Cornell University Press, 1990

Smith, Merril D. *Breaking the Bonds: Marital Discord in Pennsylvania, 1730–1830.* New York: New York University Press, 1991

Smith, Thomas Adams. Papers. Western Historical Manuscript Collection. Columbia: University of Missouri Archives,

Sobel, Mechal. *Trabelin' on: The Slave Journey to an Afro-Baptist Faith.* Westport, CT: Greenwood Press, 1979

Soltow, Lee. "Inequality Amidst Abundance: Land Ownership in Early Nineteenth Century Ohio." *Ohio History* 88 (Spring 1979): 133–151

Soltow, Lee. "Kentucky Wealth at the End of the Eighteenth Century." *Journal of Economic History* 43 (September 1983): 617–633

Sparks, Randy J. *On Jordan's Stormy Banks: Evangelicalism in Mississippi, 1733–1876.* Athens: University of Georgia Press, 1994

Stagg, J. C. A. "Soldiers in Peace and War: Comparative Perspectives on the Recruitment of the United States Army, 1802–1815." *William and Mary Quarterly* 3rd ser. 57 (January 2000): 79–120

Stansell, Christine. *City of Women: Sex and Class in New York 1789–1860*. Urbana: University of Illinois Press, 1982

St. Clair, Arthur. Arthur St. Clair Papers, 1746 through 1882. Microfilm. 8 rolls. Columbus: Ohio Historical Society, 1976

Steffen, Charles G. *The Mechanics of Baltimore: Workers and Politics in the Age of Revolution, 1763–1812*. Chicago: University of Illinois Press, 1984

Steuben, Baron de. *The Soldier's Monitor: Being a System of Discipline for the Use of the Infantry of the United States; Comprising Chiefly the Regulations of Baron De Steuben*. Rutland, VT: Fay & Davison, 1814

Stevenson, Brenda E. *Life in Black and White: Family and Community in the Slave South*. New York: Oxford University Press, 1996

Stoddard, Amos. Papers. St. Louis, MO: Missouri Historical Society, 1796–1812

Stokes, Melvyn, and Stephen Conway, eds. *The Market Revolution in America: Social, Political, and Religious Expressions, 1800–1880*. Charlottesville: University of Virginia Press, 1996

Stuckey, Sterling. *Slave Culture: Nationalist Theory and the Foundations of Black America*. New York: Oxford University Press, 1987

Sugden, John. *Tecumseh: A Life*. New York: Holt, 1997

Sutton, William R. *Journeymen for Jesus: Evangelical Artisans Confront Capitalism in Jacksonian Baltimore*. University Park: Pennsylvania State University Press, 1998

Sweet, John Wood. *Bodies Politic: Negotiating Race in the American North, 1730–1830*. Baltimore, MD: Johns Hopkins University Press, 2003

Tanner, Helen Hornbeck. "The Glaize in 1792: A Composite Indian Community." *Ethnohistory* 25 (Winter 1978): 15–39

Taves, Ann. *Fits, Trances, and Visions: Experiencing Religion and Explaining Experience from Wesley to James*. Princeton, NJ: Princeton University Press, 1999

Taylor, Alan. "Agrarian Independence: Northern Land Rioters After the Revolution." In Alfred Young, ed. *Beyond the American Revolution: Further Explorations in the History of American Radicalism*, 221–245. Dekalb: Northern Illinois University Press, 1993

Taylor, Alan. *The Divided Ground: Indians, Settlers, and the Northern Borderland of the American Revolution*. New York: Vintage, 2006.

Taylor, Alan. *William Cooper's Town: Power and Persuasion on the Frontier of the Early American Republic*. New York: Alfred A. Knopf, 1995

Taylor, George R. *The Transportation Revolution, 1815–1860*. New York: Rinehart, 1951; Armonk, NY: M. E. Sharpe, 1989

Tomlins, Christopher L. *Law, Labor, and Ideology in the Early American Republic.* New York: Cambridge University Press, 1993

Tomlins, Christopher L., and Bruce H. Mann, eds. *The Many Legalities of Early America.* Chapel Hill: University of North Carolina Press, 2001

Toulmin, Harry. *Collection of All the Public and Private Acts of the General Assembly of Kentucky.* Frankfort, KY: William Hunter, 1802

Townsend, Camilla. *Tales of Two Cities: Race and Economic Culture in Early Republican North and South America.* Austin: University of Texas Press, 2000

Trist, Elizabeth. "The Diary of Elizabeth House Trist." Edited by Elizabeth Kolody. In William Andrews et al., eds. *Journeys in New Worlds: Early American Women's Narratives*, 181–232. Madison: University of Wisconsin Press, 1990

Trollope, Frances. *Domestic Manners of the Americans.* New York: Penguin, 1997

Trommler, Frank, and Elliott Shore. *The German-American Encounter: Conflict and Cooperation Between Two Cultures, 1800–2000.* New York: Berghahn Books, 2001

Tullos, Allen. *Habits of Industry: White Culture and the Transformation of the Carolina Piedmont.* Chapel Hill: University of North Carolina Press, 1989

Tunis, Edwin. *Colonial Craftsmen and the Beginnings of American Industry.* Baltimore, MD: Johns Hopkins University Press, 1965

Turbin, Carole. "Beyond Conventional Wisdom: Women's Wage Work, Household Economic Contribution, and Labor Activism in a Mid-Nineteenth-Century Working-Class Community." In Carol Groneman and Mary Beth Norton, eds. *"To Toil the Livelong Day": America's Women at Work, 1780–1980*, 47–67. Ithaca, NY: Cornell University Press, 1987

Turner, Nat. *The Confessions of Nat Turner, the Leader of the Late Insurrection, in Southampton VA.* Baltimore, MD: Thomas R. Gray, 1831

Ulrich, Laurel Thatcher, ed. *A Midwife's Tale: The Life of Martha Ballard, Based on Her Diary, 1785–1812.* New York: Vintage, 1990

Usner, Daniel H. Jr. *American Indians in the Lower Mississippi Valley: Social and Economic Histories.* Lincoln: University of Nebraska Press, 1998

Vanderworth, W. C. *Indian Oratory: Famous Speeches by Noted Indian Chieftains.* Norman: University of Oklahoma Press, 1971

Vickers, Daniel. "Competency and Competition: Economic Culture in Early America." *William and Mary Quarterly* 3rd ser. 47 (January 1990): 3–29

Wade, Richard. *The Urban Frontier: The Rise of Western Cities, 1790–1830.* Cambridge, MA: Harvard University Press, 1959

Waldstreicher, David. *In the Midst of Perpetual Fetes: The Making of American Nationalism, 1776–1820*. Chapel Hill: University of North Carolina Press, 1997

Wallace, Anthony F. C. *The Death and Rebirth of the Seneca*. New York: Alfred A. Knopf, 1969

Wallace, Anthony F. C. *Jefferson and the Indians: The Tragic Fate of the First Americans*. Cambridge, MA: Harvard University Press, 1999

Wallace, Anthony F. C. *The Long, Bitter Trail: Andrew Jackson and the Indians*. New York: Hill and Wang, 1993

Ward, Matthew C. *Breaking the Backcountry: The Seven Years' War in Virginia and Pennsylvania, 1754–1765*. Pittsburgh, PA: University of Pittsburgh Press, 2003

Waselkov, Gregory A. *A Conquering Spirit: Fort Mims and the Redstick War of 1813–1814*. Tuscaloosa: University of Alabama Press, 2006

Watson, Harry. *Andrew Jackson vs. Henry Clay: Democracy and Development in Antebellum America*. Boston: Bedford/St. Martin's, 1998

Welter, Barbara. "The Cult of True Womanhood: 1820–1860." *American Quarterly* 18 (Summer 1966): 151–174

West, Thomas G. *Vindicating the Founders: Race, Sex, Class, and Justice in the Origins of America*. Lanham, MD: Rowman and Littlefield, 1997

Wharton, Mary E., and Roger W. Barbour. *Bluegrass Land and Life: Land Character, Plants and Animals of the Inner Bluegrass Region of Kentucky, Past, Present, and Future*. Lexington: University Press of Kentucky, 1991

Wheeler, William Bruce, and Susan D. Becker, eds. *Discovering the American Past: A Look at the Evidence*, Volume 1, 5th ed. Boston, MA: Houghton Mifflin Company, 2002

White, Deborah. "Female Slaves: Sex Roles and Status in the Antebellum Plantation South." In Catherine Clinton, ed. *Half Sister of History: Southern Women and the American Past*, 56–75. Durham, NC: Duke University Press, 1994

White, Richard. *"It's Your Misfortune and None of My Own": A History of the American West*. Norman: University of Oklahoma Press, 1991

White, Richard. *The Middle Ground: Indians, Empires, and Republics in the Great Lakes Region, 1650–1815*. New York: Cambridge University Press, 1991

White, Richard. *The Roots of Dependency: Subsistence, Environment, and Social Change Among the Choctaws, Pawnees, and Navajos*. Lincoln: University of Nebraska Press, 1983

White, Shane. *Somewhat More Independent: The End of Slavery in New York City, 1770–1810*. Athens: University of Georgia Press, 1991

Whitman, T. Stephen. *The Price of Freedom: Slavery and Manumission in Baltimore and Early National Maryland*. Lexington: University Press of Kentucky, 1997

Wigger, John H. *Taking Heaven by Storm: Methodism and the Rise of Popular Christianity in America*. New York: Oxford University Press, 1998

Wilentz, Sean. *Chants Democratic: New York City and the Rise of the Working Class, 1788–1850*. New York: Oxford University Press, 1984

Wilentz, Sean. "Artisan Republican Festivals and the Rise of Class Consciousness in New York City, 1788–1837." In Michael H. Frisch and Daniel J. Walkowitz, eds. *Working-Class America: Essays on Labor, Community, and American Society*, 37–77. Urbana: University of Illinois Press, 1983

Williams, Isaac. *Aunt Sally: or, The Cross the Way of Freedom. A Narrative of the Slave-life and Purchase of the Mother of Rev. Isaac Williams of Detroit, Michigan*. Cincinnati, OH: American Reform Tract and Book Society, 1858

Williams, James. *Life and Adventures of James Williams, a Fugitive Slave, with a Full Description of the Underground Railroad*. San Francisco, CA: Women's Union Print, 1873

Williams, William H. *The Garden of American Methodism: The Delmarva Peninsula, 1769–1820*. Wilmington, DE: Scholarly Resources, 1984

Wilson, Carol. *Freedom at Risk: The Kidnapping of Free Blacks in America, 1780–1865*. Lexington: University Press of Kentucky, 1994

Wilson, David A. *United Irishmen, United States: Immigrant Radicals in the Early Republic*. Ithaca, NY: Cornell University Press, 1998

Wood, Betty. *Gender, Race, and Rank in a Revolutionary Age: The Georgia Lowcountry, 1750–1820*. Athens: University of Georgia Press, 2000

Wood, Gordon S. *The Creation of the American Republic, 1776–1787*. Chapel Hill: University of North Carolina Press, 1969

Wright, Conrad Edick. *The Transformation of Charity in Postrevolutionary New England*. Boston, MA: Northeastern University Press, 1992

Wright, Donald R. *African Americans in the Early Republic*. Arlington Heights, IL: Harlan Davidson, 1993

Wright, Franklin W. "The Haitian Revolution." *American Historical Review* 105 (February 2000): 103–115

Wright, J. Leitch. *The Only Land They Knew: American Indians in the Old South*. Lincoln: University of Nebraska Press, 1999 (Originally printed 1981)

Wyatt-Brown, Bertram. *The Shaping of Southern Culture: Honor, Grace, and War, 1760s–1880s*. Chapel Hill: University of North Carolina Press, 2001

Wyckoff, William. *The Developer's Frontier: The Making of the Western New York Landscape*. New Haven, CT: Yale University Press, 1988

Young, Alfred F. "George Robert Twelves Hewes (1742–1840): A Boston Shoemaker and the Meaning of the American Revolution." In Herbert G. Gutman and Donald H. Bell, eds. *The New England Working Class and the New Labor History*. Urbana: University of Illinois Press, 1987

Young, Jeffrey Robert. *Domesticating Slavery: The Master Class in Georgia and South Carolina, 1670–1837*. Chapel Hill: University of North Carolina Press, 1999

Young, Mary. "The Cherokee Nation: Mirror of the Republic." *American Quarterly* 33 (Winter 1981): 502–524

Zagarri, Rosemarie. *Revolutionary Backlash: Women and Politics in the Early American Republic*. Philadelphia: University of Pennsylvania Press, 2007

Zagarri, Rosemarie. "The Rights of Man and Woman in Post-Revolutionary America." *William and Mary Quarterly* 3rd ser. 55 (April 1998): 203–230

Zakin, Michael. *Ready-Made Democracy: A History of Men's Dress in the Early Republic, 1760–1860*. Chicago: University of Chicago Press, 2003

Zilversmit, Arthur. *The First Emancipation: The Abolition of Slavery in the North*. Chicago: University of Chicago Press, 1967

Zonderman, David A. *Aspirations and Anxieties: New England Workers and the Mechanized Factory System, 1815–1850*. New York: Oxford University Press, 1992

Index